Kubernetes Secrets Handbook

Design, implement, and maintain production-grade
Kubernetes Secrets management solutions

Emmanouil Gkatziouras

Rom Adams

Chen Xi

Kubernetes Secrets Handbook

Group Product Manager: Preet Ahuja

Publishing Product Manager: Suwarna Rajput

Senior Editor: Arun Nadar

Technical Editor: Irfa Ansari

Copy Editor: Safis Editing

Project Coordinator: Uma Devi

Proofreader: Safis Editing

Indexer: Tejal Daruwale Soni

Production Designer: Shankar Kalbhor

Marketing Coordinator: Rohan Dobhal

First published: January 2024

Production reference: 1120124

Published by
Packt Publishing Ltd.
Grosvenor House
11 St Paul's Square
Birmingham
B3 1RB

ISBN 978-1-80512-322-4

www.packtpub.com

To my father. A mentor for life and the best teacher I had. At every milestone reached, you have your own share of credit.

– Emmanouil Gkatziouras

To my grandmother for her kindness, my grandfather for his wisdom, and my partner and best friend, Mercedes Adams, for her love, patience, and continuous support.

– Rom Adams

To my wife. A beacon of love and strength in my life. Your support and care have shaped every success I've achieved. In every moment, your presence is a blessing beyond measure.

– Chen Xi

Foreword

In today's digital landscape, the orchestration of containers has revolutionized how we build, deploy, manage, monitor, and scale cloud-native applications. Among the myriad tools available, Kubernetes has emerged as the de facto platform for container orchestration, empowering teams to streamline development and deployment processes like never before.

However, as we venture deeper into this realm of agility and efficiency, the critical aspect of security often becomes a concern relegated to the background. The management of Secrets – those sensitive pieces of information ranging from credentials, API keys, and other sensitive data – is a paramount challenge to organizations. Mismanagement of these Secrets can lead to substantial cyberattacks that jeopardize not just an organization's data but also its reputation and trust. Even the accidental mismanagement of Secrets, such as Secrets being mistakenly stored in a code repository such as GitHub, can greatly increase the attack vector on both Kubernetes platforms and the applications that they host.

This book stands as a beacon in the sea of Kubernetes knowledge, guiding practitioners and enthusiasts alike through the intricate landscape of security and Secrets management within Kubernetes. It is a comprehensive guide that not only illuminates the potential vulnerabilities but also offers robust strategies and best practices to fortify your cloud-native applications and Kubernetes platforms.

With a meticulous approach, the authors delve into the core concepts of Kubernetes security, dissecting every layer of its architecture to unveil potential vulnerabilities and common pitfalls. Furthermore, they navigate the complex terrain of Secrets management, presenting battle-tested methodologies and tools to safeguard these invaluable assets.

From encryption in transit and encryption at rest to Secrets integration with CI/CD pipelines and mechanisms for identity and access management, this book thoroughly details the arsenal of security features Kubernetes offers, empowering you to craft and deliver a robust security strategy. It will arm you with practical insights and real-world examples, providing a hands-on approach to managing your Kubernetes Secrets against ever-evolving cyber threats.

As cloud-native application development continues its rapid evolution, the importance of securing our digital environments and artifacts cannot be overstated. This book is an indispensable companion, a guiding light for anyone navigating the Kubernetes ecosystem, ensuring that security and Secrets management remain at the forefront of their endeavors. It will cover Secrets management across multiple cloud providers and secure integration with other third-party vendors.

Prepare to embark on a journey that not only enhances your knowledge but also empowers you to fortify the foundation of your digital endeavors. When it comes to Kubernetes Secrets management, security should be built in, not bolt-on, and this book will arm you with the tools, techniques, and processes to ensure that your Secrets remain just that…secret!

Chris Jenkins, Principal Chief Architect, Global CTO Organization, Red Hat Inc.

Contributors

About the authors

Emmanouil Gkatziouras started his career in software as a Java developer. Since 2015, he has worked daily with cloud providers such as GCP, AWS, and Azure, and container orchestration tools such as Kubernetes. He has fulfilled many roles, either in lead positions or as an individual contributor. He enjoys being a versatile engineer and collaborating with development, platform, and architecture teams. He loves to give back to the developer community by contributing to open source projects and blogging on various software topics. He is committed to continuous learning and is a holder of certifications such as CKA, CCDAK, PSM, CKAD, and PSO. He is the author of *A Developer's Essential Guide to Docker Compose*.

Rom Adams (né Romuald Vandepoel) is an open source and C-Suite advisor with 20 years of experience in the IT industry. He is a cloud-native expert who helps organizations to modernize and transform with open source solutions. He is advising companies and lawmakers on their open and inner-source strategies. He has previously worked as a principal architect at Ondat, a cloud-native storage company acquired by Akamai, where he designed products and hybrid cloud solutions. He has also held roles at Tyco, NetApp, and Red Hat, becoming a subject matter expert in hybrid cloud. He has been a moderator and speaker for several events, sharing his insights on culture, process, and technology adoption, as well as his passion for open innovation.

Chen Xi is a highly skilled Uber platform engineer. As a tech leader, he contributed to the secret and key management platform service, leading and delivering Secrets as a service with a 99.99% SLA for thousands of Uber container services across hybrid environments. His cloud infrastructure prowess is evident from his work on **Google Kubernetes Engine** (**GKE**) and the integration of Spire-based PKI systems. Prior to joining Uber, he worked at VMware, where he developed microservices for VMware's Hybrid Kubernetes management platform (Tanzu Mission Control) and VMware Kubernetes Engine for multi-cloud (Cloud PKS). Chen is also a contributing author to the **Certified Kubernetes Security Specialist (CKS)** exam.

About the reviewers

Brad Blackard is an industry veteran with nearly 20 years of experience at companies such as Uber, Microsoft, and Boeing. At Uber, Brad led multiple technical initiatives as a leader in the Core Security organization, including Secrets management at scale. Most recently, Brad has served as head of engineering for DevZero, a start-up focused on securely improving developer experience and productivity, and he continues to serve there as an advisor.

Ethan Walton is a staff security engineer with a background in Kubernetes, DevOps, and cloud security. He has been active in the space since 2019, with work spanning platform engineering, cloud infrastructure consulting at Google, and leading cloud security initiatives within growing engineering organizations. Ethan is certified as a Google Cloud Professional Cloud Network Engineer and is an avid technology enthusiast. Outside of work, Ethan is also heavily invested in Venture Capital and helping to discover transformational technology start-up companies that will help shape the future.

I'd like to thank my family and especially my mother, father, and better half, Alexandra, for understanding the time and commitment it takes to continue pursuing my passion in the ever-changing world of technology. Day in and day out, this would not have been possible without them every step of the way. Thank you, and thanks to all the great technology trailblazers who continue to make every day an exciting day to work in this field.

James Skliros, a seasoned lead engineer, has shaped the digital landscape for over two decades, and he is renowned for spearheading projects and showcasing exceptional expertise in DevOps, the cloud, and Kubernetes. His adeptness at developing innovative initiatives and enhancing operational efficiency in DevOps is evident throughout his career. Evolving from a system administration background, he now focuses on architecture and solution design, emphasizing a passion for cloud security. Beyond his professional endeavors, he remains dedicated to technology, contributing insightful blogs and articles to his employer and personal platform.

I want to extend my deepest gratitude to my incredible wife, who has been my unwavering support during both the highs and lows of my career journey. Her steadfast encouragement has allowed me to persist in achieving my goals. Additionally, I appreciate Innablr for providing a growth-oriented workplace. Their support has played a key role in my career progression, and I am sincerely thankful for the opportunities they've offered.

Table of Contents

Part 2: Advanced Topics – Kubernetes Secrets in a Production Environment

5

Security, Auditing, and Compliance 83

6

Disaster Recovery and Backups 97

Part 3: Kubernetes Secrets Providers

10

Exploring Cloud Secret Store on GCP   161

11

Exploring External Secret Stores   173

14

Conclusion and the Future of Kubernetes Secrets Management   249

Preface

Kubernetes Secrets management is a combination of practices and tools that help users to securely store and manage sensitive information, such as passwords, tokens, and certificates, within a Kubernetes cluster and keep them safe and secure. Securing Secrets such as passwords, API keys, and other sensitive information is critical for protecting applications and data from unauthorized access. Developers who understand Kubernetes Secrets management can help ensure that Secrets are managed securely and effectively, reducing the risk of security breaches. Many industries and regulatory frameworks have specific requirements for managing sensitive data. By learning Kubernetes Secrets management practices, developers can ensure that their applications comply with these requirements and avoid potential legal or financial penalties.

Who this book is for

This book is for software and DevOps engineers and system administrators looking to deploy and manage Secrets on Kubernetes. Specifically, it is aimed at the following:

- Developers who are already familiar with Kubernetes and are looking to understand how to manage Secrets effectively. This could include individuals who are already using Kubernetes for application deployment, as well as those who are new to the platform and looking to learn more about its capabilities.

- Security professionals who are interested in learning how to securely manage Secrets within a Kubernetes environment. This could include individuals who are responsible for securing applications, infrastructure, or networks, as well as those who are responsible for compliance and regulatory requirements.

- Anyone who is interested in using Kubernetes to deploy and manage applications securely, and who wants to understand how to effectively manage Secrets within that environment.

What this book covers

Chapter 1, Understanding Kubernetes Secrets Management, introduces you to Kubernetes and the importance of Secrets management in applications deployed on Kubernetes. It gives an overview of the challenges and risks associated with managing Secrets, the objectives, and the scope of the book.

Chapter 2, Walking through Kubernetes Secrets Management Concepts, covers the basics of Kubernetes Secrets management, including the different types of Secrets; their usage scenarios; how to create, modify, and delete Secrets in Kubernetes; and secure storage and access control. It also covers how to securely access Secrets with RBAC and Pod Security Standards, as well as auditing and monitoring secret usage.

Chapter 3, Encrypting Secrets the Kubernetes-Native Way, teaches you how to encrypt Secrets in transit and at rest in etcd, as well as key management and rotation in Kubernetes.

Chapter 4, Debugging and Troubleshooting Kubernetes Secrets, provides guidance on identifying and addressing common issues that arise when managing Secrets in Kubernetes. It covers best practices for debugging and troubleshooting Secrets, including the usage of monitoring and logging tools, ensuring the security and reliability of Kubernetes-based applications.

Chapter 5, Security, Auditing, and Compliance, focuses on the importance of compliance and security while managing Secrets in Kubernetes. It covers how to comply with security standards and regulations, mitigating security vulnerabilities, and ensuring secure Kubernetes Secrets management.

Chapter 6, Disaster Recovery and Backups, provides you with an understanding of disaster recovery and backups for Kubernetes Secrets. It also covers backup strategies and disaster recovery plans.

Chapter 7, Challenges and Risks in Managing Secrets, focuses on the challenges and risks associated with managing Secrets in hybrid and multi-cloud environments. It also covers strategies for mitigating security risks in Kubernetes Secrets management, guidelines for ensuring secure Kubernetes Secrets management, and the tools and technologies available for Kubernetes Secrets management.

Chapter 8, Exploring Cloud Secret Store on AWS, introduces you to AWS Secrets Manager and KMS and how they can be integrated with Kubernetes. It also covers monitoring and logging operations on Kubernetes Secrets with AWS CloudWatch.

Chapter 9, Exploring Cloud Secret Store on Azure, teaches you how to integrate Kubernetes with Azure Key Vault for secret storage, as well as the encryption of Secrets stored on etcd. It also covers monitoring and logging operations on Kubernetes Secrets through Azure's observability tools.

Chapter 10, Exploring Cloud Secret Store on GCP, introduces you to GCP Secret Manager and GCP KMS and how they can be integrated with Kubernetes. It also covers monitoring and logging operations on Kubernetes Secrets with GCP monitoring and logs.

Chapter 11, Exploring External Secret Stores, explores different types of third-party external secret stores, such as HashiCorp Vault and CyberArk Secrets Manager. It teaches you how to use external secret stores to store sensitive data and the best practices for doing so. Additionally, the chapter also covers the security implications of using external secret stores and how they impact the overall security of a Kubernetes cluster.

Chapter 12, Integrating with Secret Stores, teaches you how to integrate third-party Secrets management tools with Kubernetes. It covers external secret stores in Kubernetes and the different types of external secret stores that can be used. You will also gain an understanding of the security implications of using external secret stores and how to use them to store sensitive data using different approaches such as init containers, sidecars, CSI drivers, operators, and sealed Secrets. The chapter also covers the best practices for using external secret stores and how they can impact the overall security of a Kubernetes cluster.

Chapter 13, Case Studies and Real-World Examples, covers real-world examples of how Kubernetes Secrets are used in production environments. It covers case studies of organizations that have implemented Secrets management in Kubernetes and lessons learned from real-world deployments. Additionally, you will learn about managing Secrets in CI/CD pipelines and integrating Secrets management into the CI/CD process. This chapter also covers Kubernetes tools to manage Secrets in pipelines and the best practices for secure CI/CD Secrets management.

Chapter 14, Conclusion and the Future of Kubernetes Secrets Management, gives an overview of the current state of Kubernetes Secrets management and future trends and developments in the field. It also covers how to stay up to date with the latest trends and best practices in Kubernetes Secrets management.

To get the most out of this book

You should understand Bash scripting, containerization, and how Docker works. You should also understand Kubernetes and basic concepts of security. Knowledge of Terraform and cloud providers will also be beneficial.

Software covered in the book	Operating system requirements
Docker	Windows, macOS, or Linux
Shell scripting	
Podman and Podman Desktop	
minikube	
Helm	
Terraform	
GCP	
Azure	
AWS	
OKD and Red Hat OpenShift	
StackRox and Red Hat Advanced Cluster Security	
Trivy from Aqua	
HashiCorp Vault	

If you are using the digital version of this book, we advise you to type the code yourself or access the code from the book's GitHub repository (a link is available in the next section). Doing so will help you avoid any potential errors related to the copying and pasting of code.

Download the example code files

You can download the example code files for this book from GitHub at `https://github.com/PacktPublishing/Kubernetes-Secrets-Handbook`. If there's an update to the code, it will be updated in the GitHub repository.

We also have other code bundles from our rich catalog of books and videos available at https://github.com/PacktPublishing/. Check them out!

Conventions used

There are a number of text conventions used throughout this book.

Code in text: Indicates code words in text, database table names, folder names, filenames, file extensions, pathnames, dummy URLs, user input, and Twitter handles. Here is an example: "The kms provider plugin connects kube-apiserver with an external KMS to leverage an envelope encryption principle."

A block of code is set as follows:

```
apiVersion: apiserver.config.k8s.io/v1
kind: EncryptionConfiguration
resources:
  - resources:
      - secrets
    providers:
      - aesgcm:
          keys:
              - name: key-20230616
                secret: DlZbD9Vc9ADLjAxKBaWxoevlKdsMMIY68DxQZVabJM8=
      - identity: {}
```

When we wish to draw your attention to a particular part of a code block, the relevant lines or items are set in bold:

```
apiVersion: v1
kind: ServiceAccount
metadata:
  annotations:
    eks.amazonaws.com/role-arn: "arn:aws:iam::11111:role/eks-secret-
reader"
  name: service-token-reader
  namespace: default
```

Any command-line input or output is written as follows:

```
$ kubectl get events
...
11m          Normal    Pulled                      pod/
webpage                             Container image "nginx:stable"
already present on machin
```

Bold: Indicates a new term, an important word, or words that you see onscreen. For instance, words in menus or dialog boxes appear in **bold**. Here is an example: "Another notable tool provided by GCP to improve the security posture of a GKE cluster is the **GKE security posture** dashboard."

> **Tips or important notes**
> Appears like this.

Get in touch

Feedback from our readers is always welcome.

General feedback: If you have questions about any aspect of this book, email us at customercare@packtpub.com and mention the book title in the subject of your message.

Errata: Although we have taken every care to ensure the accuracy of our content, mistakes do happen. If you have found a mistake in this book, we would be grateful if you would report this to us. Please visit www.packtpub.com/support/errata and fill in the form.

Piracy: If you come across any illegal copies of our works in any form on the internet, we would be grateful if you would provide us with the location address or website name. Please contact us at copyright@packtpub.com with a link to the material.

If you are interested in becoming an author: If there is a topic that you have expertise in and you are interested in either writing or contributing to a book, please visit authors.packtpub.com.

Share Your Thoughts

Once you've read *Kubernetes Secrets Handbook*, we'd love to hear your thoughts! Scan the QR code below to go straight to the Amazon review page for this book and share your feedback.

https://packt.link/r/1-805-12322-X

Your review is important to us and the tech community and will help us make sure we're delivering excellent quality content.

Download a free PDF copy of this book

Thanks for purchasing this book!

Do you like to read on the go but are unable to carry your print books everywhere?

Is your eBook purchase not compatible with the device of your choice?

Don't worry, now with every Packt book you get a DRM-free PDF version of that book at no cost.

Read anywhere, any place, on any device. Search, copy, and paste code from your favorite technical books directly into your application.

The perks don't stop there, you can get exclusive access to discounts, newsletters, and great free content in your inbox daily

Follow these simple steps to get the benefits:

1.   Scan the QR code or visit the link below

https://packt.link/free-ebook/9781805123224

2.   Submit your proof of purchase
3.   That's it! We'll send your free PDF and other benefits to your email directly

Part 1: Introduction to Kubernetes Secrets Management

In this part, you will be provided with a foundational understanding of Kubernetes Secrets and their importance in managing sensitive data in applications deployed on Kubernetes. By the end of this part, you will have learned the basics of the purpose, function, and usage of Kubernetes Secrets with real-world examples.

This part has the following chapters:

- *Chapter 1, Understanding Kubernetes Secrets Management*
- *Chapter 2, Walking through Kubernetes Secrets Management Concepts*
- *Chapter 3, Encrypting Secrets the Kubernetes-Native Way*
- *Chapter 4, Debugging and Troubleshooting Kubernetes Secrets*

1

Understanding Kubernetes Secrets Management

This chapter will provide you with a refresher about containers, as well as a comprehensive overview of Kubernetes and its Secrets management implementation. By the end of this first walk-through, all personas (developers, platform, and security engineers) will know how to design and implement these topics with a set of hands-on examples. While going through these examples, we will highlight the respective security concerns that this book will address by covering a series of use cases that will lead to a production-grade solution for hybrid multi-cloud scenarios, including the business continuity perspective.

In this chapter, we will cover the following topics:

- Understanding Kubernetes' origins and design principles

- Setting up our first Kubernetes testing environment

- Exploring Kubernetes `Secret` and `ConfigMap` objects

- Analyzing why Kubernetes Secrets are important

- Unveiling the challenges and risks associated with Kubernetes Secrets management

- Mapping the objectives and scope of this book

Technical requirements

To complete the hands-on parts of this chapter, we will be leveraging a series of tools and platforms that are commonly used to interact with containers, Kubernetes, and Secrets management. For this first chapter, we will be setting up this environment together and ramping up with a friendly desktop graphical solution for the first set of examples. Don't worry – we have you covered with our Code in Action and GitHub repository, which contains the macOS installation example. Here is the list of required tools:

- **Docker** (`https://docker.com`) or Podman (`https://podman.io`) as a container engine. Both are OK, although I do have a personal preference for Podman as it offers benefits such as being daemonless for easy installation, rootless for added security, fully **Open Container Initiative (OCI)**-compliant, Kubernetes ready, and has the ability to integrate with `systemd` at the user level to autostart containers/Pods.

- **Podman Desktop** (`https://podman-desktop.io`) is an open source software that provides a graphical user interface for building, starting, and debugging containers, running local Kubernetes instances, easing the migration from containers to Pods, and even connecting with remote platforms such as Red Hat OpenShift, Azure Kubernetes Engine, and more.

- **Golang** (`https://go.dev`) or Go is a programming language that will be used within our examples. Note that Kubernetes and most of its third-party components are written in Go.

- **Git** (`https://git-scm.com`) is a version control system that we will be using to cover this book's examples but will also leverage in our discovery of Secrets management solutions.

This book's GitHub repository contains the digital material linked to this book: `https://github.com/PacktPublishing/Kubernetes-Secrets-Handbook`.

Understanding Kubernetes' origins and design principles

While the evolution from one platform to another might be obvious, the compelling event and inner mechanics might not be. To safely handle sensitive data within Kubernetes, we have to understand both its historical and architectural evolutions. This will help us implement a secure production-grade environment for our critical business applications.

The next few sections will describe a series of concepts, explore and practice them with a simple container runtime and Kubernetes cluster, and establish their direct relationships with security concerns that this handbook will address.

> **Important note**
> While we expect you to perform the hands-on examples while reading along, we understand that you might not have the opportunity to do so. As such, we have provided briefings and debriefings for each hands-on example.

From bare metal to containers

Four decades ago, deploying applications was done on a physical server, usually referred to as a *bare metal* installation. This approach allowed workloads to have direct access to physical resources with the best native performance possible. Due to out-of-the-box limitations for resource management from a software perspective, deploying more than one application on a physical server has always been an operational challenge that has resulted in a suboptimal model with the following root causes:

- **Physical resource utilization**: A reduced set of applications is deployed on a physical machine to limit the potential degradation of services due to the lack of proper resource management capabilities that would have helped address applications hogging all the compute resources.

- **Scalability, flexibility, and time to market**: The lead time in weeks or even months to procure, rack and stack, provision the physical machine, and have the application installed, which impacts business growth.

- **The total cost of ownership (TCO) versus innovation**: The procurement, integration, operations, and life cycle of physical servers, along with underutilized resources with limited prototyping due to high costs and lead time, slows down the organization's innovation capabilities.

Then, in the early 2000s, virtualization or *hypervisors* became available for commoditized open systems. A hypervisor is a piece of software that's merged into the operating system, installed on bare metal, that allows the IT department to create virtual machines. With this, operations teams were able to create and tailor these virtual machines to the application's precise requirements with the ability to adapt the compute resources during the application's life cycle and their usage by the business. Thanks to proper resource management and isolation, multiple virtual machines could run on a single server without having noisy neighbors causing potential service degradations.

This model provided tremendous optimizations that helped accelerate the digitalization of services and introduce a new market aside from the traditional data center business – cloud computing. However, the virtualization model created a new set of challenges:

- The never-ending increase of virtual machines thanks to continuous innovation. This exponential growth of assets amplifies the operational burden to maintain and secure operating systems, libraries, and applications.

- The increasing need for automation to perform daily **Create, Read, Update, and Delete (CRUD)** operations at a large scale involving complex infrastructure and security components.

- The need for a well-thought governance that's enforced to address the life cycle, security, and business continuity for thousands of services to support the business continuity of the organization's critical applications.

Finally, containers made their way as the next layer of optimization. Although the construct of containers was not new, as with virtualization, it required a major player to invest in the commoditized open systems to organically make it the next (r)evolution.

Let's think about a container as a lightweight virtual machine but without the need for a full operating system, which reduces the overall footprint and operational burden related to the software development life cycle and security management. Instead, multiple applications, as containers, share the underlying physical host from a software and hardware level without the overhead of the hypervisor benefiting from nearly machine-native performance. The container provides you with the following benefits:

- A well-defined standard by the OCI (`https://opencontainers.org`) to ease with building, (re)distributing, and deploying containers to any platform that's compliant with the specifications of the OCI

- A highly efficient, predictable, and immutable medium that's application-centric and only includes the necessary libraries and the application runtime

- Application portability thanks to an infrastructure and platform-agnostic solution

- An organic separation of concerns between the developers and platform engineers as there is no need to access the physical or virtual host operating system to develop, build, test, and deploy applications

- Embracing an automation-first approach and DevOps practices to address the infrastructure, application, and security management

Not mentioning a few challenges would be wrong, so here are some:

- Most IT organizations have difficulties embracing a new paradigm from both an architectural and management perspective

- Considering the organic serparation of concerns between the developers and platform engineers as a support to silos

- There's an overhype around microservices, which leads to potential suboptimal application architecture with no performance optimization but added complexity

The following diagram shows the bottom-up stack, which shows the potential application density per physical server with their respective deployment type:

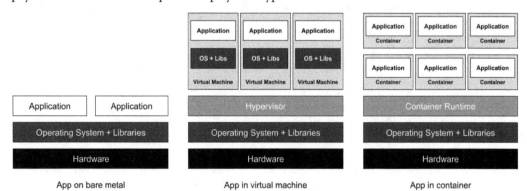

Figure 1.1 – Layer comparison between bare metal, virtual machines, and containers

We've already cited a series of benefits, and yet, we should emphasize additional ones that help with rapid prototyping, faster deployment, easy live functional testing, and so on:

- A smaller code base to maintain and enrich per microservice with easier rollout/rollback

- The capability to run in a degraded mode when one of the microservices fails but not the others

- The ability to troubleshoot misbehaving microservices without impacting the entire application

- It's faster to recover from failure as only the related microservice must be rescheduled

- Granular compute resource allocation and scalability

Not only do microservices help decouple large monolithic applications but they also introduce new design patterns to accelerate innovation.

This sounds fantastic, doesn't it? It does, but we still have a major missing element here: container runtimes such as Docker or Podman do not provide any resiliency in case of failures. To do so, a container runtime requires an additional software layer providing the applications with high availability capabilities. Managing hundreds of microservices at scale demands a robust and highly resilient orchestrator to ensure the business continuity of the applications while guaranteeing a high level of automation and abstraction toward the underlying infrastructure. This will lead to frictionless build, deploy, and run operations, improving the day-to-day responsibilities of the IT staff involved with the workloads that are deployed on the application platforms.

This is a big ask and a challenge that many IT departments are facing and trying to solve, even more so with legacy patterns. The answer to this complex equation is Kubernetes, a container platform or, as we should call it, an application platform.

Kubernetes overview

There are no better words to describe what Kubernetes is all about than the words from the Kubernetes project maintainers: *"Containers are a good way to bundle and run your applications. In a production environment, you need to manage the containers that run the applications and ensure that there is no downtime. For example, if a container goes down, another container needs to start. Wouldn't it be easier if this behavior was handled by a system?*

That's how Kubernetes comes to the rescue! Kubernetes provides you with a framework to run distributed systems resiliently. It takes care of scaling and failover for your application, provides deployment patterns, and more." (`https://kubernetes.io/docs/concepts/overview/#why-you-need-kubernetes-and-what-can-it-do`)

The same page lists the following benefits of Kubernetes:

- Service discovery and load balancing
- Storage orchestration
- Automated rollouts and rollbacks
- Automatic bin packing
- Self-healing
- Secret and configuration management

While reading through this handbook, we will explore and practice all of these benefits while designing a production-grade Secrets management solution for critical workloads.

Kubernetes design principles

We have established the context regarding the evolution and adoption of containers with the need for Kubernetes to support our applications with resiliency, scalability, and deployment patterns in mind. But how is Kubernetes capable of such a frictionless experience?

Here is my attempt to answer this question based on having experience as a former cloud architect within the Red Hat Professional Services organization:

- From a workload perspective, every infrastructure requirement that an application will consume is simply defined in a declarative way without the need for there to be a domain specialist in networking, storage, security, and so on. The YAML manifest describing the desired state of `Pod`, `Service`, and `Deployment` objects is then handled by Kubernetes as a service broker for every specific vendor who has a Kubernetes integration. In other words, application teams can safely write a manifest that is agnostic of the environment and Kubernetes distribution on which they will deploy the workloads.

- From an infrastructure perspective, every component of the stack has a corresponding Kubernetes API object. If not, the vendor can introduce their own with the standard Kubernetes API object called `CustomResourceDefinition`, also known as **CRD**. This guarantees a common standard, even when interacting with third-party software, hardware, or cloud vendors.

When Kubernetes receives a request with a valid object definition, the orchestrator will apply the related CRUD operation. In other words, Kubernetes introduces native automation and orchestration. The same principles should apply to every Kubernetes component running as a container so that they benefit from self-healing, resiliency, and scalability while being agnostic of the underlying software, hardware, or cloud provider.

This approach supports the portability not only of containerized applications but of the entire application platform while reducing the need for technology domain specialists to be involved when deploying an application, maintaining the platform, and even enriching the Kubernetes project with new features or components.

The concept of a YAML manifest to define a Kubernetes API object has been floating around for a while. It is time to look at a simple example that shows the desired state of a `Pod` object (a logical grouping for one or multiple containers):

```
apiVersion: v1
 kind: Pod
 metadata:
   name: hello-app
 spec:
   containers:
   - name: hello-world
     image: hello-path:0.1
     ports:
     - containerPort: 8080
```

This `Pod` object's definition provides the necessary information for Kubernetes to do the following:

- Define the desired state for a `Pod` object with the name `hello-app`.
- Specify that there are `containers` and that one of them is called `hello-world` and uses a container image of `hello-path`. For this, we want version `0.1` to be pulled from a container registry.
- Accept incoming traffic to the `hello-world` application, using port `8080` at the container level.

That's it! This is our first `Pod` definition. It allows us to deploy a simple containerized application with no fuzz and zero knowledge of the underlying infrastructure.

Kubernetes architecture

There is not much magic behind this orchestration but the work of multiple components provides a fantastic level of resilience and abstraction, as well as a frictionless experience. The following diagram provides an overview of the components that run within a Kubernetes instance:

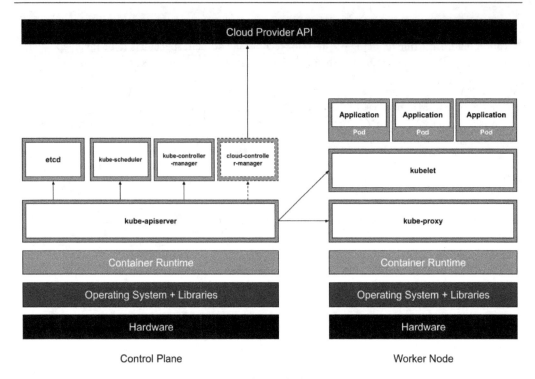

Figure 1.2 – Kubernetes components

A Kubernetes cluster can be divided into two logical groups – the control plane (some distributions refer to this as the master node) and the (worker) nodes. Let's drill down into each logical group and discover their respective components:

- Control plane:

  - kube-apiserver: This component is responsible for exposing the Kubernetes API and enabling CRUD operations regarding the object definitions and their state within etcd.

  - etcd: This component is a key value store and serves as the asset management service. A corrupted etcd results in a full disaster scenario.

  - kube-scheduler: This component tracks the desired state of Pod and will address any potential drift within the cluster. As an example, if a Pod object definition is created or modified, kube-scheduler will adjust its state so that the containers only run on a healthy node.

  - kube-controller-manager: This component runs a series of controllers that are responsible for handling the desired state of the nodes, jobs, endpoints, and service accounts. Controllers are reconciliation loops that track the difference between the desired and current state of an object and adjust the latter so that it matches the latest object definition.

- `cloud-controller-manager` (*optional*): Similar to `kube-controller-manager`, this component, when deploying Kubernetes in the cloud, enriches the cluster with additional abstractions to interact with the related cloud provider services.

- Nodes (and the control plane too!):

  - `kubelet`: This component interacts with `kube-apiserver` to verify and adjust the desired states of Pods bound to the node

  - `kubeproxy`: This component provides the basic network plumbing on each node while maintaining the networking rules to allow (or not) the internal and external network traffic to Pods

  - `container runtime`: This component runs the containers

There are additional components that should be considered as add-ons due to their direct dependency on the Kubernetes distribution. These add-ons would be responsible for handling services such as DNS, logging, metrics, the user interface, and more.

> **Important note**
>
> In a dev/test environment, a single node might be deployed to act both as a control plane and a worker node on which Pods will be scheduled. However, for resiliency purposes, a production-grade environment should consider a minimum of three control planes with dedicated worker nodes to improve resilience and separation of concerns, as well as dedicate compute resources for the applications.

Getting hands-on – from a local container to a Kubernetes Pod

The main benefits of containers are their portability and being platform agnostic. Deploying the famous *Hello World* application within a container using Docker, Podman, or Kubernetes should not require us to modify the application code. I will even go a step further and say that we should not care about the underlying infrastructure. On the other hand, there would be a large umbrella of constraints to deal with when deploying an application with a bare metal or virtualization approach.

Before we start, we assume that you have the following:

- All the technical requirements mentioned at the beginning of this chapter

- Access to this book's GitHub repository (`https://github.com/PacktPublishing/Kubernetes-Secrets-Handbook`)

- This example at hand; it is available in the `ch01/example01` folder

Let's have a look at a simple example illustrating a basic software supply chain:

- **Building the application binary**: The example is a simple Go application showcasing an HTTP service and console logging capabilities

- **Building the container image, including the application binary**: The application will be built using a Golang toolset container image; a second small footprint container image will be used to carry the application binary

- **Running the containerized application using Podman**: This first run will leverage the graphical interface of Podman Desktop to illustrate the rather simple process of running a container

- **Deploying the containerized application using Kubernetes**: This first deployment will leverage the kubectl command line to showcase how to process our first YAML manifest to create a Kubernetes Pod object

Note that this example is agnostic of the CPU architecture on which the overall process will take place. This means that you can safely perform the same exercise on different CPU targets without the need to rewrite code or change any of the configuration files.

It is interesting to note that a container runtime such as Docker or Podman is used to build the application and the container image containing our application binary. This is done via a text file called a Dockerfile, which defines all the necessary steps to build our container image:

```
FROM registry.access.redhat.com/ubi8/go-toolset@
sha256:168ac23af41e6c5a6fc75490ea2ff9ffde59702c6ee15d
8c005b3e3a3634fcc2 AS build
COPY ./hello/* .
RUN go mod init hello
RUN go mod tidy
RUN go build .
FROM registry.access.redhat.com/ubi8/ubi-micro@
sha256:6a56010de933f172b195a1a575855d37b70a4968be8edb
35157f6ca193969ad2
LABEL org.opencontainers.image.title "Hello from Path"
LABEL org.opencontainers.inage.description "Kubernetes Secrets
Handbook - Chapter 01 - Containter Build Example"
COPY --from=build ./opt/app-root/src/hello .
EXPOSE 8080
ENTRYPOINT ["./hello"]
```

The Dockerfile build steps are as follows:

1. Fetch the go-toolset image for the build.

2. Get all the application content in that image.

3. Run the Go build process.

4. Fetch the ubi-micro image as the target container.

5. Set some container image metadata.

6. Copy the binary from the build image to the target image.

7. Set a port exposure for the application. Here, this is `8080`.

8. Run the application binary.

That's it! Once the application has been built and the container image has been successfully created and pushed to the registry, the container image will be available in the localhost container registry, after which the container can be started using either Docker or Podman. This can be done through one simple command line with a few parameters, though you can leverage the Podman Desktop graphical interface.

On the other hand, running this container on an application platform such as Kubernetes requires a different approach – that is, declaratively using a YAML manifest. An example was supplied earlier in this chapter and can be found in this book's GitHub repository. This YAML manifest is submitted to `kube-apiserver` via a tool such as `kubectl`.

Here is a transactional overview of a Kubernetes `Pod` object's creation:

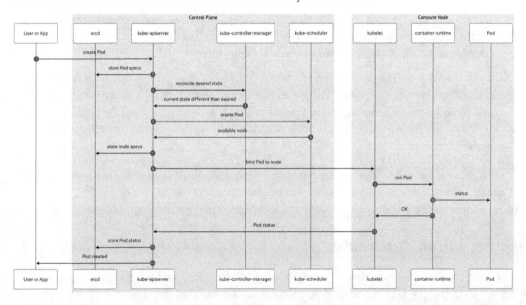

Figure 1.3 – Kubernetes Pod creation

As we can see, the `etcd` record is continuously updated during the `Pod` object's creation. The desired state is saved; the current status of every component involved in the process is also saved, which generates a sort of audit trail. Such a design allows for easier debugging when the desired outcome is not achieved.

As soon as the `Pod` object is registered within `etcd`, all the Kubernetes components are on a mission to converge toward the desired state, regardless of potential issues such as network partitioning, node failure, and more. This is the difference between running containers on a single machine with a local container runtime such as Docker or Podman and orchestrating containers at scale with a container platform such as Kubernetes.

Here's some food for thought:

- I wrote "*running the containerized applications*" and "*deploying the containerized application*" to illustrate the difference between a container runtime such as Docker or Podman running a containerized application and Kubernetes scheduling containers and orchestrating other resources such as networking, storage, Secrets, and more. Note that there is a Kubernetes object called `Deployment` that addresses release management and scalability capabilities. For more details, see `https://kubernetes.io/docs/concepts/workloads/controllers/deployment/`.

- Performing such an exercise even in a non-production environment using virtual machines could take days, even weeks.

- Developing applications using containers, for both monolithic or microservice application architecture, allows for a truly agile development cycle calling for everything to be continuous (development, integration, improvement, and deployment).

- Using YAML manifests to deploy applications will trigger an organic usage of Git repositories that will spark another practice – GitOps. In short, every desired state definition of an application and its infrastructure management lands in a Git repository, providing the *application* and *infrastructure* teams with a central point of configuration management, including, by default, authorization, peer review, and organization.

With that, we've transitioned from running the target application through a local container to running it through a Kubernetes Pod. By doing so, we acquired an understanding of how a Pod is created, which Kubernetes components are involved, the interactions that are involved, and more.

Secrets within Kubernetes

In this section, we had a refresher on containers and Kubernetes, and we also proceeded with a hands-on example that helped us establish key concepts, such as the following:

- The evolution of application deployment through times and technologies

- Why containers and Kubernetes

- The architecture and principles of Kubernetes

- Building and running containers using Podman Desktop and Kubernetes

With the knowledge we've acquired, we can start looking at the more advanced concept of Secrets within Kubernetes. We will dive into the details of how Secrets are stored on Kubernetes, how they are injected into a Pod, which is the smallest execution unit, and the security concerns that we have to tackle.

Secrets concepts

Interestingly enough, during my time designing and deploying Red Hat OpenShift, this topic was always considered irrelevant to the customer and partner teams that I was working with. Reflecting, I concluded that this is linked to the legacy patterns we have been working with for the last two or three decades.

In a traditional environment, both with physical and virtual machines, there is a clear outcome from the separation of concerns principle. The infrastructure teams care about the infrastructure and the application teams care about applications. This includes managing Secrets such as credentials, tokens, license keys, certificates, and more. No one from the application teams will share credentials for a MySQL database with the infrastructure teams.

When it comes to Kubernetes, these concerns are, by design, merged into a point of entry: the application platform. Despite the separation of concerns, the Kubernetes integration with external API-driven services requires credentials, tokens, or certificates to authenticate and trust themselves. These Secrets have to stay within the platform to ensure resiliency, scalability, and orchestration for both the cluster and applications.

When it comes to the container image's design, Secrets cannot be hardcoded or included in the container image. By hardcoding Secrets, they become available to all internal and external stakeholders with access to the container image registry. If the container image is pushed to a public registry, which is common to ease with redistribution, it will make the Secrets available to an even wider audience.

This is the reason why Kubernetes has a Secrets management framework built into it with a dedicated API object called `Secret`. Here is an overview of what a `Secret` object definition would look like:

```
apiVersion: v1
kind: Secret
metadata:
  name: mysecret
type: Opaque
data:
  username: YWRtaW4K
  password: UGFja3QxMjMhCg==
```

Let's go through the manifest:

- We informed Kubernetes that we wanted to create a `Secret` object
- The name for this object is `mysecret` and we defined a type called `Opaque`, which means that we are defining the container of the `data` field ourselves
- The `data` field is composed of two key-value pairs

Now, let's have a closer look at these key-value pairs. What seems to be a random set of characters is data being encoded in `base64`.

Why `base64`? While we could assume the need to encrypt sensitive data such as credentials, the usage of `base64` is only to ease the processing that's done through the command line, the network, and by `kube-apiserver` to avoid us processing a truncated payload due to special characters.

These two entries can be decoded on every operating system or website offering a `base64` encoding/decoding tool. So, should we assume that `kube-apiserver`, when saving the payload within the `etcd` key store, will encrypt the data? Well, this handbook has already given you a good hint that it doesn't!

Another API object has a similar data field that can be used to share sensitive data with an application: `ConfigMap`. While `ConfigMap` was designed to carry out environment variables and application arguments, its usage has been rapidly adopted by developers to also include advanced application configuration, similar to a license key file. This object's content could be leveraged by a malicious hacker to access containers, gain access to other workloads either inside or outside the platform, and even gain control of the Kubernetes cluster. As such, `ConfigMap` should be carefully handled, just like `Secret` objects. Here is an overview of a `ConfigMap` object:

```
apiVersion: v1
kind: ConfigMap
metadata:
  name: app-environment
data:
  appversion1: dev
```

As you can see, there is a major difference between the `data` field of `Secret` and the `data` field of `ConfigMap` – the encoding part. The `data` field specification of `ConfigMap` expects UTF-8 strings while the `Secret` one expects key-value pairs with the value encoded in `base64`. This example shows a way to set an application to `dev` mode, thus enabling extra instrumentation for debugging purposes.

Storing Secrets on Kubernetes

Now is a good time for a second hands-on example so that we can understand the differences between Secrets and the other Kubernetes objects, such as `ConfigMap`. Before we start, we assume that you have the following:

- All the technical requirements mentioned at the beginning of this chapter

- Access to this book's GitHub repository: `https://github.com/PacktPublishing/Kubernetes-Secrets-Handbook`

- The example at hand; it is available in the `ch01/example02` folder

Let's have a look at what we are accomplishing with this example:

1. First, we are creating a `Secret` object using the provided YAML manifest, a secret definition similar to the one we created for `mysecret` earlier. We are also checking its status and how to recover its definition from Kubernetes. This is always handy when we want to recover the current state of an object so that we can create it again later. We are also decoding the `base64` payload to reveal the key-value pairs.

2. Then, we are recovering the YAML manifest from Kubernetes to show a very simple way to get back our `Secret` object and its sensitive data. In other words, if malicious hackers succeed in interacting with `kube-apiserver`, then they can extract some or all `Secret` objects from a Kubernetes cluster.

3. Next, we are creating a new `Secret` object from scratch by encoding the key-value pairs in `base64`, writing the YAML manifest, and pushing it via the command line. Here is a transactional overview of a Kubernetes `Secret` object's creation:

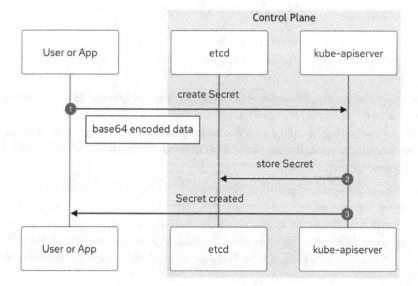

Figure 1.4 – Secret creation

4. The next step is to access the `Secret` payload from a `Pod` object. In this example, we are using a special type of container called `busybox` that provides a small footprint environment that's ideal for performing testing/debugging. The `Pod` manifest includes the reference to our newly created `Secret` object and assigns the value to an environment variable that we will `echo` from `busybox`. This will appear within container logs. Here is a transactional overview of a Kubernetes `Pod` object being created, including the `Secret` object being injected:

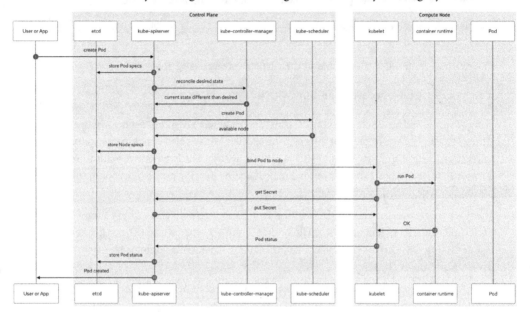

Figure 1.5 – Injecting Secret into Pod

5. Note that the `kubelet` component will be responsible for decoding the `base64` payload. This is to ensure that the payload is transported between the different components and across the wire.

6. Then, we access the `etcd` key store via its API. This shows that the data that's retrieved via such a method is not encrypted nor `base64` encoded! At this stage, malicious hackers who have successfully breached the `etcd` Pod have full access to Kubernetes asset management and can control the entire destiny of the application platform up to a cloud provider account if it's deployed in such a setup.

7. Finally, we are going one step further by extracting the `etcd` file locally and examining it to retrieve our last created `Secret` object. This seems to be a far-fetched scenario but think about filesystem access or backups taken of the Kubernetes cluster, which includes the `etcd` file. Even if the Kubernetes cluster is well-hardened with limited security exposure, malicious hackers who breach the storage and/or backup system(s) can retrieve all the `Secret` objects from such files.

Compared to the previous `Pod` creation workflow, we can establish the relatively low impact from a transaction perspective on the overall process. Note that our first example shows how to load the `Secret` key-value pairs as environment variables. However, other options also exist; we will be exploring their potential mitigations later in this book.

> **Important note**
>
> Only the container that has the environment variable defined within its `Pod` specs will have access to the key-value pairs. However, containers running with `privileged: true` will have access to all Secrets from the node on which it runs, resulting in a major security exposure.

Why should we care?

While Kubernetes provides a frictionless experience for both the platform and application teams, it does not provide you with a hardened solution.

The first approach to tackle this security concern would be to leverage a vault solution (the likes of HashiCorp Vault, CyberArk Conjure, or Azure Key Vault). However, this would only secure the application side. We are still exposed to taking into account the usage of `ConfigMap` or multi-cluster services such as application interconnect, which involves leveraging mutual authentication with certificates generated and deployed within the application platform.

So, let's rethink the requirements into simple layers:

- **The platform**: When Kubernetes is deployed, a series of `Secret` objects are created to allow internal components to interact with others (storage, networking, execution units, controllers, and so on). Third-party components being deployed later on to enrich the platform's capabilities will follow the same model. These `Secret` objects should not be offloaded to a vault solution for resilience purposes. If there is any type of partitioning with the external Vault solution, the Kubernetes cluster will start collapsing, along with all the workloads.

- **The application**: While accessing internal or external services (such as a database, S3 bucket, and so on) requires Secrets, these could be offloaded into an external Vault or similar solutions. However, applications might require a `ConfigMap` object, an encryption key for their volumes, TLS certificates, and so on.

  Similar to the observation about platform-related `Secret` objects, these should be stored within Kubernetes to ensure the scheduling, self-healing, and operability capabilities of the application platform.

By design, Kubernetes will not become a storage system or an encrypted Vault to protect sensitive data. Instead, Kubernetes will provide the necessary framework to interconnect and leverage the expertise of third-party solutions addressing each domain's specific needs.

Considering these aspects, addressing the security concerns for Secrets Management in Kubernetes is not as simple as ticking a box.

Security exposures

In this chapter, we have established the benefits of containerized applications running on Kubernetes but also the security challenges of Secrets Management on such application platforms.

Through our hands-on examples, we have acknowledged how unsafe our sensitive data is within `Secret` and `ConfigMap` objects. We can also list a series of security exposures to be exploited to compromise the application platform, including external services:

- **kube-apiserver**: This is the main component of Kubernetes and malicious hackers can leverage this first point of entry to the application platform
- **etcd**: This manages Kubernetes assets and has multiple security exposures:
  - **The database file**: `etcd` does not provide any encryption capabilities. The database file is a binary file that can be easily read.
  - **The API service**: As for the `kube-apiserver` component, `etcd` is an API-driven service and any access or network trace can expose the data.
  - **Pod**: Accessing the `Pod` object means accessing the filesystem on which the database file is written.
- **The Kubernetes nodes**:
  - **The node filesystem**: The `etcd` Pod has its filesystem hosted on a volume to provide persistent storage. This volume is attached to the node, and by accessing the node, the data can also be accessed through the attached volume.
- **Backups**:
  - The Kubernetes cluster backups include the `etcd` file. Accessing the backup can expose the data.

There are various ways that Secrets can be exposed. For example, you can interact with Kubernetes components such as `kube-apiserver` and `etcd` to do this or go through a physical level such as direct node access or access to backups.

Summary

In this chapter, we introduced containers, Kubernetes, and Secrets. We provided an overview of the history so far, going through the concepts of bare metal, virtual machine, and container-based deployments. We had the opportunity to understand the benefits of containerization and introduce container orchestration engines. We learned more about Kubernetes and its components, which made it possible for us to run our first Kubernetes secret example and also have a deep dive into the Kubernetes components involved to facilitate secret usage. This helped us identify the security and robustness concerns that come with the usage of Kubernetes Secrets.

In the next chapter, we will focus on the different types of Kubernetes Secrets, their usages, and the cross-cutting concerns that Secrets come with, such as auditing and access permissions.

2

Walking through Kubernetes Secrets Management Concepts

In the previous chapter, we had a good overview of Kubernetes, the components that Kubernetes consists of, and how configurations are applied and stored. Also, we built a Golang application and managed to run this application on Kubernetes. As expected, Secrets had to be added to our application's configuration. Secrets management comes with various concerns. From creation to modification to deletion, we need to tackle security concerns as well as scalability and resiliency.

In this chapter, we will cover the following topics:

- What are Kubernetes Secrets, and how do they differ from other Kubernetes objects?

- Different types of Secrets and their usage scenarios

- Creating, modifying, and deleting Secrets in Kubernetes

- Kubernetes Secrets configuration in different deployment scenarios

- Requirement for managing Secrets, including secure storage and access control

- Securing access to Secrets with RBAC

- Auditing and monitoring Secret usage

Technical requirements

To link concepts to hands-on examples, we will leverage a series of tools and platforms commonly used to interact with containers, Kubernetes, and Secrets management. For this chapter, we will ramp up with a friendly desktop graphical solution:

- **Podman Desktop** (`https://podman-desktop.io`) is an **open source software** (**OSS**) that interacts with containers, runs local Kubernetes instances, and even connects with remote platforms such as Red Hat OpenShift, **Azure Kubernetes Service** (**AKS**), and more. We will use the Go programming language in this chapter. To install Go on your system, you can follow the instructions from the official documentation (`https://go.dev/doc/install`).

- In this chapter, **minikube** will also be used. To install minikube on your system, you can follow the instructions from the official documentation (`https://minikube.sigs.k8s.io/docs/start/`).

- All of the code examples in the book are available on our dedicated GitHub repository with a clear structure and instruction set, with corresponding folders for each chapter (`https://github.com/PacktPublishing/Kubernetes-Secrets-Handbook`).

What are Kubernetes Secrets, and how do they differ from other Kubernetes objects?

One of the fundamental building blocks of Kubernetes is Kubernetes objects. Through Kubernetes objects, we can represent the state of the system. An application running on Kubernetes consists of the actual program, the resources the application uses, and the configurations of the application such as health checks. With regard to other cross-cutting concerns such as security, there are configurations for **role-based access control** (**RBAC**); these include cluster-wide roles, namespace roles, and the role bindings to a user or entity. Furthermore, Kubernetes objects include namespaces, which act as logical containers, and network policies, which are cluster-wide traffic rules. By creating Kubernetes objects, we declare the desired state of the cluster. Kubernetes is responsible for and will work toward ensuring that the actual state of the system matches the state defined by the objects we create.

A typical Kubernetes object has certain mandatory fields: `apiVersion`, `kind`, `metadata`, and `spec`.

We can see its YAML representation as follows:

```
apiVersion: apps/v1 #version of Kubernetes api
kind: Deployment     #type of Object
metadata:            #metadata information
  name: example-deployment
spec:                #the state the object should be
```

The most common Kubernetes objects that a Kubernetes user will stumble upon are the following:

- Pod
- Deployment
- StatefulSet
- Cronjob
- Service
- Ingress
- NetworkPolicy
- ConfigMap
- Secret

The preceding objects can be logically grouped into objects representing workloads. Objects such as Pod, Deployment, StatefulSet, and Cronjob are used to define computing resources that will execute certain tasks; those can be running a server, executing a cronjob, or even setting up a distributed memory grid. Objects such as Service, Ingress, and NetworkPolicy specify networking aspects of our application; this can be load balancing traffic internally, exposing Kubernetes services to the internet, as well as blocking traffic internally between applications. So far, the Kubernetes objects mentioned are targeted toward application deployments to compute resources and traffic routing between applications.

ConfigMap and Secret are different in their usage since they are targeted toward configuration storage. ConfigMap and Secret are objects consumed by applications running on Kubernetes. ConfigMap can be used for storing configurations. Common examples of configurations can be an nginx configuration stored in nginx.conf, a JSON-based configuration, or an application configuration based on YAML. Secret objects are for sensitive data. Take, for example, a **mutual TLS (mTLS)**-enabled nginx configuration; we need a TLS key stored in a .key file and a certificate stored in a .pem file. Both are sensitive files and need to be handled securely. This secure handling should also apply to credentials such as usernames and passwords or access tokens. Essentially, Kubernetes Secrets are Kubernetes objects used in order to store sensitive configuration data, thus access should be restricted and the information stored in Secrets should be handled securely.

Different types of Secrets and their usage scenarios

Kubernetes provides us with various types of Secrets. Behind the scenes, it uses the same storage mechanism that we saw in *Chapter 1, Understanding Kubernetes Secrets Management*; Secrets, once created, will be serialized and stored on etcd. What differs is how those Secrets are handled when used. There are various types of Secrets; let us examine them one by one.

Opaque

An Opaque secret is the default secret type. Whenever we want to add a sensitive configuration, whether it is a file or a variable, it will be created as an Opaque secret.

Opaque Secrets can be used by providing key values:

```
$ kubectl create secret generic opaque-example-from-literals --from-literal=literal1=text-for-literal-1
$ kubectl get secret opaque-example-from-literals -o yaml
apiVersion: v1
data:
  literal1: dGV4dC1mb3ItbGl0ZXJhbC0x
kind: Secret
...
type: Opaque
```

Opaque Secrets can also be executed by applying a YAML file:

```
$ kubectl create secret generic opaque-example-from-literals --from-
literal=literal1=text-for-literal-1
$ kubectl create secret generic secretfile --from-file=secret-file.
txt=./secret.file.txt
kubectl get secret secretfile -o yaml
apiVersion: v1
data:
  secret-file.txt: QSBmaWxlIHdpdGggc2Vud210aXZlIGRhdGE=
kind: Secret
metadata:
...
type: Opaque
```

The examples for Opaque Secrets are available in the ch02/secret-types/opaque folder. The opaque.sh script will run the Bash commands needed to achieve the end result.

Kubernetes service account token

A Pod is a unit of work on Kubernetes; a Pod that needs to interact with the Kubernetes API is in need of an identity. A service account is an identity that can be mapped to Pods directly or transitively through a deployment. A Pod can interact with the Kubernetes API, provided it has a service account attached. The service account attached is authorized to access resources of interest. On startup, the Pod with a service account configured has a service account token attached to its filesystem.

Long-lived access token

On Kubernetes, prior to version v1.27, a service account token would be accessible as a Kubernetes secret managed by Kubernetes. This is called a long-lived access token.

It's still possible to create a long-lived access token in the latest versions. This can be achieved by creating an empty secret and putting an annotation with the name of the service account:

```
apiVersion: v1
kind: Secret
metadata:
  name: service-account-secret
  annotations:
    kubernetes.io/service-account.name: example-service-account
type: kubernetes.io/service-account-token
```

As we can see, we note the service account in the `annotations` section. By running the `apply` command, we should see that a token has been generated:

```
$ kubectl create sa example-service-account
kubectl apply -f service-account-secret.yaml
kubectl get secret service-account-secret -o yaml
apiVersion: v1
data:
  ca.crt: ...==
  namespace: default
  token: eyJhbGxffQ.eyJhdWQ3RlbTpdW50In0.0LyJWAc2M9SdA3g
kind: Secret
metadata:
  annotations:
...
type: kubernetes.io/service-account-token
```

Instructions to create long-lived access tokens are available in the following script: `ch02/secret-types/service-account/long-live-access-token.sh`

Service account token mounted on Pod

We've seen a service account as a secret; let us see how a service account token is mounted to a Pod.

A Pod with a service account should look like this:

```
apiVersion: v1
kind: ServiceAccount
metadata:
  name: example-service-account
---
apiVersion: v1
kind: Pod
...
spec:
  ...
  serviceAccountName: example-service-account
```

Once we apply the preceding YAML manifest, we can run a command within the Pod we just scheduled. We will print the service account token mounted as follows:

```
$ kubectl exec -it busybox -- cat /var/run/secrets/kubernetes.io/
serviceaccount/token
eyJhbGdkxfTlUifQ.eyJhdWQidwid3RlbTpdW50In0.0LyJWAc2M9SdA3g
```

As we can see, it is a **JSON Web Token (JWT)** token.

Instructions to create a Pod with a service account are available in the following script: ch02/ `secret-types/service-account/service-account-with-pod.sh`

Docker config

By using an image on a Pod, we might want to pull images from an alternative container registry. For this purpose, we want to mount the Docker configuration so that it is possible to communicate with the registry of our choice. One of the ways we can test this is by just using our local Docker configuration.

We will use the following template to generate a YAML manifest:

```
apiVersion: v1
kind: Secret
metadata:
  name: registry-docker-config
type: kubernetes.io/dockercfg
data:
  .dockercfg: |
     REPLACE_WITH_BASE64
```

You can see the `REPLACE_WITH_BASE64` string; this would be replaced with the Docker config from Docker Hub.

In the `docker-credentials` folder, there is already a Docker config file for that purpose at ch02/ `secret-types/docker-credentials/config.json` without any actual credentials:

```
{
  "auths": {
    "https://index.docker.io/v1/": {}
  }
}
```

We will issue a login and use our Docker Hub credentials:

```
$ docker --config ./ login --username=dockerhub-username
--password=dockerhub-password
```

The file will contain the basic authentication needed to connect with Docker Hub:

```
{
...
    "auth": "token"
...
}
```

We will use this config to mount it as a Kubernetes secret:

```
$ DOCKER_CONFIG=$(cat ./config.json|base64)
$ cat docker-credentials-template.yaml|sed "s/REPLACE_WITH_
BASE64/$DOCKER_CONFIG/" > docker-credentials.yaml
```

In our next steps, we will upload the credentials to Kubernetes by applying the YAML manifest we created:

```
$ kubectl apply -f docker-credentials.yaml
```

Then, we will create a Pod that pulls from the registry:

```
apiVersion: v1
kind: Pod
metadata:
  name: nginx
spec:
  containers:
  - name: nginx
    image: nginx:1.14.2
    ports:
    - containerPort: 80
  imagePullSecrets:
  - name: docker-credentials
```

The image will be pulled using the credentials specified.

The preceding instructions have been orchestrated in the following script: ch02/secret-types/docker-credentials/docker-credentials.sh

Basic authentication

Basic authentication consists of a key secret combination for the username and password. It gives us the option to be more declarative when specifying a basic authentication secret.

The YAML manifest should contain a value for the username and password keys:

```
apiVersion: v1
kind: Secret
metadata:
  name: basic-auth-secret
type: kubernetes.io/basic-auth
stringData:
  username: a-user
  password: a-password
```

Once we apply the preceding YAML manifest, the result will be very similar to the Opaque Secrets.

The preceding instructions have been orchestrated in the following script: `ch02/secret-types/basic-authentication/basic-auth-secret.sh`

TLS client or server

TLS Secrets are used to store SSL/TLS certificates. TLS Secrets can be used in order to be more declarative when it comes to mounting TLS certificates. However, a TLS secret can have direct usage when it comes to specifying an Ingress.

An Ingress acts as an external load balancer to your system, serving HTTP/HTTPS traffic. Traffic needs to be secured using SSL.

An SSL secret has the following format:

```
apiVersion: v1
kind: Secret
metadata:
  name: ingress-tls
type: kubernetes.io/tls
data:
  tls.crt: CRT
  tls.key: KEY
```

By using the `ch02/secret-types/ssh/tls.sh` script, we will create a certificate and key that can be used on an HTTP server. The secret created will be named `ingress-tls`. The script used as a certificate will have a `webpage.your.hostname` host.

Let's create an Ingress using TLS certificates we created previously:

```
apiVersion: networking.k8s.io/v1
kind: Ingress
...
spec:
  tls:
  - secretName: ingress-tls
    hosts:
      - webpage.your.hostname
  rules:
  - host: webpage.your.hostname
...
```

By using the Ingress, we can define hosts and the SSL for the hosts.

Note on minikube users

If you used minikube throughout the `minikube.sh` script, you should enable Ingress on your workstation as follows:

```
$ minikube addons enable ingress
```

We can now test the Ingress. Be aware that the Ingress needs to get an IP assigned:

```
$ kubectl get ing
NAME              CLASS    HOSTS                   ADDRESS          PORTS       AGE
webpage-ingress   nginx    webpage.your.hostname   192.168.49.2     80,
443    79s
```

Since this IP might belong to an internal VM, we need to issue a `minikube tunnel` command, which will forward the traffic to our Ingress:

```
$ minikube tunnel
```

By navigating to `https://localhost/`, we can see the certificate:

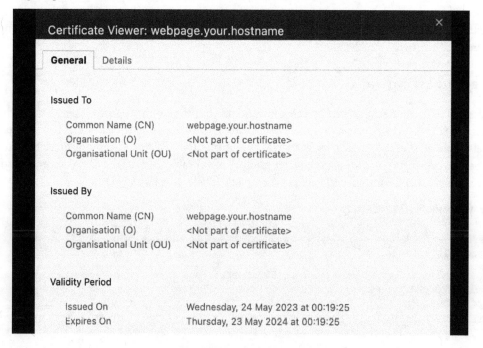

Figure 2.1 – SSL certificate

Also, if we want to validate the Ingress routing, we can change `/etc/hosts` and map the `webpage.your.hostname` DNS to `localhost`.

Token data

This type of secret is a bootstrap token. It looks like the usual bearer token that we use on REST APIs; in the case of Kubernetes, it is used specifically for the bootstrap process of a Kubernetes cluster. When initializing a Kubernetes cluster, a bootstrap token is created and can then be used to join new nodes to the cluster.

Conclusion

We had a deep dive into Kubernetes Secrets. We identified different types of Secrets and ran examples of each secret type, depicting their usage and peculiarities. For the latest developments in Secrets, you can always refer to the official documentation (`https://kubernetes.io/docs/concepts/configuration/secret/#secret-types`). Throughout this section, the provisioning of the Secrets was done through the `kubectl` command line. In the next section, we will explore our options for managing Secrets, creating them, deleting them, and modifying them.

Creating, modifying, and deleting Secrets in Kubernetes

Previously, we focused on creating Secrets and displaying their usage. We will proceed further on administrating Secrets and identify the available commands and options for provisioning Kubernetes Secrets.

data and stringData

We applied plaintext Secrets either by using a YAML file or through the command line. Behind the scenes, the Secrets that we applied in plaintext were converted to a `base64` format. We can either apply Secrets in plaintext or apply them using `base64`; eventually, they will end up residing on Kubernetes in a `base64` format. When we apply a secret using plaintext values, we use the `stringData` field. Kubernetes will handle the encoding and decoding of the values we provided.

Take, for example, the following secret:

```
apiVersion: v1
kind: Secret
metadata:
  name: plain-text
type: Opaque
stringData:
  value: non-base64
```

Once we create the secret, we will retrieve it. It should be in `base64`:

```
$ kubectl apply -f plain-text.yaml
$ kubectl get secret plain-text -o yaml|grep value
  value: bm9uLWJhc2U2NA==
```

The value was stored in a base64 format. This is a convention that Kubernetes follows for storing Secrets. This is especially useful if we consider the different variations a secret can have. A secret can have a complex value; for example, a large YAML file or even a binary.

For the complex situations described previously, we have the option of the data field. When we apply Kubernetes Secrets using a base64 format, we use the data field:

```
apiVersion: v1
kind: Secret
metadata:
  name: base64-encoded
type: Opaque
data:
  value: bm9uLWJhc2U2NA==
```

Now that we have acquired knowledge on creating Secrets, we will proceed with other operations such as update and delete.

Updating Secrets

When it comes to Kubernetes objects, there are some basic commands that we can use to manage them. Those commands apply also to Secrets since they are Kubernetes objects too.

Editing Secrets

Editing a secret is done by using the edit command of kubectl. kubectl comes with a preconfigured editor. By default, the editor is Vim:

```
$ kubectl edit secret plain-text
```

As we can see, the secret when editing will be presented in a base64 format. If we try to change the secret using plaintext, we will fail. When we edit a secret, we must provide a base64 value.

An option when editing a secret using kubectl is to record the command that causes the change using the —record=true argument:

```
$ kubectl edit secret plain-text --record=true
$ kubectl get secret plain-text -o yaml
...
    kubernetes.io/change-cause: kubectl edit secret plain-text
--record=true
...
```

As we can see, the edit command that we issued is recorded.

For backup purposes as well as for keeping track of the previous state, when editing we can use the —save-config=true argument:

```
$ kubectl edit secret plain-text --save-config=true
$ kubectl get secret plain-text -o yaml
...
kubectl.kubernetes.io/last-applied-configuration: |
      {"apiVersion...."type":"Opaque"}
...
```

In the last-applied-configuration field, we will back up the previous configuration.

So far, we have edited Secrets and managed to keep track of the commands that caused the Secrets to change but also keep track of the last applied configuration. This is not always the case; sometimes, we might want Secrets to be immutable, which is something we will achieve in the next section.

Immutable Secrets

In certain cases, we might want our Secrets to remain unchanged; for example, we want to prevent accidental editing. Here's how we can achieve that:

```
apiVersion: v1
kind: Secret
metadata:
  name: immutable-secret
type: Opaque
stringData:
  value: non-base64
immutable: true
```

If we try to edit the following secret, once we try to save, we will face the following error message:

```
data: Forbidden: field is immutable when `immutable`is set
```

Also, if we make an existing secret immutable, then it is not possible to edit it; the secret becomes permanently immutable. To change an immutable secret, the only way is to delete the secret and re-apply it. Next, we will learn how to delete Kubernetes Secrets.

An example of showcasing immutable Secrets is provided at ch02/secret-types/secret-management/immutable/immutable-secret.sh.

Deleting Secrets

The command for deleting a Kubernetes object also applies to Secrets.

The following example will delete a Kubernetes secret if it exists:

```
kubectl delete secret immutable-secret
```

By deleting a secret, it is permanently removed from our system. The only way to be able to retrieve it is either by restoring an `etcd` backup, provided it contains the secret, or applying a manual backup that was taken using the following command:

```
kubectl get secret immutable-secret -o yaml
```

Conclusion

In this section, we went one step further on managing Kubernetes Secrets. We updated Secrets, kept track of our changes, and also took a backup of the previously existing configuration. Furthermore, we created immutable Secrets in order to prevent accidental editing, and last but not least, we deleted Secrets we did not need anymore. In the following section, we will focus on concerns surrounding secret usage in different environments.

Kubernetes Secrets configuration in different deployment scenarios

Throughout the **software development life cycle (SDLC)**, a team might use different environments to test their increments before releasing them to production. Just as with a production deployment, any other deployment on another environment will have certain configuration requirements, including Secrets.

Secret usage among environments

When it comes to Secrets, we need to ensure their durability and integrity regardless of the environment. Having different handling of Secrets in different environments can cause issues in the long term, and the team will not be able to fully validate the security implications of choices on secret handling.

Provided the environments have differences due to cost-saving requirements or because a full installation brings more overhead, Secrets need to be securely stored. There might be cases where Secrets might be shared. An example can be a proprietary key of an external SaaS service that needs to be shared between environments. Another example is when multitenant cloud accounts host multiple environments.

From development to deployment

To deploy a secret, sensitive information needs to reside somewhere. This information at some point will be inserted by an individual to a system and applied to Kubernetes. Companies nowadays store their sensitive information on various systems designed specifically to host this type of information. Briefly, secure storage is required to host Secrets.

The life cycle of deploying something as sensitive as a Kubernetes secret starts from retrieving the certificate from the secure storage, creating the YAML file needed for the secret, and applying it to Kubernetes.

In the case of CI/CD jobs, most CI/CD providers provide us with the option to use secret values on our jobs. This can assist us in providing credentials to our CI/CD jobs to interact with the secret storage.

Another paradigm is GitOps. Argo CD is an extremely popular tool that can have a secret deployment customized to be able to apply a secret after it has been decrypted.

Conclusion

When it comes to different environments, our handling of Secrets should be treated the same regardless of the environment. This helps with automation as well as consistency.

Requirement for managing Secrets, including secure storage and access control

In terms of responsibilities, a Kubernetes cluster has a responsibility to securely contain Secrets and prevent unauthorized access. Every secret that is hosted on Kubernetes has been stored by an individual or an automated process. At some point in time, this secret that now resides on Kubernetes was in another system. This makes it important to store Secrets securely before they reach Kubernetes.

Secure storage

There are various tools dedicated to the purpose of secure storage. Take, for example, HashiCorp Vault, **Google Cloud Platform** (**GCP**) Secret Manager, and **Amazon Web Services** (**AWS**) Secrets Manager. These are external Secrets management solutions.

The benefit of those solutions is that they can be used as a standalone Secrets management system but can also be used directly from Kubernetes. It is feasible to use secure storage during development or even on CI/CD jobs.

A thing these types of solutions have in common is that they tackle cross-cutting concerns such as management, versioning, encryption, and access-control capabilities.

Access control

Access control is essential to have our secret storage secured. Durability, encryption at rest, and encryption in transit make our interactions with a secure storage system secure, but it is not enough. We need to have fine-grained control when it comes to accessing Secrets.

We need to distinguish between users and their role in an organization. Also, permissions might differ per environment. Another aspect is auditing and identifying whether there was an incident of unauthorized access.

Git and encryption

Apart from using a secure storage system, another popular option is to store Secrets in an encrypted form. By storing Secrets encrypted on a Git repository, various aspects are feasible through Git's capabilities. For example, versioning is by default enabled through commit history, access control is satisfied through the access control rules of Git, and the resiliency and durability of storage are based on the provider's guarantees. As for encryption, this can be as good as the solution chosen. Data can be encrypted in various forms, from a **Pretty Good Privacy (PGP)** key (`https://www.openpgp.org/`) to a hardware security module to a modern **cloud key management service (cloud KMS)** solution. An extremely popular tool based on this is **Mozilla Secrets OPerationS (SOPS)**: `https://github.com/mozilla/sops`. Mozilla SOPS utilizes KMSs provided by cloud providers as well as PGP.

Conclusion

Just as with every secret, their access should be limited, and they should not be available to be accessed to unauthorized personnel in any circumstances. For these reasons, apart from where we keep Secrets, we need to provide proper access control.

Securing access to Secrets with RBAC

A cross-cutting concern when it comes to Kubernetes objects is authorized access. Overall, the state of a system is something sensitive. You should have authorized access for operations such as changing the number of replicas for a deployment or changing the autoscaling rules for a deployment. The security mechanism that Kubernetes provides us with is RBAC.

RBAC introduction

RBAC consists of the following Kubernetes objects:

- Roles
- Role bindings
- Cluster roles
- Cluster role bindings

We will check each component separately and see how they are combined with Kubernetes Secrets.

Roles

Roles are a set of permissions that take effect only on the namespace where the role resides. By specifying a role, we define operations that can be executed upon a Kubernetes resource. Roles have the following format:

```
apiVersion: rbac.authorization.k8s.io/v1
kind: Role
metadata:
  namespace: default
  name: secret-viewer
rules:
- apiGroups: [""]
  resources: ["secrets"]
  verbs: ["get","list","watch"]
```

verbs are the actions that we should be able to execute, and resources are the targets for those actions. apiGroups points to the API group of the resources we will interact with; by setting an empty value, it indicates the core API group.

The preceding Role object enables the actor with that role to get, list, and watch Secrets for the default namespaces. Let us proceed and bind that role to an actor.

Role bindings

By checking how a Role object is represented using YAML, we identify the action and the target. Role bindings help us to define the actor. An actor can be a user (individual or a group) or a service account. Role bindings have the following YAML manifest:

```
apiVersion: rbac.authorization.k8s.io/v1
kind: RoleBinding
metadata:
  name: secret-viewer-binding
  namespace: default
roleRef:
  apiGroup: rbac.authorization.k8s.io
  kind: Role
  name: secret-viewer
subjects:
- kind: ServiceAccount
  name: secret-viewer
  namespace: default
```

A namespace is present when defining a role binding. This is because role bindings take effect only on the namespace in which they reside. On roleRef, we define a role that should be on the same namespace. On `subjects`, we define a list of actors that will have access to that role. Take note that the subjects can come from different namespaces.

Cluster roles

Cluster roles are close to roles: they do define a set of permissions; however, they take effect cluster-wide and are not limited to one namespace. They have the following YAML representation:

```
apiVersion: rbac.authorization.k8s.io/v1
kind: ClusterRole
metadata:
  name: secret-admin-cluster
rules:
- apiGroups: [""]
  resources: ["secrets"]
  verbs: ["*"]
```

This is almost identical to the `Role` object except for the namespace not being present since those rules apply cluster-wide. The preceding `ClusterRole` role enables the actor with that role to administer Secrets from all namespaces we have on the Kubernetes clusters. We can now proceed with binding that `ClusterRole` object to an actor.

Cluster role bindings

By using cluster role bindings, we bind a cluster role to a list of users and service accounts. A cluster role binding has the following YAML representation:

```
apiVersion: rbac.authorization.k8s.io/v1
kind: ClusterRoleBinding
metadata:
  name: secret-admin-cluster-binding
subjects:
- kind: ServiceAccount
  name: secret-admin
  namespace: default
roleRef:
  kind: ClusterRole
  name: secret-admin-cluster
  apiGroup: rbac.authorization.k8s.io
```

Now that we have been introduced to RBAC and how we can utilize it to secure Secrets, we can proceed to an end-to-end example.

RBAC and Secrets

In the previous example, we created roles and cluster roles for our cluster's secret resources. We focused on a viewer role and an administrator role for Secrets, but it is worth seeing if there are more options.

We can identify which verbs are related to Secrets by using an `api-resources` call:

```
$ kubectl api-resources -o wide|grep secrets
secrets v1 true Secret [create delete deletecollection get list patch
update watch]
```

Now that we know what our options are, we will create our own RBAC configuration for our Secrets.

ClusterRole

We will create a cluster role for administering Secrets using the `ClusterRole` specification in the YAML file we created earlier:

```
$ kubectl create sa secret-admin
$ kubectl apply -f ./secret-admin-cluster.yaml
```

This should create a cluster role able to administer Secrets cluster-wide. We will use a Pod with the `ClusterRole` object attached and check the secret creation:

```
apiVersion: v1
kind: Pod
metadata:
  name: kubectl-create-secret
spec:
  containers:
  - name: kubectl
    image: bitnami/kubectl:latest
    args:
    - create
    - secret
    - generic
    - test
    - --from-literal=literal1=text-for-literal-1
  serviceAccount: secret-admin
  serviceAccountName: secret-admin
```

By checking the logs, we should see the following message:

```
secret/test created
```

The Pod was configured with the service account, and the service account has a cluster binding to a `ClusterRole` object with admin permissions upon Secrets.

Role

We will use the role we created earlier that provides viewer permissions over Secrets:

```
$ kubectl create sa secret-viewer
$ kubectl apply -f ./secret-viewer.yaml
```

We should now have a viewer role for Secrets on the default namespace. We will run a Pod to retrieve the Secrets:

```
apiVersion: v1
kind: Pod
metadata:
  name: kubectl-get-secrets
spec:
  containers:
  - name: kubectl
    image: bitnami/kubectl:latest
    args:
    - get
    - secret
    - secret-toview
  serviceAccount: secret-viewer
  serviceAccountName: secret-viewer
```

Conclusion

In this section, we introduced RBAC for Secrets. We identified available actions for Secrets within a cluster and the distinction between `ClusterRole` and `Role` objects. We then proceeded to secure secret usage within our cluster and provided fine-grained authorized access to Secrets, whether access was limited to a namespace by using a role or access was granted throughout the cluster. Since we have fulfilled the requirement for authorized access, another requirement that we should pay attention to is monitoring our secret usage.

Auditing and monitoring secret usage

To record and monitor ongoing activities on a Kubernetes cluster, we have the option of auditing. Events that happen in a Kubernetes cluster are sent to the output stream or saved as logs; this makes it feasible to identify what happened in our system.

In our case, we want to monitor our secret usage. To avoid the overhead of other activities, we will focus only on audits generated for Secrets.

The audit configuration to enable audits on Secrets should be the following:

```
apiVersion: audit.k8s.io/v1
kind: Policy
omitStages:
  - "RequestReceived"
rules:
  - level: Metadata
    resources:
    - group: ""
      resources: ["secrets"]
```

On a Kubernetes installation, this can be achieved by using the `--audit-policy-file` flag and passing it when running `kube-apiserver`:

```
kube-apiserver --audit-policy-file=/path/to/audit-policy.yaml
```

minikube note

In the case of minikube, we need to pass the audit configuration when starting minikube.

We have summed up those actions in the `minikube-script.sh` script:

```
minikube start \
  --extra-config=apiserver.audit-policy-file=/etc/ssl/certs/audit-policy.yaml \
  --extra-config=apiserver.audit-log-path=-
```

Since we enabled auditing, let's check the logs:

```
$ kubectl logs -f kube-apiserver-minikube -n kube-system | grep audit.k8s.io/v1
```

To trigger an audit event, we can issue a secret operation:

```
$ kubectl get secret
```

Eventually, we will receive the following log:

```
{"kind":"Event",...,"verb":"list","user":{"usernam
e":"minikube-user","groups":["system:masters","sys
tem:authenticated"]},"sourceIPs":["192.168.49.1"],-
"...,"responseStatus":{"metadata":{},"code":200},...}
```

We managed to track and monitor changes in our Secrets thanks to enabling the auditing feature of Kubernetes.

Summary

In this chapter, we had a deeper dive into Kubernetes Secrets. We learned about the different types of Kubernetes Secrets and for which occasions they are used, and we went through executing code snippets highlighting those use cases. Also, since Secrets contain sensitive information, we went further into securing access to those Secrets by applying RBAC rules. This helped us to limit access to Secrets but also provide authorized access to our Pods. Another aspect that we covered is auditing. Auditing is a very important aspect since we want to have full control over access to Secrets as well as other operations. In the next chapter, we will focus on encrypting Secrets in transit and at rest.

3

Encrypting Secrets the Kubernetes-Native Way

In the previous two chapters, we have reviewed together the foundational knowledge regarding the architecture, implementation, and usage of `Secret` objects within the Kubernetes architecture and design. We also established that `Secret` objects are not safe as-is within Kubernetes platforms due to their unencrypted nature, both in terms of key-value pair and the etcd data file, resulting in major security exposures for your business.

In this chapter, we will get closer to both Kubernetes and etcd, understanding their associated security weaknesses and how we can mitigate or reduce them. While these responses could be considered tightly coupled with the container platform deployment, thanks to the open source nature of the operating system and Kubernetes distribution, most if not all can be applied widely.

This chapter focuses on an in-platform approach, starting with the Kubernetes-native encryption design, including the possibility to connect with a **Key Management Service** (**KMS**), and concluding with an etcd hardening overview.

In this chapter, we will cover the following topics:

- Native encryption without any external components
- Native encryption with an external component
- Encryption at rest of etcd and other components

Technical requirements

To link concepts with hands-on examples, we are leveraging a series of tools and platforms commonly used to interact with containers, Kubernetes, and Secrets management. For this chapter, we are continuing with the same set of tools used in the earlier chapters:

- **Docker** (`https://docker.com`) and Podman (`https://podman.io`) can both be used as a container engine. Both are OK, although I do have a personal preference for Podman as it offers benefits such as being daemonless for easy installation, rootless for added security, fully OCI compliant, and Kubernetes-ready, and it integrates with `systemd` at the user level to autostart containers/Pods.

- **Podman Desktop** (`https://podman-desktop.io`) is an open source software providing a graphical user interface to build, start, and debug containers, run local Kubernetes instances, ease the migration from container to Pod, and even connect with remote platforms such as Red Hat OpenShift, Azure Kubernetes Engine, and more.

- **Golang** (`https://go.dev`) or Go is a programming language used within our examples. Note that Kubernetes and most of its third-party components are written in Go.

- **Git** (`https://git-scm.com`) is a version control system that we will be using to recover the book examples and also leverage in our discovery of Secrets management solutions.

In addition, the following tools will be looked at:

- **HashiCorp Vault** (`https://www.vaultproject.io/community`) is a community vault with an enterprise offering to safely store credentials, tokens, and more

- **Trousseau** (`https://trousseau.io`) is a KMS provider plugin to leverage external KMSs such as HashiCorp Vault, Azure Key Vault, or an AWS equivalent

The following link gives you access to the digital material linked to this book:

- The GitHub repository: `https://github.com/PacktPublishing/Kubernetes-Secrets-Handbook`

Kubernetes-native encryption

Data in payloads written in etcd is not encrypted but encoded in base64, which is almost equivalent to clear text. Encrypting the data contained in the payload will protect from the aforementioned protection mechanisms, but not replace them!

Interestingly enough, we have established that our Kubernetes key-value store, also known as etcd, does not provide any encryption capabilities except for the networking part, nor does Kubernetes provide advanced KMS capabilities as HashiCorp Vault or Azure Key Vault would.

However, the Kubernetes project has designed a KMS framework within `kube-apiserver`, the service validating and configuring data for the API objects, to leverage one of the following encryption providers:

- The `identity` provider is the default configuration, meaning no encryption is applied to the data field encoded in base64

- The `aes` provider, with two options being `aesgcm` or `aescbc`, leverages the local encryption capabilities with a random encryption key generated by the user

- The `kms` provider plugin connects `kube-apiserver` with an external KMS to leverage an envelope encryption principle

The way the KMS provider framework is configured is by enabling its capability at the `kube-apiserver` Pod's (re)start time.

We enable `kube-apiserver` with this capability as follows:

- We reference `kube-apiserver` with two configuration flags; one to enable the capability and reference a configuration file, and one to enable auto-reload when the changes are applied to the configuration file

- A configuration file is to be deployed on every control plane node where the path and the name are defined within the configuration flag itself

Let's start with the configuration file, which is based on a YAML manifest referencing the `EncryptionConfiguration` API object and looks like this:

```
apiVersion: apiserver.config.k8s.io/v1
kind: EncryptionConfiguration
resources:
  - resources:
      - Secrets
      - ConfigMap
    providers:
      - identity: {}
```

This YAML manifest is an actual explicit version of what `kube-apiserver` is configured with by default, even when the capability is disabled. The manifest can be read as follows:

- The `resources` list; a reference to the Kubernetes API objects to encrypt being either `Secrets`, `ConfigMap`, or custom resources starting within Kubernetes version 1.25

- The `providers` list with precedence; a reference to the encryption mechanism being either `identity`, `aesgcm`, `aescbc`, or `kms`

As mentioned, the providers list has a precedence construct. This means that kube-apiserver will parse the list in a sequential way, which could have an impact on your operations. This will be illustrated within the hands-on examples.

The easiest way, to begin with, is to use the preceding default definition to set up our first EncryptionConfiguration file and to make sure that it is properly deployed on every control plane node.

> **Important note**
>
> This deployment, apart from the location and method, is heavily dependent on your Kubernetes distribution and we strongly invite you to verify the respective project/vendor documentation.
>
> When using Kind from the Kubernetes projects, it can be simply referenced with an extra volume definition that we will illustrate within the hands-on examples. To ease this process, the file will be called configuration.yaml and deployed within the /etc/kubernetes/encryption folder.

Now that we've had a look at the EncryptionConfiguration file, let's have a look at the flags to enable kube-apiserver with the provider(s) referenced within our configuration file.

Here is an overview of the flags to enable the kube-apiserver Pod with encryption capabilities:

- The flag to enable and reference the configuration file is as follows:

```
--encryption-provider-config=/etc/kubernetes/encryption/
configuration.yaml
```

- The flag, available since Kubernetes 1.26, to automatically reload the changes applied to the configuration file without restarting kube-apiserver is as follows:

```
--encryption-provider-config-automatic-reload=true
```

The following Pod definition snippet shows where to place these two flags:

```
apiVersion: v1
kind: Pod
...
spec:
  containers:
  - command:
    - kube-apiserver
    - --advertise-address=10.89.0.2
    - --allow-privileged=true
...
```

```
    - --encryption-provider-config=/etc/kubernetes/encryption/
configuration.yaml
    - --encryption-provider-config-automatic-reload=true
```

Now that we have taken a look at how to enable these capabilities, let's deep dive into the provider options.

Standalone native encryption

The native encryption can be enabled without the need for any additional software, either on the control plane or externally to the Kubernetes cluster.

identity

This provider is the default `kube-apiserver` configuration, which is equivalent to not transforming any data field payload to an encrypted one before storing it within etcd.

The following diagram provides an overview of the encryption workflow:

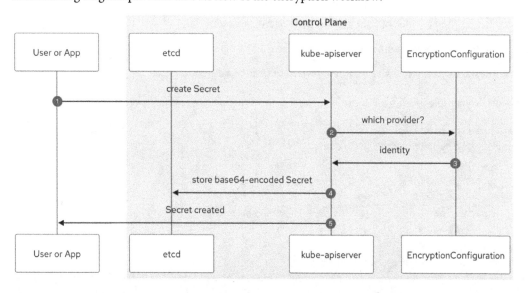

Figure 3.1 – Kubernetes workflow for the KMS identity provider

The diagram flow can be read as follows:

1. A user creates a `Secret` object.

2. `kube-apiserver` checks the `EncryptionConfiguration` provider list.

3. The provider refers to `identity`.

4. `kube-apiserver` stores the base64-encoded `Secret` in etcd.

This provider doesn't encrypt any of the `Secret` data field payload and is the default Kubernetes behavior at installation time. It can also be used to replace any encrypted Secrets with the following providers if needed.

aesgcm and aescbc

This provider uses the Golang AES encryption libraries to transform the data field payload of the listed resources to an encrypted one.

The provider leverages the **Advanced Encryption Standard** (**AES**) and offers two modes:

- CBC, considered weak but fast
- GCM, considered faster and less weak when key rotation is implemented

From an implementation perspective, we follow the same principles with both:

- Generate a 32-byte (or more) random encryption key encoded in base64
- Set up the provider of your choice, `aescbc` or `aesgcm`
- Reference the key within the `EncryptionConfiguration` configuration file
- Restart `kube-apiserver` if auto-reload is not enabled

This is fairly simple, both from a process and a `configuration.yaml` perspective:

```
apiVersion: apiserver.config.k8s.io/v1
kind: EncryptionConfiguration
resources:
  - resources:
      - secrets
    providers:
      - aesgcm:
          keys:
            - name: key-20230616
              secret: DlZbD9Vc9ADLjAxKBaWxoevlKdsMMIY68DxQZVabJM8=
      - identity: {}
```

The following diagram provides an overview of the encryption workflow when a new `Secret` object is being created:

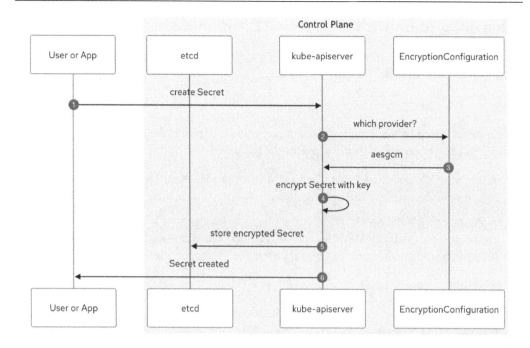

Figure 3.2 – Kubernetes workflow for the KMS aesgcm/aescbc provider

The diagram flow can be read as follows:

1. A user creates a `Secret` object.

2. `kube-apiserver` checks the `EncryptionConfiguration` provider list.

3. The provider refers to `aesgcm`.

4. `kube-apiserver` encrypts the data field payload with the provided key within the provider definition.

5. `kube-apiserver` stores the encrypted `Secret` object in etcd.

The `aesgcm` and `aescbc` providers are easy-to-implement solutions to encrypt the data field payload from the listed resources.

However, this simplicity comes with a trade-off; this solution leverages an encryption key that is again encoded in base64, referenced in a YAML manifest file, and stored on the local filesystem of each control plane node. With a system or a disk/filesystem breach, a malicious hacker can retrieve the encryption key and decrypt the payloads within the etcd data file.

Finally, these providers are subject to multiple vulnerabilities, ranging from padding oracle attacks to birthday attacks or the ability to *guess* encryption keys based on the number of times that keys have been used to write encrypted payloads, enhancing the need for a proper automated key rotation strategy.

Native encryption with an external component

The native encryption can be enabled by leveraging additional software, either on the control plane or externally to the Kubernetes cluster.

kms

The Kubernetes kms provider is a response to the security key exposure from the previous aescbc and aesgcm encryption providers by calling for the following:

- An external KMS, such as Azure Key Vault, HashiCorp Vault, or AWS Vault, to leverage the construct of the envelope encryption scheme.

- A plugin, called Kubernetes KMS provider plugin, to interconnect kube-apiserver with one or multiple external KMSs. This approach reduces the kube-apiserver development, integration, and maintenance that would be required to support every KMS vendor.

The KMS encryption is designed with an envelope encryption scheme using a two-key approach:

- A **data encryption key**, also known as a **DEK**, to encrypt the data field payloads from the listed resources. DEKs are generated locally by kube-apiserver and linked to the Kubernetes clusters.

- A **key encryption key**, also known as a **KEK**, to encrypt the DEK. A KEK is generated and hosted remotely on the KMS.

> **Important notes**
>
> While it is possible to have a single KEK hosted on a remote KMS to address multiple Kubernetes clusters, this is not recommended as it would become a single point of failure and security exposure if the remote KMS was compromised. It is advised to consider one dedicated KEK per Kubernetes cluster and potentially multiple remote KMSs.
>
> Thinking about the multi-tenancy requirement, it would make sense to even have a dedicated KEK per tenant, a feature that is currently not (yet) implemented at the time of writing.

At the time of writing, the Kubernetes project has introduced KMSv2, the latest implementation of the KMS provider for kube-apiserver.

While the high-level functional purpose is identical, the design and implementation are slightly different. These differences could be impacting your compliance and regulation needs:

- In KMSv1, each Secret object creation generates a dedicated DEK during the transaction with each DEK being encrypted with the KEK calling the KMS, which impacts the performance when operating a large Kubernetes cluster environment.

- In KMSv2, `kube-apiserver` generates a DEK at startup (or at the `EncryptionConfiguration` reload time), calls the KMS plugin to encrypt it using the remote KEK from the KMS server, caches the DEK, performs the encryption and decryption from memory, and will call the KMS for encryption only at restart or during key rotation. This redesign greatly improves the performance and resilience at a large scale.

The following diagram provides an overview of the encryption workflow for KMSv1:

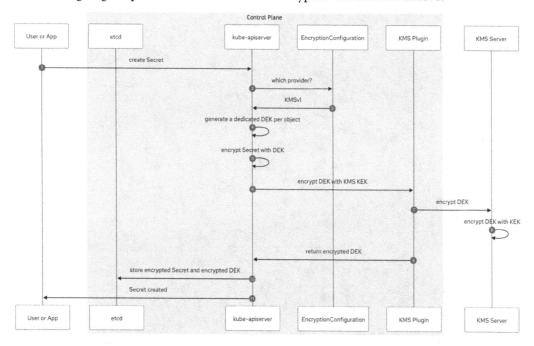

Figure 3.3 – Kubernetes workflow for the KMS plugin v1 provider

The diagram flow can be read as follows:

1. A user creates a `Secret` object.
2. `kube-apiserver` checks the `EncryptionConfiguration` provider list.
3. The provider refers to KMSv1.
4. `kube-apiserver` generates a DEK.
5. `kube-apiserver` encrypts the data field payload with the DEK.
6. `kube-apiserver` requests the DEK encryption to the KMS plugin.
7. The KMS plugin requests the KMS to encrypt the DEK with the KEK.

8. The KMS encrypts the DEK with the KEK.

9. The KMS plugin returns the encrypted DEK to `kube-apiserver`.

10. `kube-apiserver` stores the encrypted `Secret` and DEK in etcd.

The following diagram provides an overview of the encryption workflow for KMSv2:

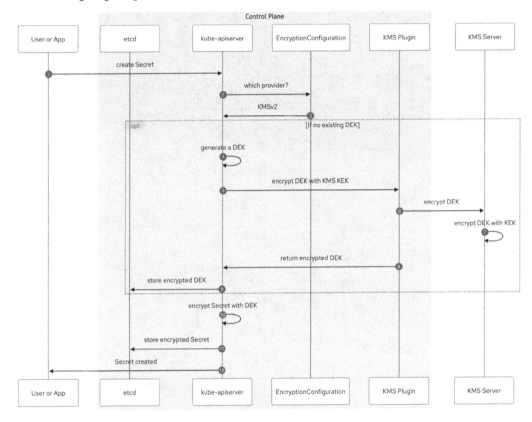

Figure 3.4 – Kubernetes workflow for the KMS plugin v2 provider

The diagram flow can be read as follows:

1. A user creates a `Secret` object.

2. `kube-apiserver` checks the `EncryptionConfiguration` provider list.

3. The provider refers to KMSv2.

4. If there is no existing DEK, `kube-apiserver` will generate one.

5. If a DEK was generated, `kube-apiserver` requests the DEK encryption to the KMS plugin.

6. The KMS plugin requests the KMS to encrypt the DEK with the KEK.

7. The KMS encrypts the DEK with the KEK.

8. The KMS plugin returns the encrypted DEK to `kube-apiserver`.

9. `kube-apiserver` stores the encrypted DEK in etcd.

10. `kube-apiserver` encrypts the data field payload with the DEK.

11. `kube-apiserver` stores the encrypted `Secret` in etcd.

The `kms` provider adds complexity in terms of configuration. This method complies with all regulations requiring external key management while addressing most if not all of our onion layers.

KMS provider plugin example

As described earlier, the `kms` provider requires an additional third-party software called a `kms` provider plugin to connect `kube-apiserver` with an external KMS, such as HashiCorp Vault or any other KMS supported by the plugin being used.

The plugin will be deployed on the control plane nodes as a local UNIX socket to interact directly with `kube-apiserver` without going through the network, which could be a potential security exposure.

A community project such as *Trousseau* (`https://trousseau.io`), among others, provides this capability to extend the `kube-apiserver` capabilities with HashiCorp Vault, Azure Key Vault, and AWS KMS.

Getting hands-on with key-value data

Within the Git repository, in the `ch03` folder, you will find a walkthrough to deploy a new Kind cluster using Podman or Docker, using a specific cluster configuration file to get a ready-to-use instance with the default `EncryptionConfiguration` configuration.

The how-to includes a quick intro to the Kind configuration file allowing us to enable specific flags for `kube-apiserver`, and explains how to mount a specific folder to the Pod with a configuration file. This will help you in the future to interact with other Kubernetes distributions leveraging the same principles.

From there, you will have a chance to implement each provider and create and replace `Secret` objects with their new revisions being encrypted with the provider in question. This approach will highlight the capability to move from one provider to another without a major operational burden.

Finally, the hands-on examples will help you to verify that each `Secret` object has been encrypted with the appropriate combination of provider, key, and version if applied by dumping the entries directly from the etcd data store.

Precedence

As previously mentioned, the provider list has a precedence evaluation or, in other words, a sequential order to consider during implementation:

1. When creating a new `Secret`, `kube-apiserver` will use the first provider listed to encrypt or not, if the provider is `identity`, the data field payload for the listed resources.

2. When reading an existing `Secret`, `kube-apiserver` will check the Secret header to define the KMS provider, its version, and the associated key:

    *   If there is a match, it will try to decrypt the `Secret` data field payload

    *   If there is no match, an error will be returned

3. All existing Secrets could be replaced with a newer revision by changing the provider list order. The most common example would be to introduce a new KMS provider, such as `aesgcm`, and replace all unencrypted Secrets with a newer revision that will be encrypted with the `aesgcm` provider. This particular case is illustrated within the hands-on example.

This implementation example of a `kms` provider showcases the usage of an external KMS service. Note that the `kms v1` provider is deprecated with version 1.28 of Kubernetes in favor of a more resilient `kms v2` that's capable of sustaining network partitioning.

Going further with securing etcd

The previous section described the native encryption capabilities provided by Kubernetes at the application layer or, in other words, how to secure sensitive data from `Secret` and `ConfigMap` objects being processed by the Kubernetes API server.

Depending on the deployment type, whether on-premises or in the cloud, other layers can benefit from encryption to avoid or reduce security exposures:

*   When self-deploying on-premises or in the cloud using physical or virtual machines, the Kubernetes `EncryptionConfiguration` API object is stored as a file on disk; accessing this configuration file, as well as the etcd data file, will compromise all sensitive data recorded as part of the API objects in etcd.

*   When consuming a managed Kubernetes instance from a cloud provider, the control plane becomes their responsibility. However, not all services are equal and some require a thorough review of the configuration to ensure that the cloud provider you are selecting is handling the encryption at rest on its infrastructure level and allows you to enable the Kubernetes native encryption.

Considering the following onion diagram, we can list the illustrated components as potential exposure points to be addressed to mitigate unauthorized access to the data within etcd, including Secrets and ConfigMaps. This section provides you with an analysis of each component in terms of security risk and related mitigation(s):

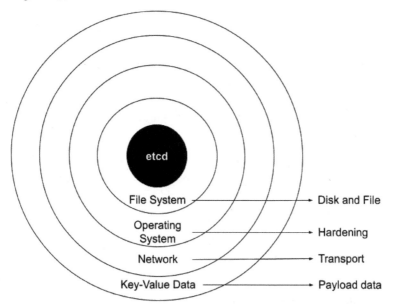

Figure 3.5 – The etcd security exposure presented as onion layers

Due to the numerous combinations of Linux and Kubernetes distributions, not to even mention the extensive cloud provider offerings, this chapter provides an extensive hands-on section on the key-value data while sharing guidance on all other components, for which the following references will help you with implementing a security and hardening profile for your systems:

- Tevault, Donald A. (2023). *Mastering Linux Security and Hardening: A Practical Guide to Protecting Your Linux System from Cyber Attacks* by *Packt Publishing.*

- Kalsi, Tajinder. (2018). *Practical Linux Security Cookbook: Secure Your Linux Environment from Modern-Day Attacks with Practical Recipes* by *Packt Publishing.*

It is also worth noting that cloud providers are doing most of the heavy lifting to encrypt at-rest disks and filesystems to mitigate related attack vectors. However, all of them advise leveraging the Kubernetes `EncryptionConfiguration` API server configuration for end-to-end encryption.

Linux system hardening

The art of operating system hardening is to reduce the access breach exploits to zero. From our context, it means no remote access via the operating system to the etcd data file.

It is important to appreciate the effort from Linux distributions to include the concept of security profiles, leveraging standards such as SCAP at the early stage of system installation, and helping with relevant and consistent hardening based on your organization's needs. A series of industry-specific profiles, such as CIS Benchmarking and NIST, are offered at the deployment time, helping to configure the operating system with the necessary rules to comply with the chosen regulation. These rules are explained when using the graphical user interface or can be found within the vendor documentation. No matter your preferred installation method – text, graphical, or kickstart – all can benefit from such hardening automation.

This approach helps to reduce the pressure on the Ops team. By automating the relevant 100+ specific configuration rules, complying with a regulatory profile such as PCI-DSS can easily be achieved without reading its 360 pages of requirements. This would complement the 190+ pages of the Red Hat Security Hardening reference guide.

Once the system has been deployed with the appropriate security policy relevant to your organization's industry, the OpenSCAP bench toolset can be used to scan your entire install base to provide you with the following:

- A tailor-fit audit per Linux distribution
- A shareable audit file including a risk-scoring system
- A mitigation strategy with the most common toolsets (Shell script, Puppet, Ansible, and so on)

See the following for reference:

- OpenSCAP: `https://www.open-scap.org/`
- OpenSCAP PCI-DSS rules: `http://static.open-scap.org/ssg-guides/ssg-rhel9-guide-pci-dss.html`
- Red Hat Enterprise Linux security hardening: `https://access.redhat.com/documentation/en-us/red_hat_enterprise_linux/9/html-single/security_hardening`

Hardening a Linux system includes tasks pre- and post-installation. To avoid redeploying your operating system, enable the appropriate security profile and disk encryption during the installation process. Most Linux distributions, such as the Red Hat Enterprise Linux 9, have a graphical user interface to set a specific security profile and provide you with a list of mandatory configuration changes to comply with the chosen profile.

The GitHub repository has two examples within the ch03 folder demonstrating the hardening of a Linux system using the installer graphical interface and a kickstart file.

Linux data encryption

Stealing a disk or a server is a serious concern, and it happens more often than we could believe. But it is not only for on-premises infrastructure; cloud virtual disks could be stolen too thanks to hypervisor exploits that could leak the disk file, which means all your business-critical systems have their credentials leaked too.

Since etcd does not offer any encryption capabilities (at the time of writing), the data file that will be stored on the control plane node filesystem can be accessed and easily read to recover our Secret object payload, as shown in *Chapter 1, Understanding Kubernetes Secrets Management*. This means that any physical deployment scenarios colocated on-premises and with edge computing would result in security exposures when an attacker steals the disk(s) or node(s).

To address this concern, the disk and filesystem will need to be encrypted. Why both, you ask? While a **full disk encryption** (**FDE**) might seem to be an easy solution to tick the box, a diverse range of attacks has been proven successful in accessing data both with and without stealing the entire system. Adding a filesystem encryption will reduce the chances of a data leak including Secret objects used to access your cloud, application, and storage accounts.

Disk encryption

FDE, sometimes referred to as **self-encrypting disk** (**SED**), is an interesting starting point to provide a fully offloaded encryption process from the host, reducing the attack surface. It is transparent to both the operating system and the applications (no drivers or libraries to maintain). FDE guarantees a high level of compatibility, supportability, and portability across different hardware and software combinations.

All FDE/SED disks are delivered with a zero-length authentication key/password to ease the initial setup, especially if there is no user requirement to do so. When defining an authentication key or password, the DEK is stored on the disk and protected with the defined custom user key.

The benefits of this workflow are as follows:

- Protection from physical theft of the disk(s)
- Protecting the data even before boot time
- Enabling re-key options for compelling events and compliance purposes

The pitfalls are the following:

- Booting requires user interaction to input the authentication key
- Losing the key means losing the data
- Hacking is still a possibility

Indeed, the effectiveness of these disks could be challenged, with different approaches demonstrating how to access and compromise the data on these disks provided by these two references:

- *Hardware-based Full Disk Encryption (In)Security* by Tilo Müller, Tobias Latzo, and Felix C. Freilling from System Security Group at Friedrich-Alexander Universität: `https://www.cs1.tf.fau.de/research/system-security-group/sed-insecurity/`

- Perform an internet search with the following terms: `NSA disk firmware hack`

Note that most professional-grade disks (mechanical or chip-based) offered in servers and storage arrays are delivered with such technology. This is the first hardware layer of protection to consider.

Filesystem encryption

When it comes to encrypting a Linux filesystem, multiple approaches could be considered, including both open source and proprietary options. For this section, we will have a look at three open source solutions, from easy to complex, from the perspective of requirements.

Plain device-mapper encryption

The usage of device-mapper encryption with `dm-crypt` is an obvious and simple choice as it performs a block-level encryption on an unpartitioned disk. This technique provides disk-level encryption that could be accessible with a so-called garbage random data introducing a deniable encryption method.

The benefits of using device-mapper encryption are as follows:

- Full disk encryption is provided

- No partition tables are exposed, nor are the UUID or LABEL

- It provides a robust solution in case of a disaster (in a LUKS setup, if the header is destroyed, the data is lost)

The pitfalls are the following:

- A high level of mastery of device mapping is required to ensure proper configurations

- A single passphrase with no key rotation is a potential issue with specific compliance/regulation requirements

- There is no key derivation function that would reduce the vulnerability to brute-force attacks when passphrases are generated with a lack of entropy

- There is no support for the TRIM command on solid-state drives

See the following for reference:

- Project: `https://www.kernel.org/doc/html/latest/admin-guide/device-mapper/dm-crypt.html`

- Implementation on Arch Linux: `https://wiki.archlinux.org/title/Dm-crypt`

Linux Unified Key Setup (LUKS)

LUKS can be considered as a universal disk encryption software with secure password management implemented in its core. This allows us to overcome some if not all of the pitfalls linked to key derivation, rotation, and multiple passphrase capabilities. Along with these, LUKS is compatible with the **logical volume management** (**LVM**) and software RAID scenario for interesting solutions that would address different needs and compliance/regulation requirements. Here are a few examples where LUKS can be integrated with other solutions:

- LUKS on a partition

- LVM on LUKS

- LUKS on LVM

- LUKS with software RAID

LUKS can also be complementary to other solutions to provide additional security responses. A plain device mapper and a headerless LUKS implementation would set up a deniable encrypted device (no header). This method would also address the key rotation requirement with capabilites for key derivation and multiple passphrases. This could be the best of both worlds, a solution that I would appreciate the most when no external KMS is required.

See the following for reference:

- Project: `https://gitlab.com/cryptsetup/cryptsetup/blob/master/README.md`

- Implementation on Red Hat Enterprise Linux: `https://access.redhat.com/documentation/en-us/red_hat_enterprise_linux/9/html/security_hardening/encrypting-block-devices-using-luks_security-hardening`

Device mapper with LVM and LUKS

As listed in the LUKS section, there are multiple combinations to implement disk encryption using LUKS. However, each setup comes with benefits and trade-offs, sometimes major ones, such as the following:

- LVM on LUKS would ease the partitioning and protect the volume layout when locked, but relies on a single encryption key with all volumes being encrypted

- LUKS on LVM provides flexibility to support un/encrypted volumes while being complex to maintain and less secure by exposing the volume layout

For both the device mapper and LUKS solutions, the usage of TRIM with solid-state drives could be a security exposure or a security response.

With a plain mode `dm-crypt`, if TRIM is enabled, it will eventually expose the encryption and could leak enough data from freed blocks to discover the encryption pattern. However, if there is no hard requirement for both data and deniable encryption, then it can be safely enabled as there will be a significant performance improvement.

With LUKS, the header is stored at the beginning of the device. If there is a passphrase rotation, the previous one will be revoked and TRIM will help to free the blocks. If not, then an attacker could research the device to get the old header and decrypt the disk.

For increased security with LUKS, the usage of a (virtual) **Trusted Platform Module** (**TPM**) can be leveraged to store and handle the automatic unlocking of the drives while booting. This removes the manual typing of the passphrase but could expose the key and thus the data if the server is stolen.

To avoid complexity, rely on the risk analysis approach to define the needs regarding your specific environment and how to comply with your regulations. Then, select a filesystem encryption method that addresses your requirements and the operational team's skills.

Network-bound disk encryption (NBDE)

Key management services, also called key escrow in this context, offload the encryption key to a remote service to avoid some of the pitfalls listed in the previous solutions. Keys are stored in a vault-like data store and thus require high availability and backup strategies to guarantee the availability and survival of the encryption keys. If not, the data on the disk will be lost forever. Note that backups also need to be secured to avoid any key leaks from side channels or opportunistic hacks.

The **network-bound disk encryption** (**NBDE**) solution solves these challenges by introducing a multilayering of security:

- It uses the HTTP/HTTPS protocol to ease the network configuration.
- A set of servers created with a predefined quorum to provide encryption/decryption capabilities. If the quorum is not met, the decryption will not happen until that instance is back online. This creates the notion of network dependencies, or the network on which the disk should be connected to access all NBDE servers before allowing the exposure of its content.
- Symmetric encryption keys being split across all the NBDE servers with an easy-to-(re) distribute public key.
- Reduce key management, no vault, and no high availability and backup necessary.
- Allow transparent reboot when all conditions are met.
- Protect against a disk or server and its disks being stolen, unless the entire NBDE setup is stolen.

This solution is not as hard as it sounds to implement. Such implementation can be put in place in no time while addressing the most rigid compliance and regulation requirements.

See the following for reference:

- Example of a project for a resilient KMS for NBDE: `https://github.com/latchset/tang`

- Example of an NBDE implementation on Red Hat Enterprise Linux: `https://access.redhat.com/documentation/en-us/red_hat_enterprise_linux/9/html/security_hardening/configuring-automated-unlocking-of-encrypted-volumes-using-policy-based-decryption_security-hardening`

- Example of NBDE with Tang server implementation on Red Hat OpenShift: `https://docs.openshift.com/container-platform/4.13/security/network_bound_disk_encryption/nbde-about-disk-encryption-technology.html`

Transport

The entire Kubernetes design is based on API-driven architecture. This means that any exchange of payloads needs to be done through a secure channel using Transport Layer Security (TLS). If not, exchanges with etcd will be readable from the wire, including sensitive data from the Secrets.

Most Kubernetes distributions have TLS enabled by default and provide Ops with TLS security profile options to guarantee compatibility between services and applications interacting with each other. In Red Hat OpenShift, a granular approach allows the Ops to configure a specific TLS security profile for the ingress, the kubelet, and the control plane components, the latter including etcd.

Note that the service endpoint could also be enforced with a TLS termination handled by external network equipment or software, such as a load balancer. While this approach would secure network flow from the end user accessing the API server with a fully qualified domain name, this will not protect the internal Kubernetes network flow if left without any TLS termination. Both should be considered to guarantee an improved security posture.

See the following for reference:

- etcd transport security model: `https://etcd.io/docs/v3.5/op-guide/security/`

- Red Hat OpenShift: `https://docs.openshift.com/container-platform/4.13/security/tls-security-profiles.html#tls-profiles-kubernetes-configuring_tls-security-profiles`

Summary

While security measures depend on the organization's compliance and regulation requirements, a risk-based assessment will define the appropriate actions to harden your information systems. However, securing Kubernetes Secrets is not optional but a must.

Given the current trend of adopting hybrid multi-cloud patterns, having one cluster's etcd compromised, whether it is on the cloud or self-managed, could lead to compromising the entire environment. These types of attack leverage in-cluster network connections or a fleet management tool for which the token would be recorded within the compromised etcd. Such a scenario would lead to a viral attack infecting every connected endpoint.

As a remediation, the native Kubernetes encryption – more specifically, the kms provider – is a best practice security pattern supported by all the major cloud and software providers.

Remember, security is not a finite game but a continuous effort. Regular audits and scans of your ever-changing environment will provide you with the most current state of compliance. They will also help to build a backlog of tasks to mitigate known vulnerabilities and misconfigurations.

In the next chapter, we will look at the debugging and troubleshooting techniques to analyze unexpected behaviors when configuring and consuming Kubernetes Secrets.

4

Debugging and Troubleshooting Kubernetes Secrets

So far, we have identified the attack vectors for Kubernetes Secrets. Two of them are encryption at rest and encryption in transit. Previously, in *Chapter 3, Encrypting Secrets the Kubernetes-Native Way*, encryption at rest helped us increase our security at rest and in transit. In this chapter, we will focus on debugging issues that we might have with Secrets. Secrets play a critical role in storing and providing sensitive information used by applications and services running in a Kubernetes environment. They are crucial to our applications, and understanding how to effectively troubleshoot Secret-related issues can save lots of time and effort.

In this chapter, we will expand on the following topics:

- Discussion of common issues with Kubernetes Secrets
- Debugging and troubleshooting Secrets
- Best practices for debugging and troubleshooting Secrets

By the end of the chapter, we will have acquired the knowledge needed to tackle secret-related challenges effectively. Also, we should be able to follow certain workarounds and avoid common pitfalls when troubleshooting Secret-related issues.

Technical requirements

To link concepts with practice, we will use a series of tools and platforms commonly used to interact with containers, Kubernetes, and Secrets management. For this chapter, we need the following tools:

- **Docker** (`https://docker.com`) or Podman (`https://podman.io`) as a container engine.

- **Golang** (`https://go.dev`), or Go, which is a programming language used within our examples. Note that Kubernetes and most of its third-party components are written in Go.

- **minikube** (`https://minikube.sigs.k8s.io/docs/`) allows us to run a single-node Kubernetes cluster on our personal computers, making it perfect for learning and development purposes.

- **Git** (`https://git-scm.com`) is a version control system that we will be using to recover the book examples but also leverage our discovery of Secrets management solutions.

- **Helm** (`https://helm.sh`) is a package manager for Kubernetes that we will be using to simplify the deployment and management of Kubernetes resources.

- **GnuPG** (`https://gnupg.org/download/`) is a free open source implementation of OpenPGP. OpenPGP provides cryptographic privacy and authentication for data communication.

The following link gives you access to the digital materials used in this book:

- The GitHub repository: `https://github.com/PacktPublishing/Kubernetes-Secrets-Handbook`

Note that reference to Kubernetes distributions such as Azure Kubernetes Engine, Rancher Kubernetes Engine, and Red Hat OpenShift will be made but you don't need working instances of these to perform the hands-on exercises.

Discussion of common issues with Kubernetes Secrets

Throughout the previous chapters, we interacted with Kubernetes either through direct commands or by using YAML files. While applying those YAML specifications and applying the commands, some mistakes are very likely to occur along the way. An incorrect Secret name or YAML definition can introduce hours of troubleshooting to identify what caused the issue in the first place.

For these reasons, certain principles need to be followed:

- YAML files are structured and can create a source of truth

- Reusability of Secrets minimizes errors

- Automation removes human intervention, which is prone to error

Applying a Secret eagerly every time we want to use it through the command line makes it easy to introduce an error in the specification. By having the Secret defined through a YAML file, it is easy to check the structure through an editor and to ensure that we have the desired outcome. Also, a YAML file gives the flexibility to apply the same Secret multiple times. In case of an error, the same file can be fixed and applied.

The other principal is a Secret's reusability. The reusability can happen in multiple ways. The more you apply the creation of the same Secret each time, the more likely you will encounter an error. A Secret that can reside in a namespace can be used by various components.

Helm and Helm Secrets

When it comes to providing encryption and decryption capabilities for Secrets on Helm charts, we have the option of the Helm Secrets plugin. With Helm Secrets, we can encrypt sensitive data and the confidential information that resides on Kubernetes Secrets such as passwords, certificates, keys, and so on. There are various encryption options available when it comes to Helm Secrets. There are cloud KMS options such as AWS KMS and GCP KMS. There is also a non-vendor-based option, which is encryption through the gpg command-line tool, an implementation of the OpenPGP standard.

Creating a PGP key

One of the options to encrypt a file with Helm Secrets is to use a PGP key. PGP uses public key encryption; a public and private key pair are used. The public key is used to encrypt the data and the private key to decrypt the data. The public key can be distributed, whereas the private key should be kept secret. Information can be encrypted by anyone who has access to the public key; however, the decryption can happen only through the actor holding the encryption key.

If a PGP key is not available, we can generate one as follows:

```
$ gpg --generate-key
```

This command will generate the key with some default options, for example, expiration after one year and a default key size. By using the --full-generate-key function, there are more options during key creation.

A prompt will ask for a passphrase; ignore this prompt and leave it empty. If the passphrase is not left empty, it will be required at every step of decryption making operations difficult to automate.

We can list the keys and retrieve the key we already created:

```
$ gpg --list-keys
       00FFFE11421E1F1EED1EEE811E11E111D1111111
uid             [ultimate] test-key-2 <kubernetes@secrets.com>
sub    rsa3072 2023-08-27 [E] [expires: 2025-08-26]
```

Now that we have a key generated, we can proceed with encrypting Secrets.

Encrypting Secrets

Supposing we have this file with Helm values:

```
jwt-key:
  value: secret-key
```

Provided we already have a GPG key, Helm Secrets will use it in order to encrypt the sensitive values. We need to create a `.sops.yaml` file specifying the GPG key to be used:

```
creation_rules:
    - pgp: >-
         gpg-key
```

Then we can just encrypt the values:

```
helm secrets enc values.yaml
```

Eventually, our file should look like this:

```
jwt-key:
    value:    ENC[AES256_
GCM,data:9/OgmkCNm2DbEw==,iv:dbthtzx1t8KUHazh7v48T7ASep0rTbYJBrl/
jEw6zWE=,tag:MLVXlruHpkMxYihPvNieVQ==,type:str]
sops:
...
    pgp:
          enc: |
              -----BEGIN PGP MESSAGE-----
              -----END PGP MESSAGE-----
    version: 3.7.3
```

Helm and Helm Secrets are two of the many tools that can help us organize our Secrets in a structured format and keep them secured and encrypted on disk. Helm and Helm Secrets are examples of keeping Secrets in a YAML format and reusing them through templating.

To summarize, automation and proper Secret organization can not only give us productivity gains but also help a lot in removing the need for human intervention. Most of the time, when an error is introduced, it is highly likely to be caused by human intervention.

Secret application pitfalls

During the creation of Kubernetes Secrets, we might encounter errors, which can occur due to several reasons. An error may come from an invalid YAML syntax, invalid Secret type, missing data, or bad encoding. On the bright side, failing to apply a Secret properly gives us immediate feedback. A dry run can help us to validate our operations before executing them.

> **Important note**
>
> Take note that all the Kubernetes commands executed take effect on the default namespace unless specified otherwise or configured through the Kubernetes context. The following commands will take effect on the default namespace or the namespace that has been configured.

Dry run

Before applying a Kubernetes Secret, we can simulate the creation or update of the Secret by using the --dry-run option. By using --dry-run along with the kubectl commands, we do not actually perform any operation. It is a helpful feature for testing and validating our Secret configurations before applying them, thus saving time from troubleshooting.

For example, we want to create a Secret from literals:

```
$ kubectl create secret generic opaque-example-from-literals --from-
literal=literal1=text-for-literal-1 --dry-run=client
secret/opaque-example-from-literals created (dry run)
```

This output can confirm that our action will be successful. We can go one step further and produce a response in YAML:

```
$ kubectl create secret generic opaque-example-from-literals --from-
literal=literal1=text-for-literal-1 --dry-run=client -o yaml
secret/opaque-example-from-literals created (dry run)
apiVersion: v1
data:
   literal1: dGV4dC1mb3ItbGl0ZXJhbC0x
kind: Secret
metadata:
   creationTimestamp: null
   name: opaque-example-from-literals
```

The dry run can help us validate the operation without applying it, and we can validate the outcome of the operations without the operation taking any effect. Though the --dry-run option is extremely useful, it cannot be of help with Secrets that are successfully applied containing invalid data content. A common issue is the Base64 formatting of a Secret.

Base64

The Base64 format is used for representing Secret values. By default, when applying a Secret, if the value is in plain text, it will be encoded and stored in the Base64 format. Also, instead of supplying the value in plain text, we can submit a value already encoded in the Base64 format. This might cause an issue if the value that we want to submit is by its nature Base64-encoded.

Take, for example, an AES-256 key:

```
$ secretKey=$(openssl rand -hex 32)
$ echo "$secretKey"
80a3284da641ac728b5585fd913b0e60e9c4f61ffe2cfb6f456c16a312552e11
$ echo "$secretKey" |md5sum
6a59e95805ea05ff21a708038be9b130
echo "$secretKey"
```

The AES key printed is already encoded using Base64. Through Base64 encoding, binary data is represented in a format of printable ASCII characters. This makes it easier to pass in our codebase, for example, through environment variables. Also, we printed the MD5 hash of the Secret, and we will use the hash for troubleshooting purposes later.

Let us try now to create a Secret using the AES-256 key we created previously using the openssl command:

```
$ kubectl create secret generic aes-key --from-literal=key=$secretKey
-o yaml
apiVersion: v1
data:
  key: ODBhMzI4NGRhNjQxYWM3MjhiNTU4NWZkOTEzYjBlNjBlOWM0ZjYxZmZlMmNmY
jZmNDU2YzE2YTMxMjU1MmUxMQ==
kind: Secret
metadata:
..
type: Opaque
```

As we can see, the Secret has been encoded. If we try to mount the Secret in a Pod, it will contain the right value:

```
apiVersion: v1
kind: Pod
...
      command: ["/bin/sh","-c"]
      args: ["echo $(key) | md5sum"]
      envFrom:
        - secretRef:
            name: aes-key
```

We applied it, so let's check the logs:

```
$ kubectl logs print-env-pod
6a59e95805ea05ff21a708038be9b130  -
```

The checksums match. As you see, we preferred to use an MD5 hash over just printing the variable. Printing variables in a live environment might lead to a data leak.

We will try the same through a YAML file, but we shall not encode the key:

```
apiVersion: v1
kind: Secret
metadata:
  name: aes-key
type: Opaque
data:
  key:
80a3284da641ac728b5585fd913b0e60e9c4f61ffe2cfb6f456c16a312552e11
```

Once we try to use the key through an environment variable on a Pod, we face an issue:

```
$ kubectl apply -f base_64_example.yaml
$ kubectl logs -f print-env-pod
fc7d115eb58e428c53b346659e7604d6
```

The MD5 hash is different. This is because the key was passed to the Pod in binary format. Kubernetes identified that the Secret is in the Base64 format; therefore, by creating the Pod, it decoded the AES key and placed the binary as an environment variable. This can create confusion and hours of debugging.

Specific Secret types

Kubernetes provides us with specific Secret types. This might give us the impression that before applying a Secret, certain checks take place concerning the format of the Secrets. This behavior might vary based on the type of Secret.

TLS Secret

When we apply TLS Secrets, Kubernetes will not perform any checks with regard to the content of the Secrets. For example, we will try to create a TLS Secret using invalid certificates:

```
apiVersion: v1
kind: Secret
metadata:
  name: ingress-tls
type: kubernetes.io/tls
data:
  tls.crt: aW52YWxpZC1zZWNyZXQ=
  tls.key: aW52YWxpZC1zZWNyZXQ=
```

We might think that there would be a check when applying the Secret; however, this will not happen. The Secret will be created and eventually, it will cause issues once a resource tries to mount and use it.

Basic auth Secrets

Basic auth Secrets fall in the same category as TLS Secrets. There are no validation checks when basic auth Secrets are being applied:

```
apiVersion: v1
kind: Secret
metadata:
  name: basic-auth-secret
type: kubernetes.io/basic-auth
stringData:
  no-username: a-user
  password: a-password
  another-key: some-value
```

The Secret is applied, although it is obviously wrong. A `basic-auth` Secret should have a username and a password; however, we added variables of different names.

docker config Secret

In the case of docker config Secrets, Kubernetes will perform validation and issue an error in the case of an invalid Kubernetes configuration. We will try to apply a Secret containing an invalid Docker configuration:

```
apiVersion: v1
kind: Secret
metadata:
  name: docker-credentials
type: kubernetes.io/dockercfg
data:
  .dockercfg: |
    UkVQTEFFDRV9XSVRIX0JBU0U2NA==
```

When we run the following command, the file will not be applied. The docker config we provided is the wrong one:

```
kubectl apply -f docker-credentials.yaml
The Secret "docker-credentials" is invalid: data[.dockercfg]: Invalid
value: "<secret contents redacted>": invalid character 'R' looking for
beginning of value
```

The errors we get when applying a Secret can vary. Sometimes, we might even create an erroneous Secret without receiving any feedback.

So far, we have identified issues we could face during the application of the Secrets and how we could use dry runs to our advantage. We have also identified cases where the Secret application is correct but the content of the actual Secret is incorrect. Last, but not least, we have had an overview of the types of Secrets that Kubernetes may or may not apply any validations to. This brings us to the next section on troubleshooting Secrets.

Debugging and troubleshooting Secrets

Debugging Kubernetes Secrets is hard. This is largely because issues with Secrets materialize mainly when another component dependent on them is failing. For example, imagine an ingress deployment with bad certificates. Identifying the actual issue will be a process of inspecting multiple components until you find the root cause. In this section, we will learn tools and approaches for troubleshooting common Secret issues such as non-existent Secrets, badly configured Secrets, and more.

The describe command

So far, `kubectl get` has been our main command to retrieve information about Kubernetes resources. As a command, it can provide a quick way to retrieve information on the resources of interest and their status. The `kubectl get` function can serve us only to a certain level, however. Once more information is needed, we should utilize the `kubectl describe` command. By using the `kubectl describe` command, we can retrieve detailed information for Kubernetes resources.

Supposing we have an Nginx deployment Pod in our Kubernetes cluster, we will describe the deployment as follows:

```
$ kubectl describe deployment.apps/nginx-deployment
Name:               nginx-deployment
Namespace:          default
CreationTimestamp:      Wed, 28 Jun 2023 23:53:22 +0100
...
Pod Template:
  Labels:  app=nginx
  Annotations:      test-annotation: nginx
  Containers:
   nginx:
...
    Mounts:        <none>
  Volumes:         <none>
Conditions:
  Type           Status  Reason
  ----           ------  ------
  Available      True    MinimumReplicasAvailable
  Progressing    True    NewReplicaSetAvailable
OldReplicaSets:  <none>
NewReplicaSet:   nginx-deployment-544dc8b7c4 (1/1 replicas created)
Events:          <none>
```

The `kubectl describe` command provides us with all the information needed for the resource of interest. As we can see, it can list events, labels, annotations, and even properties that apply only to the resource examined.

Non-existing Secrets

We will utilize the `describe` command for a deployment that tries to use a Secret that does not exist. Our example will try to mount a Secret volume that is non-existent:

```
apiVersion: apps/v1
kind: Deployment
metadata:
  name: nginx
spec:
...
    spec:
      containers:
        - name: nginx
          image: nginx
          volumeMounts:
            - name: users-volume
              mountPath: /users.json
      volumes:
        - name: users-volume
          secret:
            secretName: user-file
```

Since we specified a deployment, we will not be confronted with an error immediately. Our deployment will get into a continuous `ContainerCreating` state until the Secret is available.

In this case, by using the `describe` command, we shall get the information that would assist us in identifying the problem:

```
kubectl describe pod nginx-5d66b7fbc-7cb7g
...
  Warning  FailedMount  36s (x9 over
2m44s)  kubelet                  MountVolume.SetUp failed for volume "users-
volume" : secret "user-file" not found
```

Thanks to the `describe` command, we can see that the Secret is not available.

The feedback from badly mounted volumes is not immediately visible. This is not the case when Secrets are mapped to environment variables.

Take, for example, an Nginx Pod acquiring its environment variables through a Secret that does not exist:

```
apiVersion: v1
kind: Pod
metadata:
  name: nginx-pod
spec:
  containers:
    - name: nginx
      image: nginx
      envFrom:
        - secretRef:
            name: does-not-exist
  restartPolicy: Always
```

Let us apply the configuration. After some seconds, we will see that the Pod is not able to start:

```
$ kubectl get po
NAME        READY STATUS                      RESTARTS    AGE
nginx-pod 0/1    CreateContainerConfigError   0           3s
```

We shall use the `describe` command to dig deeper:

```
$ kubectl describe pod nginx-pod
Warning   Failed 3s (x8 over 87s) kubelet Error: secret "does-not-
exist" not found
Normal    Pulled 3s               kubelet Successfully pulled image
"nginx" in 968.341209ms
```

As expected, the Pod is not able to start since the Secret is missing. This is something that we detected because of the `describe` command.

Badly configured Secrets

Badly configured Secrets are the reason you could spend hours on debugging. They can expand to multiple components in an application being affected and lead to extensive troubleshooting.

A complex scenario can be an ingress with invalid SSL certificates. We previously created an SSL certificate Secret containing invalid certificates. We will create an ingress that will use those SSL certificates and try to identify the issue.

The Secrets we shall apply are as follows:

```
apiVersion: v1
kind: Secret
metadata:
  name: ingress-tls
type: kubernetes.io/tls
data:
  tls.crt: aW52YWxpZC1zZWNyZXQ=
  tls.key: aW52YWxpZC1zZWNyZXQ=
```

The ingress is as follows:

```
apiVersion: networking.k8s.io/v1
kind: Ingress
metadata:
  name: nginx-ingress
  annotations:
    nginx.ingress.kubernetes.io/ssl-redirect: "true"
    nginx.ingress.kubernetes.io/rewrite-target: /
spec:
  tls:
    - hosts:
        - bad-ssl
      secretName: ingress-tls
  rules:
    - host: bad-ssl
      http:
        paths:
          - path: /
            pathType: Prefix
            backend:
              service:
                name: nginx-service
                port:
                  number: 80
```

At some point, the ingress will be operational. We can check this using the `kubectl get ing` command:

```
$ kubectl get ing
NAME             CLASS    HOSTS     ADDRESS         PORTS      AGE
nginx-ingress    nginx    bad-ssl   192.168.49.2    80, 443    2m36s
```

Eventually, by reaching the ingress through the browser, we will see a certificate that has been generated by Kubernetes. If we don't provide a certificate by ourselves or we provide a bad certificate configuration, Kubernetes will generate a certificate on its own.

The first step would be to check the Kubernetes events:

```
$ kubectl get events
...
11m           Normal    Pulled                 pod/
webpage                                Container image "nginx:stable"
already present on machine
```

Also, based on our previous work, we can see the events just for the ingress:

```
$ kubectl describe ing
...
Events:
  Type     Reason   Age                 From               Message
  ----     ------   ----                ----               -------
  Normal   Sync     35s (x2 over 37s)   nginx-ingress-
controller   Scheduled for sync
```

Eventually, we will have to identify the problem by checking the controller logs:

```
kubectl logs -f ingress-nginx-controller-755dfbfc65-vf7v6 -n ingress-
nginx
...
W0701 10:18:30.928989        7 backend_ssl.go:45] Error obtaining
X.509 certificate: unexpected error creating SSL Cert: no valid PEM
formatted block found
...
W0701 10:18:35.203316        7 controller.go:1348] Unexpected error
validating SSL certificate "default/ingress-tls" for server "bad-ssl":
x509: certificate is not valid for any names, but wanted to match
bad-ssl
```

The logs will lead us to the badly configured certificate. This is where our focus will be.

Troubleshooting and observability solutions

Our troubleshooting has so far involved the usage of kubectl, which is not always feasible. Depending on the organization, there can be various observability solutions integrated with a Kubernetes installation. For example, Datadog is a popular observability solution. In the case of a cloud-based Kubernetes offering, the observability tools offered by a cloud provider are integrated with the Kubernetes offering. That means tools such as CloudWatch and Google Cloud Monitoring can help us to identify the incidents without the usage of kubectl. We will see more on this topic in *Chapter 8, Exploring Cloud Secret Store on AWS, Chapter 9, Exploring Cloud Secret Store on Azure,* and *Chapter 10, Exploring Cloud Secret Store on GCP.*

We saw certain scenarios of badly configured Secrets. In order to identify the cause, we followed a process and used tools such as describe, and we checked the logs of Kubernetes.

Best practices for debugging and troubleshooting Secrets

When a Secret is wrong, it can affect us in ways that are not immediately visible. A top-down approach can be used where we start by checking the actual application that is affected. Eventually, we will reach a point where the logs will point to the misconfigured Secret. Once we reach the Secret, we should identify whether the Secret has been applied correctly or whether it is a wrong Secret.

We could make a checklist when evaluating the Secret:

1. Ensure the existence of the Secret.
2. Check the value of the Secret.
3. Decode the Secret and see whether it is the desired one.
4. Use MD5 hashing.
5. Avoid downloading Secrets locally.

The next thing to check is whether the application of the Secret is wrong. Imagine a scenario where a Secret is mounted on a Pod of a deployment incorrectly. There is the option to continuously try to change the deployment and eventually figure out along the way what is wrong. However, this might not give the best results. It is very easy to continuously apply trial and error until you figure out what is not working, but this will consume time and also make it difficult to distinguish what is happening.

There are many things that can go wrong in an application. This translates to noise that makes it difficult to identify the problem. Ruling out that the Secrets are not the problem brings us closer to a resolution. Secrets are already a complex concept.

A way to rule out that the Secret usage is wrong can be by using a simple Docker container and mounting the Secrets there. A simpler container is less complex and minimizes what can go wrong:

1. Mount the Secrets as environment variables to a Pod.
2. Mount the Secrets as a file to a Pod.
3. Use the hash algorithm of your choice to make sure they are the expected Secret.

By following this approach, the possibility of any Kubernetes issues being caused by the Secrets are minimized.

Avoiding leaking Secrets

It is essential to avoid leaking any Secrets when troubleshooting. When you have an issue with a Secret, it is very tempting to open a terminal session to a Kubernetes Pod and run troubleshooting commands. The logs generated in a container are written to the standard output (`stdout`) and standard error (`stderr`) streams. Kubernetes is integrated with many popular logging solutions such as AWS CloudWatch, Datadog, and Google Cloud Monitoring. By printing Secrets on a Pod, those Secrets are written to those streams and will end up in one of the integrated logging solutions. A logging solution can be widely accessible in an organization – more accessible than direct Secret access on a Kubernetes cluster. The outcome of this action is a data leak, and as soon as this happens, the Secrets have to be revoked causing extra overhead.

Another best practice is to avoid downloading the Secrets locally when troubleshooting. Downloading the Secrets locally could lead to a violation of the information security policies that an organization has established.

Summary

In this chapter, we went further into the details of debugging Kubernetes Secrets and focused on troubleshooting and debugging common issues faced with Secrets within our Kubernetes clusters. We learned how essential it is to keep Secrets organized and follow best practices, and how human error can introduce hours of troubleshooting. We also went through the process of identifying issues with Secrets and tools that we could use to get to the root of the problem. In the next chapter, we will focus on security and compliance when it comes to Kubernetes Secrets.

Part 2: Advanced Topics – Kubernetes Secrets in a Production Environment

In this part, you will explore more advanced topics related to Kubernetes Secrets, including security and compliance considerations, risk mitigation strategies, and disaster recovery and backup plans. Toward the end, you will learn more about mitigating security risks and how to establish a disaster recovery plan and backup strategies for Kubernetes Secrets.

This part has the following chapters:

- *Chapter 5, Security, Auditing, and Compliance*
- *Chapter 6, Disaster Recovery and Backups*
- *Chapter 7, Challenges and Risks in Managing Secrets*

5

Security, Auditing, and Compliance

In the previous chapters, we established the foundations from a design, implementation, and operational perspective to address the challenges of Kubernetes Secrets management. We also highlighted key areas of concern by peeling each layer of our full-stack infrastructure onion while considering paths to reduce or even mitigate security exposures. However, no matter how much effort we put into motion, the following questions will always float around:

- How can our IT environments be secured enough?
- What are the best practices from a control and audit perspective?
- What are my **Chief Information Security Officer (CISO)** requirements?

This chapter kicks off the advanced topics of this handbook with a reversed approach based on the last question, "*What are my CISO team requirements?*" The answer is usually in the form of another question, such as "*What are the regulations that my organization has to comply with?*", which implies a legal perspective.

In this chapter, we will expand on the following topics:

- Understanding cybersecurity versus cyber risk management
- The most common compliance standards
- Best practices for controlling, auditing, and mitigating security risks

By the end of this chapter, you will know how to address the security concerns at the people, process, and technology levels through a simple reusable blueprint.

Technical requirements

To complete the hands-on parts of this chapter, we will be leveraging a series of tools and platforms that are commonly used to interact with containers, Kubernetes, and Secrets management. For this chapter, we will be continuing with the same set of tools:

- **Docker** (`https://docker.com`) or Podman (`https://podman.io`) as a container engine. Both are ok, although I do have a personal preference for Podman as it offers benefits such as being daemonless for easy installation, rootless for added security, fully OCI compliant, Kubernetes ready, and the ability to integrate with `systemd` at the user level to autostart containers/Pods.

- **Podman Desktop** (`https://podman-desktop.io`) is open source software that provides a graphical user interface for building, starting, and debugging containers, running local Kubernetes instances, easing the migration from containers to Pods, and even connecting with remote platforms such as Red Hat OpenShift, Azure Kubernetes Engine, and more.

- **Git** (`https://git-scm.com`) is a version control system that we will be using to cover this book's examples but also leverage in our discovery of Secrets management solutions.

- **Kube-bench** (`https://github.com/aquasecurity/kube-bench`) is a community tool that can measure your Kubernetes cluster against the CIS Benchmarks.

- **Compliance Operator** (`https://github.com/ComplianceAsCode/compliance-operator`) is a community tool that measures and remediates security controls on the Kubernetes cluster.

- **HashiCorp Vault** (`https://www.vaultproject.io/community`) is a community Vault with an Enterprise offering for storing credentials, tokens, and more safely.

- **Trousseau** (`https://trousseau.io`) is a KMS provider plugin that leverages external KMSs such as HashiCorp Vault, Azure Key Vault, and their AWS equivalents.

This book's GitHub repository contains the digital material linked to this book: `https://github.com/PacktPublishing/Kubernetes-Secrets-Handbook`.

Cybersecurity versus cyber risk

While (cyber)security and cyber risk have more than enough publications, they are often mistaken to be the same thing.

The purpose of this section is to help you reflect on reshaping the traditional understanding of *doing* security from an IT-centric perspective to *practicing* security while having a holistic understanding of the organization's needs and requirements. This will help you perform a dynamic risk management assessment for appropriate security measure implementation.

Cybersecurity

Most organizations assign the security domain to their respective IT departments by designating a set of limited individuals almost working in isolation. Doing so introduces three limitations to their cybersecurity mission:

- A limited scope only related to the infrastructure stack with no or limited consideration to critical business applications
- Limited knowledge of the organization's business continuity plan
- The operations team has limited capabilities to respond appropriately to a security incident

This model has a twofold approach:

- Incident-driven or reactive
- Lock everything down to address the reduced capabilities to monitor and discover security breaches

Since security is seen as a constraint by all IT staff, from developers to operations of all domains, drastic changes will be made either on an internal incident basis or when there is a public reference within the same industry.

Some argue that they have monitoring and processes in place that help identify and drive incidents to resolution. They also agree that there is a lack of fire drills to train their IT staff, a similar situation to the **Disaster Recovery Plan (DRP)**.

In our fast-paced digital economy, this cybersecurity model does not respond appropriately to our three questions:

- How can our IT environments be secured enough?
- What are the best practices from a control and audit perspective?
- What are my CISO's requirements?

A typical example of ensuring security within this model would be implementing a strong login credential policy, including a 30-day password update with additional multi-factor authentication with limited integration with the organization's resources. This solution might fit an engineering team working on development but not the business team, who mainly uses web-based solutions that time out within a short period.

Cyber risk

A different approach must be considered here: risk management from a business angle to address the governance and compliance requirements of each organization department. This will help prioritize the design and implementation of security measures while acquiring the appropriate skills at the organizational level. This approach demands an understanding of the organization's mechanics, from finance to post-sales support, to prevent technical experts under/over-investing in security tools that are inefficient for the different business units.

Like a DRP, cyber risk management is about defining the minimal set of requirements to enable the organization to achieve its business goals, even in the case of a cyber-attack. When building such governance, not only must we answer the three aforementioned questions but also get the board to ask each executive the following:

- **CEO**: What would be the brand damage of a security breach?
- **CFO**: What would be the financial impact of a security breach?
- **CISO**: Are we prioritizing our investment to improve our security posture?
- **COO**: Would our customers/partners trust doing business with our organization?

While cybersecurity is seen as a cost, cyber risk management provides the reporting capabilities to show the business value of security investments and associated posture with a near-real-time response.

A typical example of security within this model would be implementing a strong login credential policy using a one-time password method. This solution offers sufficient security for the organization's employees who are using web-based solutions. An additional multi-factor authentication with security auditing could be implemented when an employee wants to have access or push changes to the application source code.

Compared to the cybersecurity approach, the cyber risk assessment addresses different risk levels with corresponding measures from a security, compliance, and usability perspective and additional measures when interacting with critical assets.

Conclusion

Doing (cyber)security for the sake of ticking a box will not provide any benefit to the organization and will frustrate all members of staff, including the IT department, resulting in security measures being disabled and shadow infrastructure being built.

Governance brings vision, mission, and execution in terms of how to operate within the digital economy regarding cyber-attacks. Adding a risk management framework will organically introduce the *security* part within your DevOps practice. At this point, we can embrace a model that will allow us to identify, protect, detect, respond to, and recover from security breaches while considering the necessary level of effort per risk to the organization.

As a follow-up to this topic, the following references provide more details about the frameworks that aid in this area:

- National Institute of Standards and Technology (2018), *Framework for Improving Critical Infrastructure Cybersecurity*. Self-Publishing.

- European Union Agency for Cybersecurity (2023), *Good Practices for Supply Chain Cybersecurity*. Self-Publishing.

- Brown, J. (2023), *Executive's Cybersecurity Program Handbook*, Packt Publishing.

Compliance standards

The concept of compliance is about how an organization will operate respectfully while considering a set of laws and policies that are specific to its industry, headquarters location, and the countries it may do business with to ensure privacy and security. Compliance requirements will dictate most of the requirements of an organization's governance.

Any business might have to comply with more than one regulation, depending on their activities. A good example would be a US-based software company leveraging **artificial intelligence (AI)** within the healthcare sector, with **Software-as-a-Service (SaaS)** and on-premises offerings for medical practice across the globe. This implies the following legal compliance:

- The United States **Health Insurance Portability and Accountability Act (HIPAA)**, for handling patient records

- The **European Union General Data Protection Regulation (GDPR)**, a European Union regulation for collecting, processing, and storing personal user data from third parties

- The **Payment Card Industry Data Security Standard (PCI-DSS)**, an international industry standard when transacting payment cards

- Additional legal compliance, such as the European Union AI Act, which regulates the use of AI, the Cyber Resilience Act, which addresses the secure software supply chain, the Data Act, which supports the portability of data across cloud providers, and the **Network Information System 2 (NIS2)** directive, which ensures security and incident management best practices for critical infrastructure

- Do not (in)directly (re)sell a solution with any sanctioned country listed by, and not limited to, the United States Department of Commerce

Navigating the overall compliance obligations could be overwhelming. However, most regulations have overlapping security control rules that can be leveraged for a simplified or even unified approach. This is why the **Center for Internet Security (CIS)** created a comprehensive benchmark per digital platform (operating system, mobile device, server software, cloud, virtualization, container, and so on).

The CIS Benchmarks help any organization's IT department measure its current security posture from a security control perspective and related technical configurations, including exploit and mitigation details. These controls map with the most common regulatory frameworks, such as HIPAA, PCI DSS, SWIFT, ISO 27000, SOC 2, and NIST. Here is a mapping example of the CIS Benchmarks with NIST 800-53: `https://www.cisecurity.org/insights/white-papers/cis-controls-v8-mapping-to-nist-800-53-rev-5`.

From a Kubernetes perspective of the CIS Benchmarks (`https://www.cisecurity.org/benchmark/kubernetes`), which is version 1.7.0 at the time of writing, here is an overview of the controls to be considered to secure Secrets:

- **Rule 1.2.29**: Ensure that the `--encryption-provider-config` argument is set as appropriate:

  - This control description is about encrypting the `etcd` key-value store by using the remediation that we explored in *Chapter 3, Encrypting Secrets the Kubernetes-Native Way*, in the *Key value data* section

  - The benchmark also includes an audit by checking if `kube-apiserver` is running with the `--encryption-provider-config` flag

- **Rule 1.2.30**: Ensure that encryption providers are configured appropriately:

  - This control description is about making sure that the encryption provider set up for rule 1.2.29 is currently set using `aescbc`, `aesgcm`, or `kms`

  - The benchmark also includes an audit that checks the configuration content from the file referenced by the `--encryption-provider-config` flag

- **Rule 3.2.2**: Ensure that the audit policy covers key security concerns:

  - This control description is about making sure that an audit policy is in place to confirm appropriate implementation for rules 1.2.29 and 1.2.30.

  - The benchmark also includes an audit overview of the required configuration to track access to, modify, and use `Secret`, `ConfigMap`, and `TokenReview` via `Pod` and `Service`

- **Rule 5.4.1**: Prefer using Secrets as files over Secrets as environment variables:

  - This control description is about avoiding injecting `Secret` as a `Pod` environment variable due to its potential exposures within the node's memory and application logs

  - The benchmark also includes an audit overview to help you perform a search about environment variables related to Secrets within the logs

- **Rule 5.4.2**: Consider external secret storage:

  - This control description is about leveraging an external vault solution from a third party instead of the embedded `etcd` key-value store, a subject that will be explored in *Chapter 11, Exploring External Secret Stores*

  - The benchmark also includes an audit overview to help you review appropriate Secrets management implementation with this third-party solution

Note that some regulations might include physical security controls, such as data center and physical server access, which are not covered within the CIS Benchmarks. However, from our onion perspective and its security analysis in *Chapter 3, Encrypting Secrets the Kubernetes-Native Way*, these controls are relevant.

It is time to update our onion diagram so that it includes new layers representing the continuous effort to ensure compliance with regulatory obligations and standards that are described within the organization's governance:

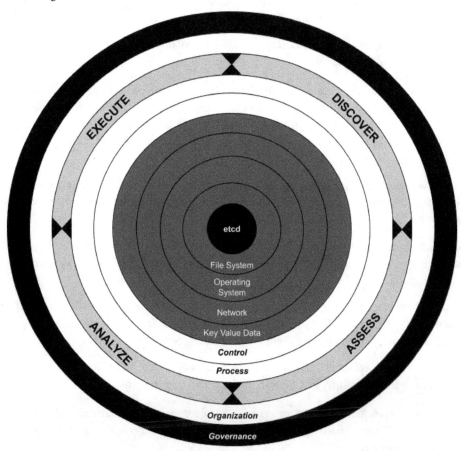

Figure 5.1 – The security posture framework for Kubernetes Secrets management

Considering the organization's governance and this cyber risk assessment model, these additional layers provide continuous discovery, assessment, analysis, and (mitigation) execution so that we can define and improve the current security and compliance posture.

Adopting a DevSecOps mindset

In the previous sections, we drafted a series of best practices that could be summarized with the following key points:

- Consider the organization's governance, which includes the regulatory frameworks they must comply with

- Adopt a cyber risk management mindset to customize the security controls to be implemented that are appropriate to each business unit instead of a rigid one-size-fits-all cybersecurity policy

- Consider security as a continuous improvement effort of discovering, analyzing, and reporting during all operational activities

We've used the term *security posture* a couple of times in this handbook. Let's define what it is while utilizing the NIST 800-37 specifications: "*The security status of an enterprise's networks, information, and systems based on information assurance resources (for example, people, hardware, software, and policies) and capabilities in place to manage the defense of the enterprise and to react as the situation changes. This is synonymous with security status.*"

Once you have established your current security posture against a framework such as the CIS Benchmarks for Kubernetes, then it will be easier to identify the gaps and continuously improve your posture with the current and future missing controls.

Embracing this approach introduces a change of mindset, which helps with continuously reviewing the organization's security posture and highlighting the gaps to mitigate. This is also referred to as DevSecOps practices.

At this stage, a DevSecOps adoption will organically infuse the governance and compliance requirements within the entire DevOps cycle. This will shorten the feedback loop for the relevant teams to work on mitigation, and thus improve compliance, security response, and posture before deploying to production.

Do not consider the DevSecOps practices as a separate framework; instead, see them as complementary to the DevOps model. All security practices are tied together within each step:

- **Planning**: This includes security, governance, and compliance requirements within the initial project scope. The pitfall would be to consider these requirements as the last validation before releasing the application.

- **Development**: This infuses security into the organization's coding governance to help mitigate common exposures. It includes code analysis tooling to help identify vulnerabilities before the code is committed.

- **CI/CD**: This involves performing security testing to scan code and container images for vulnerabilities. This helps with detecting and remediating these exposures before they make their way into production.

- **Continuous monitoring/auditing**: This helps with detecting and responding in near real-time to security exposures. This can also help with risk-based approaches, where some security exposures might be considered acceptable to carry on with but should be closely monitored.

Adding security within the DevOps flow will encourage all teams to collaborate and promote a culture of shared responsibility and accountability toward high-quality and secure software delivery by catching security exposures earlier in the development process.

Tools

From our Kubernetes perspective and based on its dedicated CIS Benchmarks, the Secrets management part will require us to do the following:

- Enable encryption capabilities for the `etcd` service
- Define and enforce resource access policies for sensitive data payloads such as `Secret` but also `ConfigMap` objects
- Consider an external Secrets management solution to enhance the platform's security posture
- Audit all interactions that are done with these objects within and outside of the platform

To do so, you'll require a set of tools that help you discover, analyze, and mitigate potential security exposures. We will explore five tools:

- **Trivy, from Aqua Sec**: This will help you not only scan container image vulnerabilities but also secret-related security exposures.
- **kube-bench**: For assessing the CIS Benchmarks.
- **Compliance Operator**: For assessing supported OpenSCAP profiles and providing mitigating paths.
- **StackRox**: For assessing supported security profiles for your clusters, container images, and networking flows. StackRox has a comprehensive user interface with a useful risk-based dashboard that ranks exposures by risk level.
- **Kubernetes logging**: For harvesting all information and audit trails related to the interaction between the platform, the applications, and users.

Let's have a look at the capabilities of these tools while illustrating their usage. All these tools help you comply with regulations and initiate the DevSecOps model while continuously improving your security posture.

Trivy

Due to the immutable nature of container images, it is important to continuously track vulnerabilities with a scanner such as Trivy. This tool also has a particular interest in Secrets management as it can target specific security severity related to Secrets.

Using the Trivy Kubernetes CLI, a scanning process can be triggered specifically for Secrets via the following command:

```
trivy k8s –severity-checks=secret –report=summary cluster
```

See the `chapter 5` folder in this book's GitHub repository for an example of how to implement Trivy on a local `kind` Kubernetes cluster.

kube-bench

Your IT department might have already invested in a security suite for your entire organization's infrastructure, but let's consider surgical tools versus generic ones.

When it comes to measuring your environment against the CIS Benchmarks, `kube-bench` from Aqua Security Software might be one of the most interesting tools to run on your Kubernetes cluster(s). The benchmark job can be configured using a standard YAML manifest; you can customize it so that it's relevant to your organization's governance.

Here is an example of a check:

```yaml
---
controls:
id: 1
text: "Master Node Security Configuration"
type: "master"
groups:
- id: 1.1
  text: API Server
  checks:
    - id: 1.1.1
      text: "Ensure that the --allow-privileged argument is set
(Scored)"
      audit: "ps -ef | grep kube-apiserver | grep -v grep"
      tests:
      bin_op: or
      test_items:
      - flag: "--allow-privileged"
        set: true
      - flag: "--some-other-flag"
        set: false
      remediation: "Edit the /etc/kubernetes/config file on the master
node and
      set the KUBE_ALLOW_PRIV parameter to '--allow-
privileged=false'"
      scored: true
```

This control example assesses if privileged containers – that is, containers bypassing any limitations from the `cgroup` controller – can elevate to the user root within the container, which also means the root on the operating system.

This example shows how to disable a control by introducing the `skip` definition:

```
---
controls:
id: 1
text: "Master Node Security Configuration"
type: "master"
groups:
- id: 1.1
  text: API Server
  checks:
    - id: 1.1.1
      text: "Ensure that the --allow-privileged argument is set
(Scored)"
      Type: "skip"
      scored: true
```

See the `chapter 5` folder in this book's GitHub repository for an example of how to implement `kube-bench` on a local `kind` Kubernetes cluster.

Compliance Operator

Another way to utilize the capabilities of `kube-bench` on a Red Hat OpenShift Container Platform and Kubernetes distributions that support operators would be **Compliance Operator**. This tool runs compliance checks against the CIS Benchmarks and other **Security Content Automation Protocol (SCAP)** profiles, such as the **Australian Cyber Security Centre's (ACSC's)** Essential Eight.

This tool not only assesses security exposures but also provides remediation capabilities. Like scanning, each mitigation has a YAML definition and can be applied one at a time or in batches, which allows for granular testing and validation phases. This can also be done on existing clusters for late implementations.

> **Important notes**
> Both `kube-bench` and Compliance Operator require specific elevated privileges to run that might not fit a production environment. A good practice would be to run these scans and remediations on a test environment that reflects your production environment before retrofitting the security rules on a production environment.

StackRox

The open source StackRox project is designed to address security challenges linked to the increased usage of containerized applications orchestrated by Kubernetes. Its fast adoption creates a growing space for security exposures, which requires a platform to offer a series of comprehensive capabilities so that it can do the following:

- Manage the vulnerabilities of container images with a remediation path. This reduces the known security exposures at runtime.

- Secure the container runtime by monitoring the application patterns and detect any potential signs of malicious processes, also called mutations. Responses can be informative or isolated from the workload.

- Secure the networking flows by providing a graphical view of how containers in the same and different namespaces could communicate and provide mitigation paths with network policies to limit lateral movements from malicious workloads.

- Audit and comply by scanning against the top industry and regulatory standards, helping organizations to baseline, improve, and maintain their security posture.

- Integrate with development pipelines by leveraging an API-driven approach, thereby enabling continuous security checks as early as possible within the development process.

Available as an open source project and integrated within the OpenShift Container Platform from Red Hat, StackRox plays a significant role in comprehensive platforms to ease the security part of the DevSecOps workflow.

See the `chapter 5` folder in this book's GitHub repository for an example of how to implement StackRox on a `kind` Kubernetes cluster.

Kubernetes logging

While this is a must from a compliance and best practices perspective, the diverse landscape of solutions available to accomplish these tasks is overwhelming. As such, we will address this using the `Audit` object definition from the Kubernetes standard API.

Kubernetes comes with an easy way to provide security-relevant records within its audit logs by enabling the relevant resources to be monitored. Here is an example of the `Secret` and `ConfigMap` objects:

```
apiVersion: audit.k8s.io/v1

kind: Policy
rules:
  - level: Metadata
    resources:

    - group: ""
      resources: ["secrets", "configmaps"]
```

Save the preceding code into a file called `auditlog-secrets.yaml` and apply this configuration against your cluster using `kubectl apply -f auditlog-secrets.yaml`.

Summary

While security and compliance can be overwhelming and considered to be constraining, this chapter drafted guidance for an organization to adopt a DevSecOps mindset with the support of standard and integrated tools.

It is important to acknowledge that the concept of security and compliance is not a finite state, with no single and simple recipe to protect your organization from digital threats. (Cyber)security will be welcomed by the entire organization when it's tailored to the business using a risk assessment approach, removing the feeling of constraints linked to operating in a so-called secured environment. When designed well, all stakeholders will organically participate in the continuous efforts of assessing, analyzing, executing, and discovering new policies, vulnerabilities, and potential ongoing attacks.

In the next chapter, we will address the business continuity aspect by introducing and implementing the disaster recovery and backup strategies of Kubernetes Secrets.

Disaster Recovery and Backups

In this chapter, we delve into the world of disaster recovery and backups for Kubernetes Secrets. The importance of robust backup and recovery strategies cannot be overstated, especially given the sensitive nature of Secrets and the demands of data integrity and availability. By the end of this chapter, you'll understand the critical importance of disaster recovery and backups in Secrets management, considering service availability, potential security implications, and stringent regulatory requirements. Moreover, you'll be equipped to formulate a disaster recovery plan that aligns with your organization's infrastructure and strategy, enhancing your capability to counteract potential disasters and challenges.

In this chapter, we will cover the following topics:

- Why disaster recovery and backups matter

- Backup strategies

- Security in backups

- Designing a disaster recovery plan

By the end of this chapter, you'll possess a deep understanding of the best practices, strategies, and tools available to back up your Kubernetes Secrets against disasters. These insights will position you to ensure the security, availability, and resilience of your Secrets, establishing a foundation for a more secure and efficient Kubernetes environment.

Technical requirements

In this chapter, we will delve into backup and recovery strategies for Kubernetes Secrets, a critical element of resilient applications. To fully understand and execute the concepts discussed, we'll be working with a set of industry-standard tools. These tools represent a common tech stack used in real-world scenarios, and understanding how to utilize them for Secrets management will enhance your ability to design a robust, secure Secrets system.

Here are the tools we'll need:

- **minikube** (`https://minikube.sigs.k8s.io/docs/`): This tool allows us to run a single-node Kubernetes cluster on our personal computers, making it perfect for learning and development purposes

- **HashiCorp Vault** (`https://www.vaultproject.io/`): We will use Vault, a secure external Secrets management system, to demonstrate how to back up and restore Secrets

- **Helm** (`https://helm.sh/`): Helm is a package manager for Kubernetes that we'll use for deploying applications and services

Introduction to Secrets disaster recovery and backups

The Kubernetes ecosystem offers various possibilities for managing sensitive data and credential info, commonly known as *Secrets*. In this dynamic and complex environment, the concept of disaster recovery and backups has become extremely critical. When speaking of backups, it could mean multiple things, depending on the architecture of the Secrets management.

One approach to Secrets management in Kubernetes is using Kubernetes' built-in *key-value store*. All the cluster data, including Secrets, are stored in etcd. If a disaster occurs, a backup of etcd can help restore the entire cluster state, including the Secrets. However, the restoration process in this case could be complex and might have limitations, especially when considering the sensitive nature of Secrets.

Another approach is to use a centralized Secrets management system, such as *Hashicorp Vault*, which can interface with Kubernetes. In such systems, Secrets aren't stored in etcd but in the central store that is secured and managed by the respective tool. In this case, the backup strategy would involve backing up the central store instead of etcd. This approach provides more granular control over Secrets and often includes sophisticated features for disaster recovery.

Regardless of the approach chosen for Secrets management, the essence of backups remains the same – a way to restore the Kubernetes system to a functioning state in case of a disaster. Backups should be comprehensive, regularly updated, and securely stored to ensure they serve their purpose when required.

Importance of disaster recovery and backups for Secrets management

Secrets are often considered tier-0 services in any environment. This denotes their utmost importance, as Secrets such as API keys, passwords, tokens, certificates, and so on act as the linchpin for service interactions and secure communications within a Kubernetes cluster. If they get lost or compromised, the impact can be significant and wide-ranging.

Service availability

Firstly, user applications running on the Kubernetes platform are highly dependent on these Secrets for their operation. They require Secrets to connect to databases, authenticate against internal or external services, interface with third-party APIs, and so on. If Secrets management systems were to suffer a failure or Secrets were lost, these applications may not be able to function properly. This could lead to a complete halt of operations until the Secrets are restored, thereby causing significant business disruption. Without a disaster recovery plan specifically tailored for Secrets, the restoration process might take longer than acceptable, leading to extended outages. In certain cases, this delay can result in significant business and financial impacts.

> **Note**
>
> The external secret store for Kubernetes may still create Kubernetes native secret resources and can be consumed by applications. In that case, the secret store failure should not directly impact service availability in a short period of time.

Recreation challenges

Without suitable backups, Secrets can be permanently lost in a catastrophic event, such as a system crash or a disaster. Recreating Secrets can often be a challenging process. In many cases, these Secrets can't simply be regenerated without going through additional complex procedures. For instance, Secrets obtained from third-party vendors usually require undergoing certain formalities and security checks before they are reissued. Some Secrets may be based on specific hardware or timed information and can't be recreated easily. This emphasizes the necessity of having a reliable backup in place, enabling quick restoration of Secrets in case of loss.

Security implications

Furthermore, a robust backup and disaster recovery strategy is critical from a security perspective. In the unfortunate event of a security breach where Secrets are compromised, it is paramount to have the ability to revert and dynamically update Secrets or rotate them based on a short **time to live** (TTL) to a secure state using a trusted backup. This can minimize the exposure window and potential damage caused by the misuse of compromised Secrets.

Regulatory requirements

Lastly, in many industries, the ability to recover critical systems (which would include Secrets management) is not just good practice but a regulatory requirement. Non-compliance can lead to heavy fines, not to mention the reputational damage that can result from a serious outage or data loss.

Practical case studies – the importance of backup Secrets

Inadequate secret backup strategies can cause security risks and vulnerabilities. Not managing Secrets properly can give rise to both availability and security disruptions. To understand the importance of backing up, let's delve into some practical case studies.

Case study 1 – a service disruption due to a lack of proper backups

Imagine a fast-growing e-commerce company that relies heavily on Kubernetes for managing its application deployments. It faces a significant system failure that crashes its Kubernetes clusters. While it manages to restore most of its services from backups, it realizes that the secret stored in Kubernetes (such as API keys for payment gateways and database credentials) were not backed up separately.

As a result, the e-commerce platform goes offline, resulting in thousands of transactions being halted. It takes several days for the company to regenerate Secrets, reconfigure them, and get the platform back online. In the meantime, it suffers significant financial losses due to lost sales and a decline in customer trust.

Case study 2 – a security breach due to inadequate backup security

In another scenario, consider a global tech SaaS company that used a centralized Secrets management system integrated with its Kubernetes clusters. It had a robust backup strategy in place, but the backups themselves were not encrypted or secured adequately.

In 2022, a group of cybercriminals managed to breach its backup store and gain access to the unencrypted Secrets. The hackers used these Secrets to perform unauthorized actions, from data theft to injecting malicious code into the company's services. The incident led to a massive security breach, damaging the company's reputation and causing significant financial harm.

Even though the company had a backup strategy in place, the lack of access control, and the non-existing encryption and security measures for the backups themselves, resulted in a severe incident. This highlights the need for proper security measures in not just managing Secrets but also backing them up.

In a Kubernetes environment, backup and disaster recovery strategies are integral components of Secrets management. By quickly restoring lost or inaccessible Secrets from backups, applications can resume operations with minimal disruption in the event of a system failure or disaster. Also, security is enhanced: in case of security breaches, the system can revert to a secure state using a trusted backup, minimizing potential damage. A robust backup and disaster recovery strategy mitigates risks and ensures the availability, integrity, and confidentiality of Secrets, playing a vital role in sustaining overall system operations.

We shall proceed to the next section and get to know more about backup strategies for Kubernetes Secrets.

Backup strategies for Kubernetes Secrets

Within Kubernetes, Secrets management involves dealing with highly sensitive data such as API tokens, certificates, keys, and more. Despite the relatively small volume of such data – a large transportation company might only manage less than a gigabyte of Secrets data – the sensitivity and value of this data are substantial.

Owing to the critical importance of Secrets, it's crucial to have robust backup strategies that minimize the possibility of data loss during backup processes. It's worth noting, however, that achieving zero data loss can be challenging, and mitigating strategies should aim to reduce data loss to the barest minimum.

An important distinction to make is that backups should not be conflated with audit logs. While backup strategies focus on preserving the value of the data itself, audit logs are geared toward tracking who accessed what data and providing a chronological record of events for accountability and traceability. In this section, we explore various backup strategies and highlight their advantages and potential challenges.

Geo-replication/cross-region replication

Geo-replication ensures that data is available across different geographical locations. There are two primary modes to consider:

- **Active-active replication**: In this model, data is written simultaneously to multiple regions. It offers high availability and is suited for applications with a global user base. It ensures fast data recovery and minimal data loss during a disaster.

- **Active-DR (disaster recovery) replication**: Here, one region is primarily active while the other is a standby DR region. In case of a failure in the active region, the DR region is activated. This strategy is more cost-effective than active-active replication, but might result in slightly higher data loss depending on the synchronization frequency.

Geo-replication in Secrets management systems comes with several advantages, such as geographic redundancy, which offers protection against region-specific disasters, and improved accessibility, allowing users to access data from the nearest region, thereby improving latency. However, despite its benefits, geo-replication also presents challenges. Managing data across multiple regions can introduce complexity, and the cost of replicating data, especially in the active-active model, can be significant.

Point-in-time snapshots to immutable storage

This strategy involves taking snapshots of Secrets at specific intervals and storing them in an immutable storage system. This method offers flexibility in terms of the type of backup:

- **Full backup**: This captures the entirety of the dataset each time a backup is made. While it's the most comprehensive approach, it can be resource-intensive and costly if done frequently, as it backs up every single piece of data every time.

- **Incremental backup**: Unlike a full backup, an incremental approach only backs up the data that has changed since the previous backup. This means that if users were to restore from an incremental backup, users need the most recent full backup and all subsequent incremental backups. It's more storage-efficient than a full backup when regularly backing up, but the restore process can be more intricate.

- **Differential backup**: This method backs up all changes made since the previous full backup, regardless of any incremental backups that might have been made in the interim. It strikes a balance between the previous two methods. Restoring is simpler than with incremental backups since users only need the most recent full backup and the latest differential backup. However, the amount of data stored can grow larger than incremental backups over time.

Point-in-time snapshots in data management come with notable advantages, such as data integrity, where immutable storage ensures that once data is written, it cannot be altered, offering protection against malicious attacks or accidental deletions. Additionally, they allow for the restoration of data from any previous point in time. However, adopting a point-in-time approach also presents challenges. The granularity of this method means the recovery point is limited to the latest snapshot, which may result in some data loss. Moreover, maintaining multiple snapshots over time can significantly increase storage costs.

Writing to multiple places during transit

Before the secret data reaches its final storage destination, it's first encrypted and written to an event stream (such as Kafka or a Pub/Sub system). This data is then batch-persisted into immutable storage. Adopting a real-time event streaming approach to Secrets management offers distinct advantages, such as redundancy, where multiple copies of data ensure high availability, and event-driven backup, which guarantees that all changes to Secrets are instantly backed up. However, this approach also brings its own set of challenges. Managing real-time event streams and batch processes can be complex, and there's a potential for data duplication, which can lead to increased storage costs due to storing data in multiple locations.

Secrets versioning and backup considerations

Secrets versioning is a unique challenge in data management, especially considering the sensitive nature of Secrets and the frequency with which they might change. Here are some considerations and strategies surrounding the versioning of Secrets during backups:

- **The value of versioning**:

  - **Audit and compliance**: Keeping multiple versions of Secrets allows for better auditing and compliance. It provides an immutable history of changes that can be invaluable in tracking unauthorized modifications or understanding changes.

  - **Rollbacks**: In the event of a misconfiguration or an error in a new secret value, having previous versions allows for quick rollbacks.

- **Backup of all versions**: By implementing a comprehensive backup strategy that includes all versions of a secret, users can ensure a complete historical record. This approach is particularly valuable in environments where maintaining a detailed audit trail is essential for compliance purposes. The primary drawback of this method is the increased storage overhead. However, considering that Secrets are usually small in size, this additional storage requirement might be negligible for most.

- **Backup of only the latest version**: Adopting a storage-efficient approach minimizes storage requirements and simplifies the backup process, but it also comes with the risk of potential loss of history. If only the latest version of data is backed up, all previous versions and the associated change history would be lost in the event of a data loss incident. This compromise might be acceptable in environments where historical data isn't deemed crucial.

- **Hybrid approach**: Selective versioning allows users to tailor their backup strategy depending on the importance of a secret, opting to keep multiple versions of some Secrets while maintaining only the latest version of others. Additionally, implementing retention policies can further refine this process, where older versions are either archived or deleted after a set period or upon reaching a specific version count.

- **Metadata and annotations**: These are used to track information related to Secrets, serving purposes such as tracking, auditing, and usage analysis. During backups, whether users are archiving the most recent or only selective versions, it's advantageous to back up the associated metadata and annotations. These backups provide essential context and additional data during the recovery process. Metadata and annotations can offer valuable context and insights for tracking, auditing, and analysis, and should be included in backups for effective recovery.

In summary, managing secret versions efficiently balances audit compliance and storage concerns. Strategies range from comprehensive backups of all versions for detailed records to selective or efficient approaches for specific needs, always considering the inclusion of metadata for effective recovery.

Choosing a backup strategy

Designing a robust backup strategy for Kubernetes Secrets is essential. An effective strategy protects Secrets in the face of a disaster, helping to prevent service disruptions and potential security vulnerabilities. The choice of strategy primarily depends on where the Secrets are stored. This section will outline factors to consider when deciding on a backup strategy, divided into shared considerations and storage-specific factors:

- **Granularity of backup**: The ability to restore individual Secrets without affecting others can be crucial in certain situations.

- **Encryption**: It's vital to ensure that backup data is encrypted, which can prevent unauthorized access and potential data breaches.

- **Access control**: Implement strict access controls. Limit access to the backups to only those who absolutely need it, such as a specific admin group.

- **Regulatory compliance**: Some regulations, such as the **General Data Protection Regulation (GDPR)** or the **Health Insurance Portability and Accountability Act (HIPAA)**, may dictate specific backup procedures. It's crucial to be aware of and adhere to these regulations when designing a backup strategy.

- **Storage overhead**: Full backups use more storage but are comprehensive. Incremental/differential backups save on storage by capturing only changes but make restoration slightly complex.

- **Data retention**: Periodically prune older backups that are beyond regulatory or business needs to manage storage or use data compression and deduplication to reduce backup size.

- **Long-term storage costs**: Regular backups (for example, every 10 minutes) with long retention (for example, 13 months) accumulate significant storage. Adjust based on secret criticality and change frequency. It is worth periodically analyzing storage expenses and adjusting the backup strategy if the costs outweigh the benefits. For Secrets with multiple versions, periodically remove older, unnecessary versions. Use different storage tiers based on backup age and importance. Shift older backups to cost-effective storage. Choose storage solutions offering predictable costs to manage budgets effectively.

The approach that we take to back up Secrets is heavily influenced by the way we manage Secrets. Whether we store Secrets on etcd or in an external secret store, the solutions will differ significantly.

Secrets stored in etcd

By default, Secrets on Kubernetes are stored on etcd, but the approach to backups will be more Kubernetes-oriented:

- **Kubernetes cluster backup**: When Secrets are stored in etcd, backing up the entire Kubernetes cluster will encompass all Secrets. Tools such as *Velero* can back up and restore the entire cluster, including Secrets.

- **etcd snapshot**: Periodic snapshots of etcd are another option, although this requires more technical expertise and caution, given its potential effects on the entire Kubernetes cluster.

For secret stored in etcd, there are two backup methods: full cluster backups and etcd snapshots, each with unique technical aspects and impacts.

Secrets stored in external secret stores

Many external Secrets management solutions, such as HashiCorp Vault or AWS Secrets Manager, have their own backup capabilities. Understanding these features and integrating them into the strategy is important. If the secret store is a cloud service, using backup services from the same provider may provide better integration and support.

Security guidance for backup

Once we have decided on a backup strategy, it is essential to comply with certain guidelines that ensure the security of our backups:

- **Isolated environment with access control**: To prevent unauthorized access, restrict access to the backup environment. Restricting access can be achieved with the following:

  - **IP whitelisting**: Only allow specific IPs to access the backup storage, especially if it's external.

  - **User access control**: Differentiate between general users and admins. Use roles and permissions to grant differential access.

  - **Access through a VPN**: Access to the resources that contain the backups should be permitted for individuals who are on the same network.

  - **Zero trust model**: Implement a zero trust security model where no user or device is trusted by default, whether inside or outside the network.

- **At rest encryption with rotatable encryption keys**: Encrypt backups when stored. Always use modern encryption standards. Regularly rotate the encryption keys and ensure users have a secure key management process.

- **In-transit security**: Secure the backups when they're being transferred. Employ protocols such as HTTPS or TLS to encrypt data during transit. Use VPNs or dedicated lines for secure connectivity.

- **Auditing and alert**: Implement monitoring of access patterns and set up alerts for unusual activities. Log all access and modification attempts. Set up immediate alerts for suspicious behaviors.

- **Immediate response to data breaches**: If backups are compromised, do the following:

  - Assess the impact

  - Rotate and change all keys and credentials to prevent decryption

- **Safeguard with immutable storage**: Ensure backup data remains unchanged by making it immutable. Use features such as AWS S3's Object Lock or WORM storage. Consider the balance between protection duration and storage costs.

Now that we have an understanding of the security guidelines with regard to secret backups, we shall proceed with the tools we can use to back up the Secrets that reside on a Kubernetes cluster.

Tools and solutions for backing up Kubernetes Secrets

Several tools and solutions exist to help users back up Secrets in a Kubernetes environment. The right one for users depends on the specific setup, requirements, and preferences. We will examine the tools that are available and how they can be combined with our infrastructure decisions.

Velero

Velero is a popular open source tool for managing disaster recovery and migrating Kubernetes cluster resources and persistent volumes. Velero allows users to back up and restore Kubernetes objects and persistent volumes.

Sample configuration for Velero backup is as follows:

```
apiVersion: velero.io/v1
kind: BackupStorageLocation
metadata:
  name: aws
  namespace: velero
spec:
  provider: aws
  objectStorage:
    bucket: myBucket
  config:
    region: us-west-2
```

For more details, please refer to the Velero documentation (https://velero.io/docs/v1.11/).

etcdctl

etcdctl is a command-line tool used with etcd, a distributed key-value store that provides a reliable way to store data across a cluster of machines. Kubernetes uses etcd to store all its data, including Secrets.

A sample etcdctl command for backup is as follows:

```
ETCDCTL_API=3 etcdctl snapshot save snapshot.db
```

Check the etcdctl documentation (https://github.com/etcd-io/etcd/tree/main/etcdctl#snapshot-subcommand) to learn more.

HashiCorp Vault

HashiCorp Vault is a product that provides control over access to sensitive data and Secrets across distributed applications. It includes a feature to snapshot its internal state for backup purposes.

For the open source version of Vault, users can leverage the Vault operator raft snapshot feature. Here is a sample command to create a snapshot of Vault's data:

```
vault operator raft snapshot save snapshot.hcl
```

However, this requires additional steps, such as integrating it into a sidecar deployment during the Vault deployment. Additionally, a mechanism for periodic uploading of data to a chosen storage location must be manually implemented.

For Vault Enterprise, the process is simplified as it includes a built-in feature for backups. Users can configure the backup destination to be, for example, AWS S3 GCS. After providing AWS credentials and setting up the interval (https://developer.hashicorp.com/vault/api-docs/system/storage/raftautosnapshots#interval), Vault Enterprise will automatically handle the data uploading process. Please refer to the configuration at https://developer.hashicorp.com/vault/api-docs/system/storage/raftautosnapshots#storage_type-aws-s3 for more details.

Despite this, monitoring of backup data metrics is still crucial. Alerts should be set up to trigger in case a backup fails. For more information, please refer to the HashiCorp Vault documentation (https://developer.hashicorp.com/vault/docs/commands/operator/raft#snapshot).

Following is a sample figure showing the backup sidecar container, which takes snapshots and uploads them to S3:

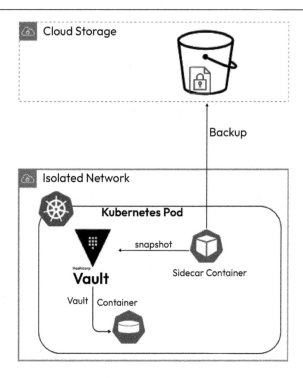

Figure 6.1 – Hashicorp Vault sidecar for backup

So, this section described the backup features of HashiCorp Vault; the open source version uses manual snapshots and data uploads, while Vault Enterprise automates these processes with features such as AWS S3 integration.

AWS Secrets Manager

AWS Secrets Manager is a Secrets management service that helps users protect access to applications, services, and IT resources. On March 3, 2021, AWS launched a new feature for AWS Secrets Manager that makes it possible for users to replicate Secrets across multiple AWS regions, which can automatically replicate a secret and access it from the recovery region to support a disaster recovery plan. For more details, see how to replicate Secrets across multiple AWS regions at `https://aws.amazon.com/blogs/security/how-to-replicate-secrets-aws-secrets-manager-multiple-regions/`.

Azure Key Vault

Azure Key Vault is a cloud service for securely storing and accessing Secrets. The `Backup-AzKeyVaultSecret` cmdlet backs up a specified secret in the Azure Key Vault by downloading it and storing it in a file. If there are multiple versions of the secret, all versions are included in the backup.

HashiCorp Vault, AWS Secrets Manager, and Azure Key Vault are forms of secret storage. Overall, they share the same qualities, which can be depicted in the following figure:

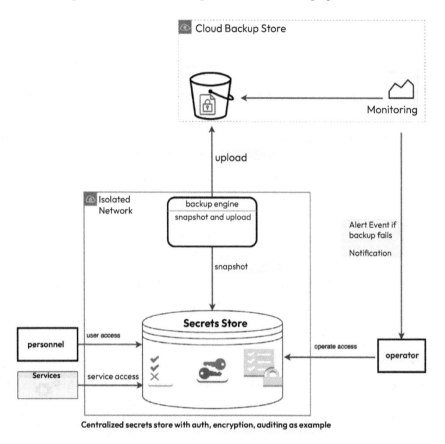

Figure 6.2 – Backup secret store

Each tool and solution has its own strengths and is suitable for different secret stores. Choose the one that fits your needs the best and always remember to consider security and compliance requirements when setting up these tools.

Next, we will talk about disaster recovery procedures for Kubernetes Secrets.

Disaster recovery for Kubernetes Secrets

A major consideration within Kubernetes Secrets management is the concept of *disaster recovery*. This involves preparing for and recovering from potential failures that may drastically affect a Kubernetes environment, particularly the Secrets it houses. In this chapter, we discuss **disaster recovery plans (DRPs)**, recovery procedures for Secrets, the associated tools, and solutions, and we examine a real-life disaster recovery scenario.

DRP in a Kubernetes environment

A DRP is a predefined and documented set of directives designed to guide organizations in recovering from potentially disastrous events. In the context of management, a well-designed DRP is instrumental in mitigating the effects of Secrets loss or exposure.

A sound DRP for a Kubernetes environment should incorporate the following elements:

- **Clear roles and responsibilities**: This involves the designation of a recovery team and an explicit detailing of what each member's roles and tasks are.

- **Defined communication strategy**: It's crucial to have a robust communication plan, covering both internal (recovery team) and external (stakeholders) communications.

- **Prepared incident response**: This includes a set of protocols for swift and effective response to minimize downtime and limit the extent of damage.

- **Recovery procedures**: These are scenario-specific steps designed to recover Secrets from various sources (e.g., etcd, external secret stores). Bear in mind that these procedures need to be tested frequently to confirm their effectiveness during actual disasters.

Additionally, due to the sensitive nature of these Secrets, their recovery should be limited to authorized personnel only, and their actions during the recovery should be auditable to maintain security and compliance standards.

Regular testing and updating

Managing Secrets in a Kubernetes environment, whether stored internally within etcd or externally, is a sensitive and crucial operation. Ensuring that backup and disaster recovery systems are functional, secure, and up-to-date is paramount. Regular testing and updating of these systems help to do the following:

- **Ensure system robustness**: Frequently test the backup and DRP systems through gamedays, which simulate real-world failure scenarios. This approach helps identify potential flaws or inefficiencies in Secrets recovery processes. The testing should encompass a range of scenarios, such as a total cluster failure for internally stored Secrets, catastrophic events at external storage locations, or the failure of the backup system itself. Gamedays provide a practical, hands-on way to assess and improve system resilience and response strategies.

- **Maintain up-to-date backups**: Secrets often change, so backup systems should be designed to update whenever there is a change to the Secrets. Regular testing can help ensure that the most recent version of Secrets is always backed up and can be restored correctly.

- **Security assurance**: Given the sensitive nature of Secrets, security is paramount. Regular penetration tests and audits should be conducted on both the Secrets storage and the backup system to uncover any potential vulnerabilities. Alerts should be set up to notify relevant personnel in case of security issues or system failures.

- **DRP relevance**: Kubernetes environments are dynamic, and changes can affect the effectiveness of existing DRPs. Regular reviews and updates of DRPs are necessary to keep them relevant to the evolving environment. As much as possible, automate the process of updating backups whenever there is a change in the Secrets.

- **Cross-team involvement**: Regularly involve relevant teams (DevOps, security, IT, etc.) in the testing and updating process to ensure a comprehensive review of systems.

Tools and solutions for disaster recovery in Kubernetes

There exist numerous tools for facilitating disaster recovery in Kubernetes. Notable mentions include Velero, Kubestr, and Kasten K10:

- **Velero**: Supports both backup and restoration operations and can handle etcd data, making it suitable for backing up Kubernetes Secrets

- **Kubestr**: Can validate the effectiveness of the backup and recovery strategy

- **Kasten K10**: Offers a comprehensive platform for managing Kubernetes application data, including backup and recovery

Onward, we shall see how all the pieces come together by examining a disaster recovery scenario.

Effective Secrets recovery scenario during a crisis

Let's look at a simplified example of an organization, *OrgX*, that successfully managed a disaster recovery scenario, specifically dealing with Kubernetes Secrets:

- **DRP**: OrgX had a DRP in place and periodically performed simulations, or "gamedays," to validate its efficacy. This practice prepared the team for actual disaster scenarios.

- **Team collaboration**: During the disaster, a cross-functional team activated the DRP. The collective efforts across different departments were key to the effective execution of the recovery plan.

- **Protecting Secrets**: As part of the recovery, the team retrieved the encrypted Secrets backups from an AWS S3 bucket. The decryption and restoration of Secrets were handled by authorized personnel using secure procedures. The Secrets were restored to a secret store, ensuring that the Secrets' integrity was maintained throughout the process.

- **Service continuity**: Quick action and adherence to the DRP enabled OrgX to restore its Kubernetes Secrets swiftly. This prompt response minimized service disruptions and ensured applications used the latest secret values.

The *OrgX* case highlights the importance of a DRP, team collaboration, security measures, and regular testing in recovering Kubernetes Secrets during a disaster.

Summary

In this chapter, we embarked on a deep exploration of disaster recovery and backup for Kubernetes Secrets. You have learned about various backup strategies, such as geo-replication, point-in-time snapshots, and writing to multiple places during transit, and how they can be applied in different scenarios. We discussed the importance of access control, encryption, and data retention in creating a robust backup strategy. We highlighted key security measures for backing up Kubernetes Secrets and how to respond swiftly and effectively to data breaches.

Through our practical examples and detailed discussions, you're now equipped with the knowledge to plan and execute a comprehensive DRP in a Kubernetes environment. You have also understood the importance of regular testing and updating of your DRP and backup systems.

As we venture into the next chapter, we'll address the challenges and security risks associated with managing Secrets in a Kubernetes environment. This will equip you with an understanding of potential pitfalls and arm you with strategies to overcome these challenges, further enhancing the security and reliability of your applications.

7

Challenges and Risks in Managing Secrets

Managing Secrets within a Kubernetes environment is a critical component of safeguarding sensitive information, such as API keys, passwords, and credentials. Effectively managing Secrets can help prevent unauthorized access to crucial information and ensure the proper functioning of services within a Kubernetes cluster. However, this task comes with its own set of challenges and potential security risks that need to be properly addressed. In this chapter, we will explore various challenges and risks associated with managing Secrets in Kubernetes and discuss mitigation strategies to enhance the security of your Secrets.

By the end of this chapter, you will have a comprehensive understanding of the challenges and risks associated with Secrets management in Kubernetes. More importantly, you will have learned practical strategies to mitigate these risks, enabling you to manage Secrets in a secure and efficient manner within your Kubernetes environment.

In this chapter, we're going to cover the following main topics:

- Understanding Kubernetes Secrets and their security risks

- Challenges and risks in different phases of Secrets management

- Mitigation strategies for security risks

This information will empower you to effectively navigate the complexities of Secrets management in Kubernetes, ensuring the confidentiality and integrity of sensitive data, and ultimately enhancing the overall security of you Kubernetes applications.

Technical requirements

To follow along with the content of this chapter and implement the strategies and practices discussed, you will need the following technologies and installations:

- **Kubernetes cluster**: You will need a working Kubernetes cluster to manage Secrets within the environment. You can use a managed Kubernetes service such as **Amazon Elastic Kubernetes Service (Amazon EKS)**, **Azure Kubernetes Service (AKS)**, or **Google Kubernetes Engine (GKE)** to set up a local cluster using minikube or Kind.

- **kubectl**: This is the Kubernetes command-line tool that allows you to interact with your Kubernetes cluster. It's essential for deploying and managing resources within your cluster.

- **Secrets management tools**: A basic understanding of how to manage Secrets using internal or external tools, or familiarity with tools such as HashiCorp Vault, CyberArk, AWS Secrets Manager, Azure Key Vault, and GCP Secret Manager is required. Additionally, it's expected that you will revisit this chapter for reference after reading *Chapters 8*, *9*, and *10*.

Grasping the complexities of Secrets management systems

Secrets management systems evolve from *simple tools to complex entities*, facing unique challenges and risks along the way. This journey encompasses a variety of phases:

- Setting up a Secrets management system

- Implementing granular access control

- Integrating with directory services

- Tackling cross-cutting concerns such as resilience, availability, and auditing

- Aligning with compliance and regulation

In the initial phase of a Secrets management system, the primary challenge is setting up a basic structure with secure storage and encryption. At this stage, access control is limited to exclusive administrative access, and the primary security risk involves the basics of secure storage and encryption. The challenge here is to establish a clear delineation of who has administrative access to Secrets.

As the system expands to accommodate users and service callers, the challenge becomes more nuanced. Implementing granular access control is essential; this must be done without creating security gaps. This phase also introduces authentication risks, especially in managing both human and machine or service authentication.

The next phase involves integration with various platforms such as **Active Directory**, **Lightweight Directory Access Protocol (LDAP)**, or **specific operators**. This introduces new challenges and risks. The integration challenge involves ensuring seamless integration without creating new vulnerabilities.

individuals as admins, causing the group to explosively grow in number. The next examples illustrate how this can occur:

- **Example of group growth**: An LDAP group that initially consisted of 10 individuals grew to 400 people, including various subgroups, losing its granularity and specificity
- **Example of admin group expansion**: External engineers are added as admins for temporary access but remain in the group, causing the admin group to grow exponentially

Risks and challenges

Indiscriminate expansion of access to Secrets carries escalating risks over time:

- **Loss of granular control**: The growth of groups from 10 to 400 people, as in the first example, leads to a loss of precise control over who has access to Secrets
- **Increased exposure to threats**: The addition of external engineers as permanent admins increases the risk of accidental disclosure or misuse of Secrets
- **Complexity in management**: Managing ballooning access rights becomes increasingly complex and time-consuming
- **Compliance issues**: The explosive growth in access may lead to violations of compliance regulations

Solutions to secret access ballooning

In order to manage the risk of ballooning secret access, several strategies can be employed. One effective measure is the implementation of strict group policies, such as preventing subgroups within admin groups, as this can help to maintain control over secret access. Furthermore, regularly scanning access rights and group memberships, perhaps every few weeks or months, can help identify any instances of ballooning access before they become problematic. In addition, the implementation of **role-based access control** (RBAC) ensures that users only have access to information necessary for their roles, which can further reduce the risk of ballooning access. And also, **just-in-time** (JIT) access is a security approach that restricts access to applications or systems to specific, needed times. Step-up authentication, on the other hand, mandates that users authenticate at a level equal to or higher than the policy protecting the resource demands.

Finally, tracking the growth of access as metrics, reflecting on any increases, and comparing these metrics to established standards can serve as early warning signs of ballooning access. This can enable organizations to take action before ballooning access becomes a security risk.

Secret valet parking

In modern technology environments, the concept of *secret valet parking* illustrates a common delegation model used in managing Secrets. Similar to entrusting your car's keys to a valet, Secrets are handed over to an integrated subsystem, which fetches the Secrets onto the host's filesystem for specific workloads or jobs.

For example, in the context of **continuous integration** (**CI**) systems, this might involve fetching all Secrets necessary for building, testing, and deploying code. While this approach simplifies workflows, it must be managed with care to ensure that Secrets are securely deleted once their purpose is fulfilled, akin to a valet returning car keys after parking a vehicle.

This delicate balance between convenience and security reflects the nuanced challenges of Secrets management and provides a vivid illustration of the trust, responsibility, and care required in handling critical assets such as Secrets.

Risks and challenges

Significant concerns and risks come along with the concept of secret valet parking:

- **Delegated identity issue**: Trusting a subsystem to manage Secrets correctly requires faith in that subsystem's ability to securely delete on-file Secrets when no longer needed. Failure to do so leaves Secrets exposed.
- **Lack of enforcement mechanisms**: Without proper checks, there is no guarantee that the integrated system will successfully delete Secrets post-usage, leading to potential unauthorized access.
- **Blast radius concerns**: If Secrets are fetched and stored for the entire host rather than only when needed, it can create a risk of widespread exposure if the host or a particular module is compromised.

Solutions to secret valet parking

To mitigate the risks associated with secret valet parking, several strategies can be employed. One effective approach is to implement dynamic Secrets, which are generated on demand and valid only for a short duration, and fetching Secrets only when required by specific workloads. After use, these Secrets are invalidated, thus minimizing the risk of unauthorized access and exposure.

A further approach is a *monitoring and verification system* that continuously observes and confirms the deletion of Secrets, ensuring compliance with expected secret handling protocols. Another approach involves *fetching Secrets* only when they are required by specific workloads. This minimizes the potential blast radius, reducing unnecessary exposure and the risk of unauthorized access. Lastly, *conducting regular reviews and audits* of Secrets management processes can ensure adherence to best practices and identify potential improvements in how Secrets are managed. By combining these strategies, organizations can reduce the risk associated with secret valet parking and improve their overall security posture.

Secret sprawl

When referring to *secret sprawl*, we are discussing the widespread distribution of Secrets across various parts of our infrastructure. These Secrets are scattered and located in numerous places, leading to significant challenges in both management and auditing for compliance. Typically, you might find a database username and password that has been hardcoded into an application's source code. It could also be present in plaintext within a configuration file, in configuration management, in version control, in a Dropbox account, or in a wiki. Essentially, these Secrets are dispersed throughout our infrastructure, existing in various locations.

Risks and challenges

Reading the preceding content is enough to start identifying things that can go wrong when Secrets are scattered throughout our infrastructure, including these aspects:

- **Lack of knowledge**: Secrets are everywhere, and tracking them becomes almost impossible

- **Limited access control**: Traditional systems don't maintain detailed logs or provide enough control over access, leading to security risks

- **Breach response**: In the event of a breach, finding the origin and dealing with it becomes complex, especially if Secrets are hardcoded in application sources

The solution to secret sprawl

The solution lies in *centralization*. By moving Secrets to a single location with tight controls, such as HashiCorp Vault and CyberArk, their management becomes more secure. Access can be restricted as needed, and audit logs provide detailed information, simplifying the response to breaches and the overall life cycle of credential management.

Secret island

A *secret island* refers to a tool or platform equipped with built-in components for managing Secrets, access control, audit, compliance, and so on, but lacks interoperability with other tools or centralized management of policies and data.

Risks and challenges

The following risks and challenges can manifest when we are utilizing a tool with the aforementioned characteristics:

- **Isolation**: It isolates subsystems, making overall Secrets management harder. Without fine-grained access control or secure storage, you must handle Secrets piecemeal without centralized oversight.

- **Lack of consolidation**: With security islands, you lose the ability to consolidate audit and control. Managing subsystems becomes chaotic, lacking a unified view of the security landscape.

- **Scalability issues**: For instance, using different Secrets for deploying applications in Jenkins CI/CD pipelines and AWS may work initially but can become unwieldy and insecure as complexity increases.

- **Human security island**: Also known as *shadow IT*, when security becomes too complicated, teams may bypass official policies, further worsening the security posture. *For example,* imagine different credentials for staging and production in Jenkins, along with AWS Secrets Manager for database Secrets and API keys. Scaling this setup becomes a struggle, with difficulties in delegation, management, and audit. Adding another team, multiple clouds, or dealing with key consistency only compounds the problem.

Now, let's look at a solution to address this challenge.

Solutions to secret islands

To mitigate the risks associated with secret islands, it is critical to implement centralized Secrets management. Centralizing Secrets management enables organizations to enforce consistent policies, streamline operations, and gain a clear view of their overall security landscape. Additionally, developing standardized security protocols and mandating their adherence across all secret islands can ensure consistency and reduce vulnerabilities. Utilizing integration tools and APIs that allow different secret islands to communicate and interact can help break down silos, leading to a more unified approach. Regular security audits and continuous monitoring are essential for detecting and rectifying inconsistencies and vulnerabilities across secret islands. Moreover, fostering communication and collaboration between the teams responsible for managing the secret islands can further enhance the organization's overall security posture. Together, these mitigation strategies can help organizations effectively manage challenges posed by secret islands.

In the critical area of managing Secrets, this part delves into several distinct but interconnected challenges and risks. From the problem of *secret zero*, where a SPOF can compromise an entire system, to the issues of *secret access ballooning*, where control over access can grow unwieldy, the complexities are multifaceted. *Secret valet parking* highlights trust and delegation issues in integrated systems, while *secret sprawl* and *secret islands* explore difficulties in maintaining cohesiveness and interoperability in increasingly complex environments. Collectively, these topics underline the nuanced and often delicate balance required to handle Secrets securely and efficiently, emphasizing the need for strategic planning, vigilance, and robust solutions.

Having navigated through the broader landscape of challenges and risks associated with general Secrets management in the previous section, we now narrow our focus to the specific context of Kubernetes (also known as K8s).

Challenges and risks in managing Secrets for Kubernetes

Kubernetes presents its unique set of challenges and risks in the realm of Secrets management. This section will dive into the specifics of managing Secrets within a Kubernetes environment, addressing the unique features and vulnerabilities of this widely used orchestration platform. Join us as we explore the intricacies of Kubernetes Secrets, recognizing both distinctive hurdles and tailored strategies for overcoming them.

Before proceeding further, it is important to clarify certain concepts related to Kubernetes and Secrets management. Kubernetes provides a native resource type known as a "*secret*," but utilizing Kubernetes' native secret resource is not the only way to manage Secrets in a Kubernetes environment.

In this section, we will discuss two different approaches to Secrets management within Kubernetes:

- **Direct use of Kubernetes native Secrets**: This approach involves using Kubernetes' built-in secret resource as the primary mechanism for Secrets management.

- **Utilizing Kubernetes native Secrets for the final state**: In this approach, Kubernetes' native secret resource is used as the final state for secret consumption within the Kubernetes platform. It is crucial to approach security risks from the perspective of Kubernetes as a platform.

Kubernetes' native Secrets resources are stored in `etcd`, the primary datastore for Kubernetes objects. By default, these Secrets are encoded using `base64`; they are not encrypted, making them vulnerable to decoding by anyone with access to `etcd`. Risks also arise from unauthorized access to the cluster's API server or to nodes that run workloads using these Secrets. To enhance security, Kubernetes allows the configuration of encryption at rest for `etcd`. For detailed instructions on enabling and configuring this encryption, please refer to the official Kubernetes documentation: *Encrypting Confidential Data at Rest* (`https://kubernetes.io/docs/tasks/administer-cluster/encrypt-data/`).

Additionally, there are scenarios where external Secrets management systems directly supply Secrets to Kubernetes workloads at runtime. In such cases, the majority of security concerns are typically delegated to Secrets management tools, and the associated security risks can vary depending on specific circumstances. For more information on general security risks associated with Secrets management, please refer to the previous section.

Security risks to manage Kubernetes Secrets

Kubernetes Secrets face several security risks, including exposure in the cluster's API server or nodes. By default, Secrets are stored in `etcd`, the primary datastore for Kubernetes objects, encoded in `base64` but not encrypted. This makes them vulnerable to anyone with access to `etcd`. Additionally, unauthorized access to the cluster's API server or nodes can lead to the exposure of Secrets.

Root exploits are another significant risk. Kubernetes does not send Secrets on a *need-to-know* basis. As a result, anyone with root access to any node can read any secret by impersonating the kubelet.

Secrets are often exposed in Kubernetes manifests. They are commonly configured using JSON or YAML files, with the secret encoded in `base64`. If these files are shared or checked into a repo, the secret is compromised.

Generally, communication from the control plane to the worker kubelet uses the TLS model, but there is no native Kubernetes feature to encrypt data in transit across nodes. It is important to use Secrets within direct Pod consumption, instead of transferring Secrets in cases where they are not in transit.

In Kubernetes, while the default Secrets management system allows for the use of RBAC to create custom roles and bindings, care must be taken to avoid granting overly broad permissions, such as "*" to all resources, including Secrets. Custom roles should be specifically tailored to control access to Secrets, defining who has the authority to view, create, edit, or delete them.

Logging and auditing issues pose additional challenges. Once a secret is accessed, it can be logged in plaintext or transmitted to an untrusted party, making it vulnerable. Moreover, Kubernetes does not offer straightforward auditing or change management for Secrets.

Finally, in Kubernetes, the absence of zero-trust mechanisms for secret access means that authorized personnel typically access Secrets in an unencrypted form. This situation indicates the necessity for a stricter access model. In such a model, even authorized personnel should handle Secrets in a manner that ensures safety for plaintext access, aligning with zero-trust principles that mandate verification at every stage.

Mitigation strategies

In securing and managing Secrets within a Kubernetes environment, several strategies should be considered.

Primarily, utilizing a centralized secret store equipped with advanced security features is recommended for managing Kubernetes Secrets. This approach not only mitigates the risk of unauthorized access but also streamlines the management process and provides a comprehensive view of the security landscape. Popular tools for this purpose include HashiCorp Vault, CyberArk, AWS Secrets Manager, and Azure Key Vault.

Additionally, Kubernetes platform-specific configurations should be used to limit potential risk factors:

- Disable the root user of a Pod, like so:

```
apiVersion: apps/v1
kind: Deployment
metadata:
  name: nginx-sample
  labels:
    app: nginx
    environment: production
spec:
  replicas: 2
  selector:
    matchLabels:
      app: nginx
  template:
    metadata:
      labels:
```

```
        app: nginx
    spec:
      containers:
      - name: nginx
        image: nginx:latest
        ports:
        - containerPort: 80
        securityContext:
          allowPrivilegeEscalation: false
          readOnlyRootFilesystem: true
          runAsNonRoot: true
      restartPolicy: Always
```

- Encrypting Secrets, both in transit and at rest, is imperative. Kubernetes native secret encryption or third-party tools can accomplish this. Encryption ensures that, even if unauthorized access occurs, the secret data remains indecipherable without the appropriate decryption keys.

Here is a sample usage to enable `EncryptionConfiguration`:

I.   Place your `EncryptionConfiguration` YAML file on the master node where the Kubernetes API server runs.

II. Modify the API server's startup parameters to include `--encryption-provider-config`, pointing to the file path of your `EncryptionConfiguration` YAML file.

Enable it by executing the following command:

```
kube-apiserver --encryption-provider-config=/etc/kubernetes/
encryption-config.yaml
```

After enabling the encryption configuration via the API server, you can now configure the use of encrypted resources such as Secrets in the Kubernetes cluster:

```
---
#
# CAUTION: this is an example configuration.
#          Do not use this for your own cluster!
#
apiVersion: apiserver.config.k8s.io/v1
kind: EncryptionConfiguration
resources:
- providers:
  - aesgcm:
      keys:
      - name: key1
        secret: c2VjcmV0IGlzIHNlY3VyZQ==
      - name: key2
```

```
                  secret: dGhpcyBpcyBwYXNzd29yZA==
         resources:
         - secrets
```

- Rigorous access controls are essential. Restricting access to Secrets through mechanisms such as RBAC is recommended. It's important to define granular permissions that explicitly indicate who can access, create, or modify Secrets.

In Kubernetes, specific auditing for secret access involves detailed logging of each interaction with secret resources. Auditing captures critical information such as who accessed the secret, when it was accessed, and the nature of the access. Auditing helps administrators determine the specifics of each action, such as what happened and when, who initiated it, and its source and destination. Monitoring and auditing are vital for overseeing secret access, timing, and purpose, aiding in the prompt investigation of suspicious activities to protect Secrets. Standard auditing records should show who accessed what and when. In Kubernetes, all access to Secrets should be logged, and these logs can be used for incident mitigation in case of potential leaks.

A sample audit log entry for secret access might look like this:

```
{
  "kind": "Event",
  "apiVersion": "audit.k8s.io/v1",
  "metadata": {
    "creationTimestamp": "2023-12-01T12:34:56Z"
  },
  "level": "Metadata",
  "timestamp": "2023-12-01T12:34:56Z",
  "auditID": "abcd1234",
  "stage": "ResponseComplete",
  "requestURI": "/api/v1/namespaces/default/secrets/mysecret",
  "verb": "get",
  "user": {
    "username": "admin",
    "groups": ["system:masters", "system:authenticated"]
  },
  "sourceIPs": ["192.0.2.0"],
  "objectRef": {
    "resource": "secrets",
    "namespace": "default",
    "name": "mysecret",
    "apiVersion": "v1"
  },
  "responseStatus": {
    "metadata": {},
    "status": "Success",
```

```
    "reason": ""
  }
}
```

To enable auditing, configure the Kubernetes API server to use this file by adding the `--audit-policy-file` flag to the API server's startup parameters, specifying the path to your audit policy file.

See this example:

```
kube-apiserver --audit-policy-file=/etc/kubernetes/policy.yaml
```

After activating the auditing policy in the Kubernetes API server, users can configure and specify the output log for particular resource access. As a quick example, let's consider access to Secrets:

```
# Log secrets access within request and response.
apiVersion: audit.k8s.io/v1
kind: Policy
rules:
- level: RequestResponse
  resources:
  - resources:
    - secrets
apiVersion: audit.k8s.io/v1
kind: Policy
rules:
- level: RequestResponse
  resources:
  - group: ""
    resources: ["secrets"]
```

Namespace isolation can be used to separate sensitive workloads. Further, network policies can be employed to restrict communication between these isolated namespaces, reducing the potential exposure of Secrets:

```
apiVersion: v1
kind: Secret
metadata:
  name: test
  namespace: test
type: Opaque
data:
  password: dGVzdA==
  username: dGVzdA==
```

Furthermore, it is vital to avoid storing Secrets in configuration files, such as JSON or YAML files, which might be checked into a repository or shared. Instead, Secrets should be stored using environment variables or a dedicated Secrets management tool.

Embracing the concept of a zero-trust system is also advisable. Implementing solutions that decrypt Secrets only when necessary and preventing direct decryption of a secret by anyone is essential.

After Secrets are accessed, it is necessary to take precautions to ensure the secret data is not logged in plaintext or transmitted to untrusted parties.

Lastly, regular rotation of keys and Secrets is essential for security, with organizations often following audit and compliance policies for rotations at set intervals, such as 30, 60, or 90 days. The **National Institute of Standards and Technology (NIST)** provides detailed guidelines for key management, including best practices and management strategies, as outlined in its *Special Publication 800-57 Part 1, Revision 5*, and *Part 2, Revision 1*. These guidelines help ensure that even if a key is compromised, its risk exposure is minimized since it remains unusable for an extended period.

By incorporating these strategies, organizations can achieve a robust and secure Secrets management system within a Kubernetes environment.

Summary

In this chapter, we focused on key concepts behind Secrets management and their importance in ensuring data protection and secure access to resources. We discussed how Secrets are created, managed, and shared among applications and services. We explored critical security risks for managing Secrets, the challenges they pose in Secrets management, and effective mitigation strategies to follow. This was followed by an in-depth analysis of Kubernetes Secrets' security risks, including exposure in the cluster's API server or nodes, root exploits, lack of encryption in transit, inadequate access controls, and more. Onward, we focused on mitigation strategies such as using Secrets management tools, encrypting Secrets, implementing access controls, and monitoring and auditing access to Secrets. In the next few chapters, we will see how to tackle these sensitive topics on popular cloud providers' Secrets management and third-party Secrets management tools.

Part 3: Kubernetes Secrets Providers

In this part, you will be introduced to external secret stores and their advantages in managing Secrets in Kubernetes, as well as how to integrate them with Kubernetes. On completion, you will understand the different types of external secret stores, how to configure external secret stores in Kubernetes, and how to integrate them with existing Secrets management solutions.

This part has the following chapters:

- *Chapter 8, Exploring Cloud Secret Store on AWS*
- *Chapter 9, Exploring Cloud Secret Store on Azure*
- *Chapter 10, Exploring Cloud Secret Store on GCP*
- *Chapter 11, Exploring External Secret Stores*
- *Chapter 12, Integrating with Secret Stores*
- *Chapter 13, Case Studies and Real-World Examples*
- *Chapter 14, Conclusion and the Future of Kubernetes Secrets Management*

8

Exploring Cloud Secret Store on AWS

A very common way to store Secrets in the cloud is to utilize the infrastructure that is provided by cloud providers. The major cloud providers have two essential pieces of infrastructure that help us with efficient Secrets management on Kubernetes: Secret Storage and KMS.

In this chapter, we shall examine AWS Secrets Manager, **Elastic Kubernetes Service** (**EKS**) integration, and secret encryption with KMS. Specifically, we will cover these topics:

- Overview of AWS Secrets Manager
- Secrets Store CSI Driver
- AWS EKS clusters and AWS Secrets Manager
- KMS for AWS Kubernetes encryption

By the end of the chapter, we should be able to use AWS Secrets Manager as an external Kubernetes secret store, encrypt Secrets on Kubernetes using AWS KMS, and search audit logs on secret operations using AWS CloudTrail and AWS CloudWatch.

Technical requirements

To link concepts with practice, we will use a series of tools and platforms that are commonly used to interact with the AWS API and Kubernetes:

- An AWS Free Tier account is required. The free tier is available to new AWS customers for a limited period. Once the period expires or the usage exceeds the free tier usage limits, pay-as-you-go service rates apply.
- The **AWS CLI** (https://aws.amazon.com/cli/) is a unified tool for managing your AWS services. Commands executed through the AWS CLI are transformed into API calls toward the AWS API.

- **Terraform** (`https://www.terraform.io/`) is infrastructure-as-code software that can be used to provision and manage infrastructure in the cloud.
- **kubectl** (`https://kubernetes.io/docs/reference/kubectl/`) is a command-line tool used for communicating with a Kubernetes cluster through the Kubernetes API.

Overview of AWS Secrets Manager

A secret is a concept that exists outside the realm of Kubernetes. Any type of application will at some point require sensitive information to be integrated with each deployment. An application deployed in the cloud requires secure secret handling. For this reason, cloud providers offer components for secret storage.

When it comes to Kubernetes, we saw in *Chapter 1*, *Understanding Kubernetes Secrets Management*, that secret information is stored on etcd. Essentially, etcd is the default secret store of Kubernetes. The crucial question is whether it is possible to have external storage for Secrets on Kubernetes apart from etcd.

This is feasible provided you actively use a cloud provider's secret storage, or you consider taking advantage of it and utilizing it on Kubernetes. Thanks to the Container Storage Interface and the workload identity, we can utilize the available secret stores.

AWS Secrets Manager (`https://aws.amazon.com/secrets-manager/`) is the secret store provided by AWS. With AWS Secrets Manager, we can store several types of credentials, such as database credentials, application credentials, and secure tokens. We will now focus on the features that make AWS Secrets Manager a good option for handling Secrets, starting with encryption.

Encryption

AWS Secrets Manager has encryption at rest as well as in transit. It uses AWS KMS to perform envelope encryption. The values stored in AWS Secrets Manager are encrypted using a data key, and the data key is encrypted using AWS KMS. The data encryption key is an AES-256 key. When a value changes on AWS Secrets Manager, a new data encryption key is generated and is used to encrypt the new value. We can also configure AWS Secrets Manager to use a different KMS key. AWS Secrets Manager also provides encryption in transit. The API calls toward Secrets Manager happen through secure private endpoints, and each call is required to be signed using X.509 certificates or a Secrets Manager secret access key.

Versioning

Versioning is another benefit of using AWS Secrets Manager. If we create a secret in AWS Secrets Manager, the secret will be stored, and a version will be assigned to it. This will be the first version of the secret. Once we update that secret, we will have an updated version of the secret, and the old version will still be available. When we access the secret, the latest version of it will be retrieved. The previous version can be configured to be automatically deleted at a certain date. This will make it impossible to retrieve it. If we want to retrieve the previous version, we must remove it from pending deletion.

Rotation

AWS Secrets Manager also permits rotation. An AWS Lambda function can be configured to execute a scheduled key rotation; the AWS documentation has a detailed guide (`https://docs.aws.amazon.com/secretsmanager/latest/userguide/rotating-secrets.html`). On invocation, the Lambda function will rotate the key based on a custom code snippet that we provided; the function templates can be found on GitHub (`https://github.com/aws-samples/aws-secrets-manager-rotation-lambdas`). During the rotation, the latest version of the key will be tested. On failure, the rotation will be retried.

Cloud-based features

Apart from tackling the storage needs of sensitive information, AWS Secrets Manager is a managed AWS component. Every AWS component comes with certain features:

- AWS IAM integration
- Logging and auditing on usage
- High availability and disaster recovery
- Integration with other AWS components

Let's look at each of these features.

AWS IAM integration

With AWS **Identity and Access Management (IAM)**, we can specify entities that can access services and resources in AWS. Those entities can be AWS users or AWS roles.

AWS users are intended to be associated with an actual human user who wants to interact with an AWS service and provision resources. AWS roles are a more flexible identity. AWS roles are used to delegate access to services, EC2 machines, and Kubernetes workloads.

The identities on AWS can be granted fine-grained permissions on AWS services.

Logging and auditing

AWS comes with CloudWatch, which is a monitoring and observability solution. CloudWatch collects real-time logs and metrics from other AWS components. In our case, with CloudWatch we can identify Kubernetes operations through logging; also, we can create custom alerts and dashboards based on the metrics provided out of the box.

CloudTrail is an AWS service targeted toward auditing. With CloudTrail, we can track actions taken by an AWS user or an AWS role. Those operations will be recorded and will be accessible through AWS CloudTrail. Take, for example, a secret retrieval by a role attached to an EC2 machine. The code running on the EC2 machine is granted permission to receive the secret, the secret is retrieved, and this action is logged to AWS CloudTrail. The EC2 machine has a role assigned with permissions to interact with AWS Secrets Manager; the role is an AWS identity, just like an AWS console user.

In the following screenshot, we can see the CloudTrail screen displaying auditing information:

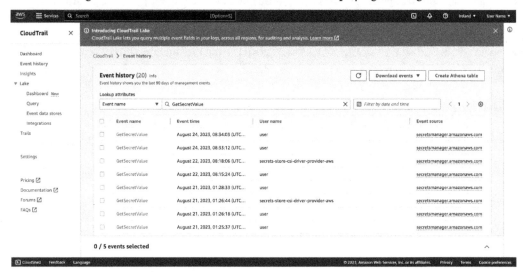

Figure 8.1 – AWS CloudTrail screen

Thanks to CloudTrail, we can identify the action that took place in AWS Secrets Manager, the identity that executed it, and at what time.

High availability and disaster recovery

Secrets provisioned on Secrets Manager are regionally highly available. This means that the secret operations will span the three availability zones that an AWS region consists of. If an availability zone becomes unavailable, requests for a secret will be served by another availability zone.

Also, with AWS Secrets Manager, we can achieve disaster recovery. By default, when we create a secret, we choose an availability zone, where this secret will reside. To protect our workloads from situations where a region is lost, we provision our infrastructure in a way that disaster recovery is feasible. AWS Secrets Manager makes this easy by enabling us to replicate a secret to another region.

Integration with other AWS components

A benefit of using the components provided by the cloud providers is how well they are integrated. AWS Secrets Manager can be integrated with other AWS components easily. In our case, we are interested in EKS, which is the managed version of Kubernetes on AWS.

We had an overview of AWS Secrets Manager and saw how it can be integrated with other AWS components. We shall proceed with integrating AWS Secrets Manager with EKS. To achieve this, we will have an overview of the tool that facilitates this integration, Secrets Store CSI Driver.

Secrets Store CSI Driver

Kubernetes CSI is a standardized interface for Kubernetes that enables us to utilize different storage providers with Kubernetes. Instead of being limited to using the default storage on Kubernetes, we have an interface providing a specification upon which we can build storage drivers. This way we can use several types of storage by implementing a new driver that complies with the CSI interface.

Here are some popular drivers for CSI:

- AWS Elastic File System
- Azure File
- Google Cloud Filestore

This is feasible for several forms of storage and is also applicable to the Secrets storage components provided by the cloud providers.

CSI drivers are provided for secret storage by the cloud providers. Secrets Store CSI Driver is a CSI interface that targets Secrets management. We can use it to mount Secrets on Kubernetes through another form of storage. Instead of consuming Secrets from etcd, thanks to Secrets Store CSI Driver, we can consume the Secrets from various external sources, and in our case, those sources are the very Secrets Storage solutions that are provided by the cloud providers.

In this section, we will focus on AWS Secrets Manager and examine how we can integrate a Kubernetes cluster into AWS to consume Secrets from the native cloud provider solution for Secrets management by using the corresponding Secrets Store CSI Driver.

How Secrets Store CSI Driver works

We have an application to be hosted on Kubernetes. That application will have to use a secret that resides on the Secrets storage solution of the cloud provider. The application will reside on a Pod since the Pod is the main compute building block of Kubernetes.

Once a Pod is created, started, or restarted, Secrets Store CSI Driver through the Secret Store CSI provider will communicate with the cloud provider's Secrets storage and retrieve the credentials. The credentials will be mounted to the Pod as a volume. The volume mounted will be attached to a directory specified.

The next question is how Secret Store CSI Driver works.

Secret Store CSI Driver is a **DaemonSet**. A DaemonSet exists on Kubernetes on every node. A DaemonSet can consist of more than one Pod.

In the case of Secret Store CSI Driver, we have the following Pods:

- `node-driver-registrar`
- `secrets-store`
- `liveness-probe`

node-driver-registrar

`node-driver-registrar` will register the CSI driver with the kubelet. A registration socket is created and exposed via the host path in the kubelet plugin registry.

secrets-store

The `secrets-store` component is responsible for mounting secret volumes during Pod creation as well as unmounting volumes during Pod deletion. It is based on gRPC implementing the CSI node service from the CSI specification.

liveness-probe

This Pod monitors the health of the CSI driver. The health liveness probe will detect any issues with the driver and will restart the Pod in order to fix the issue. In the following diagram, we can see how all the components come together:

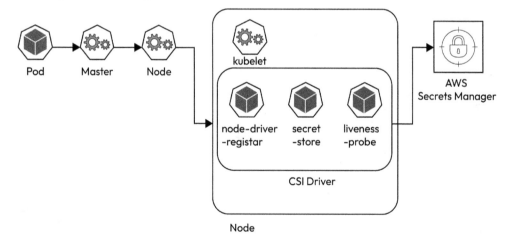

Figure 8.2 – Secrets Store CSI and AWS Secrets Manager integration

Now that we know about the CSI driver, we shall proceed with integrating it with EKS.

Integrating AWS Secrets Manager with EKS

To integrate AWS Secrets Manager with Kubernetes, we shall utilize the Secrets Store CSI Driver
. As expected, AWS provides us with Secrets Store CSI Driver (`https://github.com/aws/
secrets-store-csi-driver-provider-aws`). To integrate the driver with Kubernetes,
we will create a Kubernetes cluster.

EKS cluster on AWS

As defined earlier, **EKS** in AWS stands for **Elastic Kubernetes Service**. We have the option to set up
a Kubernetes cluster on the AWS cloud just like every other cloud. We will focus on the managed
service offering for the purpose of this chapter because it requires less maintenance and setup overhead.

If there is already an existing EKS cluster available, the Terraform setup instructions can be ignored
since the corresponding command-line arguments for AWS will be provided.

Implementing a Kubernetes cluster on AWS can require different amounts of effort based on the
installation you want to achieve. One option is to create fully private clusters with no connectivity to
the internet and everything being served internally from AWS. Another option is a cluster on a public
network. A quite common option nowadays is to deploy the nodes of the cluster on subnets that are
private and ensure that the connectivity to the internet happens through a NAT gateway. This is the
option we shall follow.

Configuring the Terraform project

A Terraform project on AWS requires us to store the state. We can store the state locally on our
filesystem, but this is not a viable option for infrastructure as code targeting a production environment.
Our option is to use a **Secure Storage Service (S3)** bucket to store the state:

```
terraform {
...
  backend "s3" {
    bucket = "state-bucket"
    key    = "eks-state"
    region = "eu-west-1"
  }
}
```

By default, the Terraform code base will use the default credentials that are configured for the AWS CLI.

We first need to initialize the Terraform project using `init`:

```
$ terraform init
```

This command will initialize our project.

With Terraform, we have the option of `plan`, which is similar to the `dry-run` command from kubectl. Instead of creating the resources, we use `plan` and identify what the state of the infrastructure would be like if the Terraform scripts had been applied:

```
$ terraform plan
```

To apply the infrastructure, we shall use the `apply` command:

```
$ terraform apply
```

Terraform basics

When using Terraform, infrastructure is defined in `.tf` files. A Terraform project involves the following operations:

- `init`
- `plan`
- `apply`
- `destroy`

So far, we have seen `init`, which is used to initialize the project and download the existing state; `plan`, which is used to evaluate the changes we perform; and `apply`, which is the command used to carry out the changes. To destroy the provisioned resource, we can use the `destroy` command.

These operations can be carried out on the project or can target a specific resource defined in the Terraform files:

```
$ terraform apply -target=aws_kms_key.a
```

In the case of existing resources, there is the option to import those resources in the Terraform state and provide them with a resource definition on the `.tf` files:

```
$ terraform import aws_kms_key.a 136c1dcb-42b0-4b9a-a569-152b9aba63e1
```

There is a recommended structure for Terraform projects. `main.tf` is the primary entry point to define resources. As the complexity of the infrastructure increases, more `.tf` files can be used. `variables.tf` contains variables that we want to be dynamic when provisioning the infrastructure and `outputs.tf` should contain the information we want to extract when we provision infrastructure with Terraform.

The Terraform project is set up, so we shall proceed with setting the VPC through Terraform.

Creating the VPC

Our cluster nodes will reside on AWS VPC. We shall use the VPC module from the `terraform-aws-modules` project (`https://registry.terraform.io/modules/terraform-aws-modules/vpc/aws/latest`):

```
module "eks_ksm_vpc" {
  source  = "terraform-aws-modules/vpc/aws"
  version = "5.0.0"
  name = "eks-ksm-vpc"
  cidr = "10.0.0.0/16"
  azs  = slice(var.availability_zones, 0, 3)
  private_subnets = ["10.0.1.0/24", "10.0.2.0/24", "10.0.3.0/24"]
  public_subnets  = ["10.0.4.0/24", "10.0.5.0/24", "10.0.6.0/24"]

  enable_nat_gateway    = true
  single_nat_gateway    = true
  enable_dns_hostnames = true
...
}
```

With this configuration, we will span a VPC among three availability zones, thus enabling us to have a highly available cluster.

We shall create a private subnet in each zone as well as public subnets.

The Kubernetes workloads will be hosted on the private subnets and external traffic will reach the Kubernetes workloads through the public network. To provide access to the internet from within the Kubernetes cluster, a NAT gateway will be configured.

Since we have the VPC configured we can now proceed and configure the EKS cluster.

Provisioning the EKS cluster

We have provisioned the VPC, so now we shall proceed with provisioning the EKS cluster. We will pick the EKS module from the `terraform-aws-modules` project (`https://registry.terraform.io/modules/terraform-aws-modules/eks/aws/latest`):

```
module "eks" {
  source  = "terraform-aws-modules/eks/aws"
  ...
  cluster_name    = var.cluster_name
  vpc_id          = module.eks_ksm_vpc.vpc_id
  subnet_ids      = module.eks_ksm_vpc.private_subnets
```

```
    cluster_endpoint_public_access = true

    eks_managed_node_group_defaults = {
      ami_type = "AL2_x86_64"
    }

    create_cloudwatch_log_group = true
    eks_managed_node_groups = {
      one = {
        ...
        min_size      = 1
      }
    }
}
```

This will create an EKS cluster. The master is managed by AWS. By creating the cluster, we specified that the nodes span the private subnets we specified previously in the VPC section. We will also create a separate log group for the EKS cluster.

To make it easy to interact with the EKS master, we shall configure the cluster endpoint to be publicly accessible. The option can be fine-tuned and specify a restricted number of IPs to be able to interact with the cluster through the kubectl tool.

Once the cluster is up and running, we can test and even run some kubectl commands.

To authenticate to the cluster, we shall use the following command:

```
$ aws eks --region eu-west-1 update-kubeconfig --name eks-ksm-cluster
```

The command will differ depending on the cluster name and the region we choose. Once this is done, we can use kubectl to point to the recently provisioned cluster:

```
$ kubectl get nodes
NAME                                  STATUS   ROLES    AGE     VERSION
ip-10-0-2-231.eu-west-1.compute.
internal    Ready    <none>   6m5s    v1.24.15-eks-a5565ad
```

Now that we have provisioned the EKS cluster, we can proceed to work with AWS Secrets Manager.

Creating Secrets on Secrets Manager

Let's create a secret using AWS Secrets Manager:

```
resource "aws_secretsmanager_secret" "ksm_service_token" {
  name = "service-token"
  replica {
```

```
    region = "eu-central-1"
  }
  recovery_window_in_days {
    ...
  }
}
```

In the `replica` block, we specify the region in which we will replicate the secret. This will give us disaster recovery capabilities. Also, the `recovery_window_in_days` block defines within how many days we can recover a secret after we set it for deletion.

Now, let's add a version for the secret we specified:

```
resource "aws_secretsmanager_secret_version" "ksm_service_token_first_
version" {
  secret_id      = aws_secretsmanager_secret.ksm_service_token.id
  secret_string = "a-service-token"
}
```

This is our first interaction with AWS Secrets Manager. We have created a secret and a version of the secret containing a string.

We will also create a role with the required IAM bindings:

```
resource "aws_iam_role" "eks_secret_reader_role" {
  name = "eks-secret-reader"
  assume_role_policy = jsonencode({
    Version = "2012-10-17",
    Statement = [
      {
        Effect = "Allow",
        "Principal": {
          "Federated": "arn:aws:iam::${data.aws_caller_identity.
current.account_id}:oidc-provider/${module.ksm_eks.oidc_provider}"
        }
        "Action": "sts:AssumeRoleWithWebIdentity",
        "Condition": {
          "StringEquals": {
            "${module.ksm_eks.oidc_provider}:aud": "sts.amazonaws.
com",
            "${module.ksm_eks.oidc_provider}:sub": "system:serviceacco
unt:default:service-token-reader"
          }
        }
      }
    ]
```

```
  })
}

resource "aws_iam_role_policy_attachment" "esrrs" {
  policy_arn = aws_iam_policy.ksm_service_token_reader.arn
  role       = aws_iam_role.eks_secret_reader_role.name
}
```

Pay close attention to the role. It is very different from what we are used to. This role is created with EKS in mind. This role is a workload identity mapped to a role in the Kubernetes cluster.

The role is limited in what it can do. We cannot use the role to perform operations on other AWS resources.

Alternatively, we can provision the Secrets using the AWS CLI:

```
$ aws secretsmanager create-secret --name service-token --secret-
string a-service-token  --add-replica-regions Region=eu-central-1
```

This will create a secret and a version.

We can also create the role and the policy using the AWC CLI:

```
...
$ aws iam create-role --role-name eks-secret-reader --assume-role-
policy-document file://eks-reader-trust-policy.json
...
$ aws iam create-policy --policy-name get-service-token --policy-
document  file://policy.json
...
$ aws iam attach-role-policy --role-name eks-secret-reader --policy-
arn arn:aws:iam::$account_id:policy/get-service-token
```

We have a role that can be attached to Kubernetes and retrieve Secrets from Secrets Manager. Our next step is to install the CSI plugin.

AWS Secrets Manager provider for CSI on EKS

It is now time to install the AWS Secrets Manager CSI provider on EKS. The first thing to do is to add the Secrets Store CSI Driver plugin to the EKS installation.

Let's start by installing the driver on EKS, since the `secrets-store-csi` driver is not available as an add-on:

```
$ helm repo add secrets-store-csi-driver https://kubernetes-sigs.
github.io/secrets-store-csi-driver/charts
$ helm install -n kube-system csi-secrets-store secrets-store-csi-
driver/secrets-store-csi-driver
$ helm repo add aws-secrets-manager https://aws.github.io/secrets-
store-csi-driver-provider-aws $ helm install -n kube-system secrets-
provider-aws aws-secrets-manager/secrets-store-csi-driver-provider-aws
```

The following will install the `secret-store-csi-driver` DaemonSet. We can validate the installation of `secret-store-csi-driver` with the following command:

```
$ kubectl get daemonset -n kube-system
NAME            DESIRED   CURRENT   READY   UP-TO-DATE   AVAILABLE   NODE
SELECTOR                  AGE       <none>                47m
...
secrets-provider-aws-secrets-store-csi-driver-provider-
aws   1             1         1       1            1           kubernetes.
io/os=linux     44s
```

We can proceed with fetching the credentials from the secret store through Kubernetes.

Fetching Secrets from Kubernetes

First, we want to map the secret through a secret provider class. In the object, we specify the name of the secret we want to fetch:

```
apiVersion: secrets-store.csi.x-k8s.io/v1
kind: SecretProviderClass
metadata:
  name: service-token
spec:
  provider: aws
  parameters:
    objects: |
        - objectName: "arn:aws:secretsmanager:eu-west-
1:1111111:secret:service_token-IJ2VLg"
```

We map a Kubernetes secret to a secret provided by AWS Secrets Manager.

Now we need a Kubernetes service account with permission to retrieve this secret:

```
apiVersion: v1
kind: ServiceAccount
metadata:
  annotations:
    eks.amazonaws.com/role-arn: "arn:aws:iam::11111:role/eks-secret-
reader"
  name: service-token-reader
  namespace: default
```

In the `eks.amazonaws.com/role-arn` section, we specify the AWS role with the permissions.

As we can see, the service account is annotated with an AWS role, which is the AWS role we created previously.

This service account, provided it is attached to a Pod, will assume this role identity by using the Kubernetes OIDC provider. More on OIDC and Kubernetes service accounts can be found in the official documentation (https://docs.aws.amazon.com/eks/latest/userguide/enable-iam-roles-for-service-accounts.html).

When the Pod is created, it will use that service account and mount that secret upon it:

```
kind: Pod
apiVersion: v1
metadata:
  name: nginx
spec:
  serviceAccountName: service-token-reader
  containers:
  - image: nginx
    name: nginx
    volumeMounts:
    - name: secret-from-asm
      mountPath: "/mnt/secrets-store"
      readOnly: true
  volumes:
    - name: secret-from-asm
      csi:
        driver: secrets-store.csi.k8s.io
        readOnly: true
        volumeAttributes:
          secretProviderClass: "service-token"
```

We can test this by printing the secret:

```
$ kubectl exec -it nginx cat /mnt/secrets-store/
arn:aws:secretsmanager:eu-west-1:274402012893:secret:service_token-
IJ2VLg
```

To summarize, we created a Pod with a service account, which was mapped to an AWS role. This service account had permission to interact with AWS Secrets Manager. As a result, we see the secret that we mounted previously. In the next section, we will focus on how we can track the actions that take place in AWS Secrets Manager, through auditing.

Auditing

We have successfully created Secrets and made sure we received them securely by utilizing AWS IAM. Since secure access has been tackled and we have fine-grained permissions, we are interested in also logging the usage of and access to our Secrets management instance.

There are two ways to evaluate the secret access that occurs in Kubernetes:

- Kubernetes Secrets access logs
- AWS Secrets Manager logs

When auditing occurs, a log message is printed in the output of a program. This is integrated with CloudWatch, the logging solution provided by AWS, and CloudTrail, the auditing solution that AWS provides.

Kubernetes logs on CloudWatch

By using CloudWatch, we can browse the Kubernetes logs. Suppose we created a secret called audit-test. We can search for any operations on Logs Insights (https://console.aws.amazon.com/cloudwatch/home?logsV2%3Alogs-insights=#logsV2:logs-insights). We can use the following log:

```
fields @timestamp, @message, @logStream, @log
| filter @message like 'audit-test'
| sort @timestamp desc
| limit 20
```

The result entries will show the actual results:

Field	Value
@message	{"kind":"Event",...,"verb":"get","user":{"user name":"kubernetes-admin", "uid":"aws-iam-authe nticator:274402012893:AIDAILH3OPGRUQEOHAR3O", "groups":["system:masters","system:authenticated"], "extra":{"accessKeyId": ["AKIAI5INYQBL233Y7J6Q"],"arn": ["arn:aws:iam::274402012893: user/ gkatzioura"],"canonicalArn": ["arn:aws:iam:: 274402012893: user/gkatzioura"], "principalId": ["AIDAILH3OPGRUQEOHAR3O"],"sessionName": [""]}},"sourceIPs":["90.221.185.67"],"userAgent": "kubectl/v1.25.4 (darwin/arm64) kubernetes/872a965","objectRef":{"resource": "secrets","namespace":"default", "name":"audit-test", "apiVersion":"v1"},"responseStatus":{"metadata":...}
@timestamp	1692687754591

This result looks familiar. It is the log we saw previously in *Chapter 2, Walking through Kubernetes Secrets Management Concepts*, when we were auditing Kubernetes Secrets.

Also, CloudWatch gives us the option to create alarms. If there are unexpected log entries that indicate access or access attempts to a secret, we can configure CloudWatch to create an alert and notify us through the communication channel of our choice, for example, email.

AWS Secrets Manager logs on AWS CloudTrail

AWS CloudTrail is a service specifically for audit logs. With CloudTrail, we can identify the retrieval of Kubernetes Secrets.

For example, we can use this URL to view the Secrets that have been recently retrieved in our AWS account: `https://console.aws.amazon.com/cloudtrail/home?#/events?EventName=GetSecretValue`.

If we navigate to the URL, the retrieval information from AWS Secrets Manager will be displayed:

```
{
    "userIdentity": {
        "type": "AssumedRole",
        "principalId": "id:secrets-store-csi-driver-provider-aws",
        "arn": "arn:aws:sts::1111111:assumed-role/eks-secret-reader/
secrets-store-csi-driver-provider-aws",
        ...
        }
    },
    "eventSource": "secretsmanager.amazonaws.com",
    "eventName": "GetSecretValue",
    ...
    "requestParameters": {
        "secretId": "arn:aws:secretsmanager:eu-west-
1:11111111:secret:service_token-93z7he"
    },
    "responseElements": null,
    ...
}
```

The user identity is the AWS role we created previously. The event name is a `GetSecretValue` event. `requestParameters` is the resource the operation is executed on.

KMS for AWS Secrets encryption

Kubernetes gives us the option to specify certain encryption providers when storing the Secrets on etcd. AWS KMS can be used as an encryption provider to encrypt the Secrets hosted on etcd.

Provisioning KMS

We shall provision a KMS key using Terraform:

```
resource "aws_kms_key" "ksm_kms_key" {
  description           = "ksm_kms_key"
  deletion_window_in_days = 30
  enable_key_rotation     = true
}
```

That key is now ready to be used standalone or with other AWS components.

Using KMS with EKS

Having created the EKS cluster, we can now specify the credentials that will decrypt the Secrets:

```
module "ksm_eks" {
  ...
  create_kms_key = false
  cluster_encryption_config = {
    resources = ["secrets"]
    provider_key_arn = aws_kms_key.ksm_kms_key.arn
  }
  ...
}
```

If we try to fetch the credentials from Kubernetes, the Secrets will be decrypted using the KMS we specified. We can use AWS CloudTrail to identify the usage. We can access CloudTrail events by following this link: `https://console.aws.amazon.com/cloudtrail/home?#/events?EventName=Decrypt`.

If we navigate to the page, the decryption operation will be displayed onscreen. Also, it will display the user responsible for the decryption operation that took place, which in our case is the role associated with the Kubernetes cluster.

The information will be in JSON format:

```
{
    "eventSource": "kms.amazonaws.com",
    "eventName": "Decrypt",
    "awsRegion": "eu-west-1",
    "sourceIPAddress": "secretsmanager.amazonaws.com",
    "userAgent": "secretsmanager.amazonaws.com",
    "requestParameters": {
        "encryptionContext": {
            "SecretARN": "arn:aws:secretsmanager:eu-west-
1:1212222223:secret:service_token-93z7he",
            "SecretVersionId": "278A157C-EA85-4211-9854-D329D3C9089F"
        },
        "encryptionAlgorithm": "SYMMETRIC_DEFAULT"
    },
    "resources": [
        {
            "ARN": "arn:aws:kms:eu-west-1:111111111:key/aaaaaaa-aaaa-
458f-b8d1-aefa58b68d8a"
        }
    ],
    "eventType": "AwsApiCall",
}
```

We managed to store our Secrets encrypted on etcd using AWS KMS. Our secret residing on etcd will be encrypted and we should be able to monitor any encryption/decryption operations.

Summary

In this chapter, we created a VPC network that spans three availability zones. On top of that network, we provisioned an EKS cluster. We managed to integrate the EKS cluster with AWS Secrets Manager. This was done securely by implementing a fine-grained role on AWS mapped to our Kubernetes workloads. We then proceeded to identify the operations that took place with regard to the Secrets stored on AWS Secrets Manager by checking CloudWatch and CloudTrail logs. Lastly, we encrypted the Secrets residing on an EKS cluster by using a managed KMS. In the next chapter, we shall focus on another popular cloud provider and its secret-handling capabilities: Microsoft Azure.

9

Exploring Cloud Secret Store on Azure

Previously, we did a deep dive into Secrets Manager on AWS. In this chapter, we shall focus on another popular cloud provider, Microsoft Azure. We will learn about Azure Key Vault, a solution provided by Azure to store Secrets and perform encryption and decryption. We will utilize Azure Key Vault in order to store Secrets and use them on our Kubernetes workloads and we also utilize Key Vault to encrypt the Secrets that reside on etcd.

In this chapter, we will cover the following topics:

- Overview of Azure Key Vault
- Introduction to Workload Identity
- AKS cluster and Azure Key Vault integration
- Auditing and logging
- Azure Key Vault for secret encryption

By the end of this chapter, we should be able to store our Secrets in Azure Key Vault, retrieve them on a Kubernetes deployment, monitor secret access through auditing, and encrypt Kubernetes Secrets using Azure Key Vault.

Technical requirements

To link concepts with hands-on examples, we are leveraging a series of tools and platforms commonly used to interact with the Azure API and Kubernetes:

- **Azure (az) CLI** (`https://learn.microsoft.com/en-us/cli/azure/`) is a multi-platform set of command-line tools used in order to create and manage Azure resources
- **Terraform** (`https://www.terraform.io/`) is an infrastructure-as-code software solution that can be used to provision and manage infrastructure on the cloud

- **kubectl** (`https://kubernetes.io/docs/reference/kubectl/`) is the command-line tool used for communicating with a Kubernetes cluster through the Kubernetes API

Overview of Azure Key Vault

Azure Key Vault is a versatile service. It can be used as a secret storage. On Azure Key Vault, we can store cryptographic keys. Also, Azure Key Vault can be used to perform encryption and decryption operations.

Since it is a managed Azure service, it benefits from the features that Azure provides by default on its services.

The features of interest are as follows:

- Azure RBAC and access policy
- High availability
- Logging, auditing, and monitoring
- Integration with other Azure components

We will take some time to examine these features that are crucial to the security of our Secrets.

Azure RBAC and access policy

Every service on Azure is protected from unauthorized usage through an identity access management layer that Azure provides. This layer comes in the form of Azure's RBAC and access policy. A security principal is an entity that has an identity on Azure and can be a user account, group account, or computer account. The legacy way of assigning permissions to security principals is through *access policies*. The recommended way to assign permissions is through **Azure role-based access control** (**Azure RBAC**). Azure RBAC will be our choice to secure Azure Key Vault as we progress through the chapter. By using Azure RBAC, we will control access to resources by creating role assignments.

High availability

When we create a Key Vault, we must specify the region where the Key Vault would be located. The contents of the Key Vault are replicated within this region. Also, the contents of the Key Vault will be replicated to a secondary region. Azure Key Vault contents are regionally highly available but also, they support disaster recovery out-of-the-box.

Imagine the scenario of a region becoming unavailable. Once the region becomes unavailable, the requests toward Azure Key Vault will be routed to the secondary region. This will happen automatically; there is no need to provision any extra Azure Key Vault resources or configure a fallback to a Key Vault residing in another region.

Logging, auditing, and monitoring

In Azure, we have the option to audit the usage of a Key Vault. By enabling auditing, we can identify who accessed the data hosted on Azure Key Vault. We can achieve this by collecting the logs through **Diagnostic settings**. Resources on Azure produce logs, and those logs contain information about the resources and the operations that take place involving each resource. Based on the resource, the content of the logs may vary.

Diagnostic settings give us the option to stream those logs to various locations. By default, the logs will be streamed to an Azure storage account. Other options are to stream the logs to the Log Analytics workspace or to the Azure Event Hub.

Integration with other Azure components

An important benefit of Azure Key Vault is the integration with other Azure components. Azure Key Vault can be integrated with the Azure Application Gateway for traffic encryption or with the SQL Server offering from Azure, to encrypt the data. One of the components of interest is the Azure Kubernetes Service.

This is enabled using the Kubernetes Secrets Store CSI Driver for Azure Key Vault. We saw in the previous chapter how the CSI Secret Store works.

The following figure shows how the integration works:

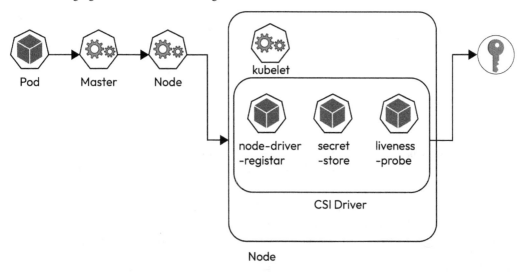

Figure 9.1 – Azure Key Vault integration

In this chapter, we will take advantage of Azure CSI Key Vault plugin and integrate it with Azure securely. The integration will involve a Kubernetes cluster in Azure using **Azure Kubernetes Service (AKS)**. To integrate these two components, Azure Key Vault and the Kubernetes cluster, it is crucial to have fine-grained permissions from the cluster toward Azure Key Vault. For this, Azure provides us with the concept of Workload Identity.

Introduction to Workload Identity

Workload Identity on AKS on Azure enables us to assign permissions to Kubernetes workloads so they can interact with Azure resources. For example, we have an Azure Key Vault that we use to store sensitive information. To interact with Azure Key Vault, we need some form of credentials. Workload Identities are machine identities representing software workloads that require identities to interact with Azure resources. Instead of creating an identity or a service principal, we can use Workload Identity by manually attaching their credentials to the service. This way, each service can have its own identity and authenticate by itself.

In Kubernetes, we can assign a Workload Identity to our Pods. By granting the RBAC permissions to this identity, we will be able to interact with Azure Key Vault.

Here is an example of how Workload Identity works:

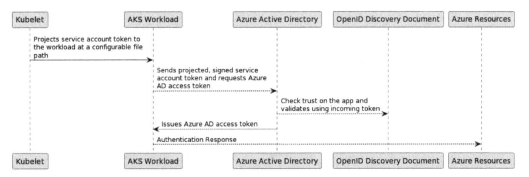

Figure 9.2 – Workload Identity behind the scenes (source: `https://learn.microsoft.com/en-us/azure/aks/workload-identity-overview?tabs=dotnet`)

The official documentation of Azure has a detailed overview of how a Workload Identity requests a token from the Azure Active Directory and then uses that token to interact with an Azure resource (`https://learn.microsoft.com/en-us/azure/aks/workload-identity-overview`).

Since we've acquired an understanding of the Workload Identity concept, we can proceed and learn more about how Azure enables the interaction between AKS and other Azure resources, such as Azure Key Vault.

Integrating an AKS cluster and Azure Key Vault

To integrate Kubernetes with Azure Key Vault, we need to have a cluster set up. There are various options to create a cluster and each choice applies to the needs of certain circumstances. We shall create a simple AKS cluster; the master will be publicly available, but the nodes will reside on a private subnet of a virtual network.

We will provide some Terraform code for the scope of creating the cluster. Also, we shall provide the commands needed in case Terraform is not applicable.

Configuring the Terraform project

While creating the Terraform project, we will configure the state. The state can be saved in a storage account:

```
terraform {
...
    backend "azurerm" {
        resource_group_name   = "resource-group"
        storage_account_name = "storage-account"
        container_name        = "tfstate"
        key                   = "aks.tfstate"
    }
}
```

By setting up the Terraform configuration, we can proceed and provision resources on Azure.

It is crucial to provision the resources for this chapter under one resource group:

```
resource "azurerm_resource_group" "ksm_resource_group" {
    name    = "ksm-resource-group"
}
```

By using a resource group, we logically separate our resources from other resources on our Azure account, specifically to the solution we want to implement.

Also, we shall create a storage account to persist logs from our services:

```
resource "azurerm_storage_account" "ksm_storage_account" {
    name = "ksmlogs"
    resource_group_name = azurerm_resource_group.ksm_resource_group.name
    ...
}
```

As mentioned in the *Overview of Azure Key Vault* section, through **Diagnostics settings**, we can enable the logs of an Azure resource to be streamed to a storage account. The storage account we provisioned will serve this purpose.

We can now proceed with creating the network.

Provisioning the network

We will create a virtual network, and we will allocate a subset of private IPs. We shall also create a subnet on which we will be able to host the Kubernetes cluster nodes:

```
resource "azurerm_virtual_network" "ksm_virtual_network" {
  name               = "ksm-virtual-network"
  ...
  address_space      = ["10.1.0.0/16"]
}
resource "azurerm_subnet" "ksm_subnet" {
  name               = "ksm-private-subnt"
  ...
  address_prefixes   = ["10.1.0.0/24"]
  enforce_private_link_endpoint_network_policies = true
}
```

The `enforce_private_link_endpoint_network_policies` option is enabled. Through this option, the applications hosted in this subnet can access Azure components through the internal network.

Provisioning the AKS cluster

We will create an AKS cluster by creating the master and adding a default node pool:

```
resource "azurerm_kubernetes_cluster" "ksm_aks" {
  name = "ksm-aks"
  ...
  dns_prefix = "private-aks-cluster"
  private_cluster_enabled = false
  oidc_issuer_enabled = true
  workload_identity_enabled = true
  role_based_access_control_enabled = true
...

  default_node_pool {
    name           = "default"
    node_count     = 1
    vm_size        = "Standard_A2_v2"
    vnet_subnet_id = azurerm_subnet.ksm_subnet.id
  }
}
```

An important thing to note is that we enable the **OpenID Connect** (**OIDC**) feature and the Workload Identity. This gives us the ability to assign roles to our Kubernetes workloads so that they can interact with Azure Key Vault.

After using the `terraform apply` command, the cluster will be provisioned:

```
$ terraform init
...
$ terraform apply
```

We have the option to implement a fully private cluster using the `private_cluster_enabled` option. In the repo, you can find the settings to create the bastion host to enable this action (`https://github.com/PacktPublishing/Kubernetes-Secrets-Handbook/blob/main/ch09/bastion.tf`).

Alternatively, if we do not want to provision the cluster through Terraform, we can use the command line:

```
$ az aks create -n ksm-aks -g ksm-resource-group --enable-addons
azure-keyvault-secrets-provider --enable-oidc-issuer --enable-
workload-identity
```

We can now successfully log in to our cluster:

```
$ az aks get-credentials --name ksm-aks \
    --resource-group ksm-resource-group \
    --subscription $subscription \
    --admin
```

By executing the preceding command, we will set up a configuration for the `kubectl` command. This configuration resides on the local `~/.kube/config` path of the workstation used to execute `kubectl` commands. Now we should be able to execute commands toward the cluster.

Creating a Key Vault

We shall proceed and create a Key Vault resource; then, on that Key Vault, we shall create a key and a secret. We will assign fine-grained permissions to make it feasible to interact with the Key Vault through RBAC permissions.

First, we create the Azure Key Vault:

```
resource "azurerm_key_vault" "ksm_key_vault" {
  name                      = "ksm-key-vault"
  ...
  sku_name                  = "standard"
  enable_rbac_authorization = true
  soft_delete_retention_days = 7
}
```

As you can see, we enabled the RBAC option. Since we enabled RBAC, we will create an identity that can be used with our Kubernetes workloads:

```
resource "azurerm_user_assigned_identity" "keyvault_reader" {
  name                 = "keyvault-reader"
  ...
}


resource "azurerm_role_assignment" "ksm_key_vault_reader" {
  scope = azurerm_key_vault.ksm_key_vault.id
  role_definition_name = "Key Vault Reader"
  principal_id         = azurerm_user_assigned_identity.keyvault_
reader.principal_id
}
...
```

We created the identity and attached the permissions enabling us to use the Secrets and view them. The next step is to set up the credentials for the federated identity. We need to use the OIDC issuer URL from the cluster we provisioned previously:

```
resource "azurerm_federated_identity_credential" "cred" {
 name   = "ksm-reader-identity"
  ...
 Issuer =azurerm_kubernetes_cluster.ksm_aks.oidc_issuer_url
 audience  = ["api://AzureADTokenExchange"]
 parent_id = azurerm_user_assigned_identity.keyvault_reader.id
  subject = "system:serviceaccount:default:service-token-reader"
}
```

Alternatively, we can create the Key Vault through the command line:

```
$ az keyvault create -n ksm-key-vault -g ksm-resource-group  -l eastus
--enable-rbac-authorization
az identity create --name keyvault-reader --resource-group
ksm-resource-group
...


az identity federated-credential create \
  --name "ksm-reader-identity" ...
```

By provisioning the identity credential, we can now interact with Azure Key Vault through Kubernetes. The federated identity credentials enable us to access resources protected by Active Directory. The federated credential that we used establishes a trust relationship with the identity provider of our AKS cluster and Active Directory. We allow the service-token-reader service account to impersonate ksm-reader-identity.

Reading Secrets from the Key Vault

We have our AKS cluster set up and our `kubectl` command is ready to execute commands to the cluster. So far, we have not had to install any plugins. This is because the plugins were enabled when creating the AKS cluster.

We can check this by running the following command on the CSI plugin:

```
kubectl get pods -n kube-system -l 'app in (secrets-store-csi-
driver,secrets-store-provider-azure)'
NAME                                   READY   STATUS    RESTARTS   AGE
aks-secrets-store-csi-driver-t6n7h     3/3     Running   0          80m
aks-secrets-store-provider-azure-htmqk 1/1     Running   0          80m
```

The CSI driver that will enable us to fetch credentials from the Key Vault is already enabled. Along with the CSI driver, we have a new object type created on Kubernetes: `SecretProviderClass`. This custom resource is used to provide driver configurations and provider-specific parameters to the CSI driver. In Kubernetes, a **custom resource** is an extension of the Kubernetes API. We specify a new kind of object that is accessed through the Kubernetes API just like all the other Kubernetes resources. We can find more information on custom resources through the official documentation (`https://kubernetes.io/docs/concepts/extend-kubernetes/api-extension/custom-resources/`).

We will create `SecretProviderClass`:

```
apiVersion: secrets-store.csi.x-k8s.io/v1
kind: SecretProviderClass
metadata:
  name: keyvault-secrets
spec:
  provider: azure
  parameters:
    usePodIdentity: "false"
    clientID: #the identity provisioned
    keyvaultName: #keyvault name
    ...
    objects:  |
      array:
        - |
          objectName: secret1
          objectType: secret
        - |
          objectName: key1
          objectType: key
    tenantId: #kubernetes tenant id
```

We can now provision the service account that will have the identity attached:

```
apiVersion: v1
kind: ServiceAccount
metadata:
  annotations:
    azure.workload.identity/client-id: #identity with Key Vault access
  labels:
    azure.workload.identity/use: "true"
  name: service-token-reader
  namespace: default
```

Essentially, the identity used is the identity that we provisioned previously with the purpose of interacting with Azure Key Vault.

After applying the following, we can set up a Pod that will use the Key Vault credentials:

```
kind: Pod
apiVersion: v1
metadata:
  name: nginx
spec:
  serviceAccountName: service-token-reader
  containers:
    - name: nginx
      image: nginx
      volumeMounts:
      - name: keyvault-secrets
        mountPath: "/mnt/secrets-store"
        readOnly: true
  volumes:
    - name: keyvault-secrets
      csi:
        driver: secrets-store.csi.k8s.io
        readOnly: true
        volumeAttributes:
          secretProviderClass: "keyvault-secrets"
```

As of now, we have achieved our main goal, which is to use Key Vault Secrets through Azure Key Vault. We did achieve access to the Key Vault Secrets, so the next thing to check is whether auditing of Key Vault access is feasible.

Auditing and logging

In the previous section, we created the Key Vault on Azure. Azure provides us with the option to enable auditing for the resources we provision.

In our case, we add a block that enables us to store the audit logs of Key Vault access to a storage account.

Let us perform the Terraform code:

```
resource "azurerm_monitor_diagnostic_setting" "ksm_key_vault_logs" {
  name                = "ksm-key-vault-logs"
  target_resource_id = azurerm_key_vault.ksm_key_vault.id
  storage_account_id = azurerm_storage_account.ksm_storage_account.id
  log {
    category = "AuditEvent"
    enabled  = true

    retention_policy {
      enabled = false
    }
  }
}
...
}
```

We've enabled Azure to capture the logs needed for auditing through a storage account.

> **Important note**
> Take note that we have set a retention policy on the log. At the time of writing, it has been announced that the **Diagnostic Settings Storage Retention** feature is being deprecated, thus the retention for logs and metrics should be configured through Azure Storage Lifecycle Management.

If we navigate to the bucket, there should be a container created on that storage account. The container will have the name `insights-logs-auditevent`, and the files in the container will be in the JSON format.

Let us examine one of the files:

```
{
  "time": "2023-08-30T09:07:19.8593007Z",
  "category": "AuditEvent",
  "operationName": "KeyGet",
  "resultType": "Success",
  "correlationId": "fa11ea42-67c0-47cd-8a6b-f7bcb349414f",
  "identity": {
```

```
      "claim": {
        "oid": "80dd018c-ede7-42f4-99a8-00e278868a7c",
        "appid": "b1967275-af7b-4d75-9804-c935ecb22226",
        "xms_mirid": "/subscriptions/.../userAssignedIdentities/
keyvault-reader",
        "xms_az_nwperimid": []
      }
    },
    "properties": {
      "id": "https://ksm-key-vault.vault.azure.net/keys/key1",
      "requestUri": "https://ksm-key-vault.vault.azure.net/keys/
key1/?api-version=2016-10-01",
      "isRbacAuthorized": true,
      ...
    },
    ...
}
```

We can see the category and the operation. Also, the identity is the one we attached to Kubernetes previously. Through audit logs, we can identify the actions that took place, the actor of those actions, and the resource upon which the actions took place, which in our case is the Key Vault we provisioned.

Azure Key Vault for secret encryption

So far, we've used Azure Key Vault to store sensitive Secrets. What we want to identify is whether we can use Azure Key Vault to encrypt the Secrets that reside on etcd.

We've already created a Key Vault. We shall use that Key Vault to create a *key* used for KMS purposes.

We will create a key first:

```
resource "azurerm_key_vault_key" "ksm_encryption_key" {
  name         = "ksm-encryption-key"
  key_vault_id = azurerm_key_vault.ksm_key_vault.id
  key_type     = "RSA"
  key_size     = 2048
    key_opts = [
    "decrypt",
    "encrypt",
    "sign",
    "unwrapKey",
    "verify",
    "wrapKey",
  ]
}
```

Take note that we can also specify a rotation policy:

```
rotation_policy {
    automatic {
      time_before_expiry = "P30D"
    }
    expire_after         = "P90D"
    notify_before_expiry = "P29D"
  }
```

When we create the Kubernetes cluster, we can use this key to encrypt the Secrets we create.

In the AKS section, we shall put this option:

```
resource "azurerm_kubernetes_cluster" "ksm_aks" {
  name = "ksm-aks"

  ...

  key_management_service {
    key_vault_key_id = azurerm_key_vault_key.ksm_encryption_key.id
    key_vault_network_access = "Public"
  }
  ...
}
```

We've successfully encrypted our Secrets on etcd using Azure Key Vault as a KMS. We can also check this through the audit logs:

```
{
  "time": "2023-09-03T11:46:27.5820050Z",
  "category": "AuditEvent",
  "operationName": "KeyDecrypt",
  "resultType": "Success",
  "identity": {
    "claim": {
      "xms_az_rid": "/subscriptions/.../managedClusters/ksm-aks",
      "xms_az_nwperimid": []
    }
  },
  "properties": {
    "id": "https://ksm-key-vault.vault.azure.net/keys/ksm-encryption-
key/0c24b95c67534a3eb85c71854dc8a7bd",
    "algorithm": "RSA-OAEP-256",
    "clientInfo": "... k8s-kms-keyvault/v0.5.0 (linux/amd64)
84fa3b7/2023-05-17-21:13",
    "httpStatusCode": 200,
    ..
    "tlsVersion": "TLS1_2"
  },
}
```

As we can see, Azure Key Vault is actively being used to decrypt the Secrets hosted on AKS. The `KeyDecrypt` operation indicates the decryption operations. An equivalent operation will take place for encrypting the Secrets on AKS. This hardens the security of our Secrets management.

Summary

In this chapter, we managed to create an AKS cluster that would be able to read Secrets from Azure Key Vault. We identified the RBAC permissions needed to achieve encrypting and decrypting of the Secrets. We also increased the security by encrypting the Secrets on etcd, using Azure Key Vault as a KMS for Kubernetes. Lastly, we could identify the usage of Azure Key Vault through the audit logs.

In the next chapter, we will focus on another popular cloud provider, Google Cloud Platform. We will explore the secret storage option on GCP and its integration with the Kubernetes offering of GCP, as well as the secret encryption options.

10

Exploring Cloud Secret Store on GCP

Previously, we did a deep dive into Azure Key Vault. We managed to store Secrets securely on Key Vault and utilized it as a key management service for the Secrets that will reside on etcd. In this chapter, we will focus on the Google Cloud Platform and will utilize the Secret Manager of Google Cloud.

We will be covering the following topics in this chapter:

- Overview of GCP Secret Manager
- Workload Identity on GKS
- GKE and GCP Secret Manager integration
- Auditing and logging
- GKE and KMS integration

By the end of this chapter, we should be able to store our Secrets to GCP Secret Manager securely, monitor secret access through auditing, and add an extra layer of security by encrypting the Secrets on etcd.

Technical requirements

To link concepts with hands-on examples, we are leveraging a series of tools and platforms commonly used to interact with the Google Cloud API and Kubernetes:

- **gcloud CLI** (`https://cloud.google.com/sdk/gcloud#download_and_ install_the`) is a set of tools to create and manage Google Cloud resources
- **Terraform** (`https://www.terraform.io/`) is infrastructure-as-code software that can be used to provision and manage infrastructure on the cloud
- **kubectl** (`https://kubernetes.io/docs/reference/kubectl/`) is the command-line tool used for communicating with a Kubernetes cluster through the Kubernetes API

Overview of GCP Secret Manager

GCP Secret Manager is the secret manager solution provided by Google Cloud. Provided that we have an application that has the need to store Secrets, the Secret Manager can be utilized. The application can be deployed on Compute Engine, Kubernetes, Cloud Functions, or any other legitimate form of deployment on Google Cloud.

Since this service is managed by Google Cloud, there are some features offered by default. We can summarize them as follows:

- IAM
- High availability
- Logging and auditing
- Integration with other Google Cloud components

Let's have a deep dive into each one.

IAM

Google Cloud comes with **identity access management** (**IAM**). Certain IAM permissions take effect on an organizational level, allowing us to manage an organization's resources. Then we have IAM permissions that apply project-wide, thus they are permissions assigned to target specific resources throughout a GCP project. The most granular level is resource-based IAM permissions. When we create a resource, we can have permissions only for that specific resource. The identities can be either users, Google Groups, or service accounts. Permissions for a specific resource can be assigned to a specific identity.

High availability

Secret Manager is a highly available solution and covers disaster recovery scenarios. By default, the Secrets can be accessed globally from different regions of Google Cloud. Behind the scenes, the Secrets are replicated in multiple regions unless specified otherwise. A reason to specify the regions is data residency limitations. If a secret cannot be stored in a certain region, we can define the regions we want the secret to be stored in and exclude any regions that should not contain any of our data.

Logging, auditing, and monitoring

Google Cloud has, by default, a logging solution that is used for application logs but also for audit logs. There is a distinction between application logs and audit logs. To be able to access audit logs on a GCP project, you need to have the Private Logs Viewer permission.

Integration with other Google Cloud components

As expected, Secret Manager is integrated with other Google Cloud components.

We can use a **key management service** (**KMS**) to encrypt the Secrets on Secret Manager and we can integrate Secret Manager with Kubernetes. As we have seen in *Chapter 8, Exploring Cloud Secret Store on AWS*, the integration with Secret Manager on Kubernetes happens through the CSI plugin.

Introduction to Workload Identity

Workload Identity on Kubernetes Engine on GCP enables us to assign permissions to Kubernetes workloads that can interact with Google Cloud resources. Google Cloud has the concept of service accounts. Service accounts are used for machines to interact with resources. A compute engine, a lambda function, or even an App Engine on Google Cloud can be assigned with a service account that has permissions to interact with Google Cloud resources. With Workload Identity, we can map service accounts on GCP with service accounts on Kubernetes.

In Kubernetes, we might use several types of deployments for our applications. We can use `Deployment`, `StatefulSet`, `DaemonSet`, and more. Behind the scenes, a Pod will be created, which is the base component for running applications on Kubernetes. The Pod can be assigned a service account. By using Workload Identity on Kubernetes and binding a Kubernetes service account to a Google Cloud service account, the Pod with the Kubernetes service account attached shall be able to interact with Google Cloud resources based on the permissions we granted on the GCP service account.

Therefore, this concept will help us with GCP Secret Manager. The access from our Kubernetes workload to Secret Manager will be authorized and feasible, thanks to the integration of Kubernetes CSI and the Workload Identity.

Now that we understand how Kubernetes and Secret Manager on Google Cloud work together, we will focus on implementing a Kubernetes cluster.

Integrating GKE and GCP Secret Manager

Thanks to the CSI Secret Store plugins, we can integrate Secret Manager solutions with our Kubernetes cluster. The Kubernetes offering on Google Cloud is the Google Kubernetes engine. We will use this Kubernetes cluster offering to integrate with Secret Manager.

There are several options to create a cluster. We will provide the Terraform code for the scope of creating the cluster. Also, we will provide other commands needed.

Configuring the Terraform project

We need to configure the Terraform provider. It will point to the GCP credentials file and also to the GCP project and the region.

The provider configuration should be like this:

```
provider "google" {
  credentials = "/path/to/credentials/file"
  project     = "your-gcp-project"
  region      = "us-central1"
}
```

To initialize, we need to run the `init` command:

```
$ terraform init
```

When we run the `init` command when a credentials file is not specified, the credentials by default will be the credentials of the user who logged in when we used the `gcloud auth login` command. Alternatively, we can specify a service account file.

Provisioning the network

We shall proceed with provisioning the network. On Google Cloud, a network is a global resource, whereas the subnets of a network are regional resources.

We will create the network, and as expected, no region will be specified since VPC is a global resource:

```
resource "google_compute_network" "vpc" {
  name                    = "${var.project_id}-vpc"
  auto_create_subnetworks = "false"
  project = var.project_id
}
```

The subnetwork will be created to host the nodes on Kubernetes. It will be mapped to the region specified:

```
resource "google_compute_subnetwork" "subnet" {
  name          = "${var.project_id}-subnet"
  region        = var.region
  network       = google_compute_network.vpc.name
  ip_cidr_range = "10.10.0.0/24"
  project = var.project_id
}
```

We can now focus on creating Secrets on Secret Manager.

Provisioning a secret on Secret Manager

GCP Secret Manager is a service; to use Secret Manager on GCP, we do not need to create a resource. Instead, we create the Secrets that will be hosted on Secret Manager.

We will get started by provisioning a secret:

```
resource "google_secret_manager_secret" "my_secret" {
  secret_id = "my-secret"
  user_managed {
      replicas {
        location = var.location
      }
      replicas {
        location = "us-east1"
      }
    }
}
```

We purposefully specified the region where the replicas will reside. The secret will be hosted in two regions, making our secret usage resilient, even during a region outage.

We created the secret, but we did not assign a specific value. For a secret, we specify a version of that secret. Let us proceed with adding the version:

```
resource "google_secret_manager_secret_version" "my_secret_version" {
  secret = google_secret_manager_secret.my_secret.id
  secret_data = "secret-data"
}
```

Also, we would like to provision a service account with permissions to retrieve the secret:

```
resource "google_service_account" "my_service_account" {
  account_id   = "read-secrets-service-account"
}
resource "google_secret_manager_secret_iam_binding" "my_secret_reader"
{
  role   = "roles/secretmanager.secretAccessor"
  secret_id = google_secret_manager_secret.my_secret.id
  members = [
    "serviceAccount:${google_service_account.my_service_account.
email}"
  ]
}
```

The secret is provisioned, and we have a service account to be used for retrieval.

Now, let's go ahead and create the GKE cluster.

Provisioning the GKE cluster

To create the GKE cluster we need to create the master, and we will also create a default node pool:

```
resource "google_container_cluster" "gke_cluster" {
  name     = "secrets-cluster"
  location = var.region
  remove_default_node_pool = true
  initial_node_count      = 1
  network    = google_compute_network.vpc.name
  subnetwork = google_compute_subnetwork.subnet.name
  ...
  workload_identity_config {
    workload_pool = "kube-secrets-book.svc.id.goog"
  }
}
```

When creating a cluster, GKE forces us to create an initial node pool by default. We can create another node pool of our choice using the `google_container_node_pool` resource. This way, we can tune more parameters of a GKE node pool in Terraform and separate the cluster and the node pool definitions. Once the new node pool is created, provided we have the `remove_default_node_pool` setting set to `true`, Terraform will remove the initial node pool. This will keep the costs low since only one node pool will be operational.

The primary node pool will be targeted toward keeping the costs low:

```
resource "google_container_node_pool" "primary_nodes" {
  name     = google_container_cluster.gke_cluster.name
  cluster  = google_container_cluster.gke_cluster.name
  version = data.google_container_engine_versions.gke_version.release_
channel_latest_version["STABLE"]
  node_count = 1
  node_config {
    oauth_scopes = [
      "https://www.googleapis.com/auth/logging.write",
      "https://www.googleapis.com/auth/monitoring",
    ]
    machine_type = "n1-standard-1"
    tags         = ["gke-node", "${var.project_id}-gke"]
    disk_size_gb = 10
    metadata = {
      disable-legacy-endpoints = "true"
    }
  }
}
```

We have been successful in creating the cluster. We can also log in to the cluster and issue some `kubectl` commands:

```
$ gcloud container clusters get-credentials secrets-cluster --region
us-central1 --project kube-secrets-book
$ kubectl get node
NAME                       STATUS    ROLES     AGE       VERSION
gke-secrets-cluster-secrets-cluster-9e54b21e-
5kxw    Ready     <none>    9m41s     v1.27.3-gke.1700
gke-secrets-cluster-secrets-cluster-b969915f-
rfjz    Ready     <none>    9m35s     v1.27.3-gke.1700
...
```

Our GKE cluster is operational and ready to serve our workloads.

Adding the CSI plugin for Kubernetes Secrets

We have an operational cluster; therefore, we will focus on setting up the CSI plugin. On a standard GKE cluster, the CSI plugin has to be installed. When it comes to GKE Autopilot, a GKE version that manages many aspects of Kubernetes out-of-the-box, the CSI plugin is installed by default.

Take note that the CSI plugin is not officially supported by Google.

First, we need to install the plugin to the cluster:

```
$ helm repo add secrets-store-csi-driver https://kubernetes-sigs.
github.io/secrets-store-csi-driver/charts
$ helm install csi-secrets-store secrets-store-csi-driver/secrets-
store-csi-driver --namespace kube-system
$ kubectl apply -f https://raw.githubusercontent.com/
GoogleCloudPlatform/secrets-store-csi-driver-provider-gcp/main/deploy/
provider-gcp-plugin.yaml
```

Then we should create a service account. The Kubernetes service account will be annotated with the ID of the GCP service account that we want our workloads to use:

```
$ kubectl create serviceaccount read-secret --namespace=default
$ kubectl annotate serviceaccount read-secret \
    --namespace=default \
    iam.gke.io/gcp-service-account=read-secrets-service-account@test-
gcp-project.iam.gserviceaccount.com
```

This way, the service account of Kubernetes will act on behalf of the service account we created previously. The service account is able to retrieve the Secrets from Secret Manager.

`SecretProviderClass` is a custom resource type providing driver configurations and parameters to the CSI driver. We shall specify `SecretProviderClass`:

```
apiVersion: secrets-store.csi.x-k8s.io/v1
kind: SecretProviderClass
metadata:
  name: app-secrets
spec:
  provider: gcp
  parameters:
    secrets: |
      - resourceName: "projects/project-i/secrets/my-secret/versions/
latest"
        path: "good1.txt"
```

The last step is to create a Pod. The Pod will use the Workload Identity and act on behalf of the `read-secrets-service-account` GCP account. Also, the Pod will use `SecretProviderClass` we created previously and mount the Secrets to the Pod as a file:

```
apiVersion: v1
kind: Pod
metadata:
...
spec:
  serviceAccountName: mypodserviceaccount
  containers:
  - ...
    volumeMounts:
      - mountPath: "/var/secrets"
        name: mysecret
  volumes:
  - name: mysecret
    csi:
      driver: secrets-store.csi.k8s.io
      readOnly: true
      volumeAttributes:
        secretProviderClass: "app-secrets"
```

What we have achieved is to mount the secret to the Pod using the CSI plugin. We can now focus on monitoring the usage of Secrets. Auditing and logging play a crucial role in identifying operations on a cloud resource or Kubernetes.

Auditing and logging

Google Cloud comes with logging and auditing out-of-the-box. Once we provision a Kubernetes cluster, all the operations will be visible through the logging console.

Suppose we create a secret on the cluster we provisioned previously:

```
$ kubectl create secret generic empty-secret
```

This action will be logged on the audit logs of GKE, and all we must do is search the logging console on GCP using the following query:

```
protoPayload.methodName="io.k8s.core.v1.secrets.create"
protoPayload.@type="type.googleapis.com/google.cloud.audit.AuditLog"
resource.type="k8s_cluster"
```

As a result, we should see all the operations upon accessing Secrets:

Figure 10.1 – Kubernetes audit logs on GKE

Apart from audit logs on Kubernetes, we can also utilize the audit logs on Secret Manager. On the logging screen of GCP, we can search specifically for audit logs:

```
resource.type="audited_resource" AND
resource.labels.service="secretmanager.googleapis.com"
```

This GCP log query filter will enable us to see the logs related to Secret Manager.

GKE security posture dashboard

Another notable tool provided by GCP to improve the security posture of a GKE cluster is the **GKE security posture** dashboard. The GKE security posture dashboard is a set of features in the Google Cloud console scanning GKE clusters and workloads, offering opinionated, actionable recommendations.

GKE security posture focuses on two sections:

- Kubernetes security posture
- Workload vulnerability scanning

Through the Kubernetes security posture dashboard, when a vulnerability is discovered, it is automatically displayed on the dashboard with the clusters and workloads affected in order to enable us to proceed with further actions:

Figure 10.2 – GKE security posture

Through workload vulnerability scanning, the container images running in the clusters are scanned for vulnerabilities. Also, there is support for scanning the actual programming language packages for vulnerabilities, making the workloads even more secure.

As expected, the findings of the GKE security posture are integrated with other cloud components such as logging and monitoring, thus making it feasible to have alerts and enable automation when it comes to tackling any security incidents.

Now that auditing and logging are in place, we can proceed with the more advanced concept of encrypting Secrets by integrating GKE and KMS.

Integrating GKE and KMS

It is feasible to use KMS to encrypt the Secrets on the Google Kubernetes Container Engine. By default, GKE will encrypt data at rest, and the encryption is managed by GCP. Apart from this secure handling of our data, we might want to have more control over the encryption of the data. In this case, we have the option to encrypt the data residing on Kubernetes by using a KMS key that we provision and maintain in our GCP project. We shall start by provisioning the KMS key:

```
resource "google_kms_key_ring" "ksm_key_ring" {
  name     = "ksm-key-ring"
  location = var.region
}
resource "google_kms_crypto_key" "ksm_secret_key" {
  name = "ksm-secret-encryption"
  key_ring = google_kms_key_ring.ksm_key_ring.id
  lifecycle {
    prevent_destroy = false
  }
}
```

We should also assign permissions in order for the Kubernetes service account to be able to perform encryption and decryption. Take note that on GKE, the master is managed by GCP, and the service account that the master nodes use is not a service account residing on our Google Cloud project, thus we need to assign permission to a service account that is not part of our project:

```
data "google_project" "project" {}
resource "google_kms_crypto_key_iam_binding" "ksm_secret_key_encdec" {
  crypto_key_id = google_kms_crypto_key.ksm_secret_key.id
  role          = "roles/cloudkms.cryptoKeyEncrypterDecrypter"
  members = [
  "serviceAccount:service-${data.google_project.project.number}@
container-engine-robot.iam.gserviceaccount.com"
  ]
}
```

We just created the KMS. In our cluster configuration, let's enable the database encryption option:

```
resource "google_container_cluster" "gke_cluster" {
  name      = "secrets-cluster"
  location = var.region
...
  database_encryption {
    key_name = google_kms_crypto_key.ksm_secret_key.id
    state = "ENCRYPTED"
  }
}
```

Instead of GCP using its own KMS key, we supply our own **customer-managed key** (**CMK**). Our Secrets on Kubernetes will be encrypted by using the KMS key we provided.

Summary

In this chapter, we had a deep dive into Secrets management on Google Cloud and GKE. We learned about Secret Manager, the GCP offering for Secrets management, and the features that come with it such as availability, auditing, and integration with other Google Cloud components. We then proceeded to provision a Kubernetes Engine on GCP using the GKE offering and integrated it with Secret Manager. Then we used KMS to encrypt the Secrets on Kubernetes at rest. Finally, by using Google Cloud monitoring, we managed to keep track of the secret operations on Kubernetes, Secret Manager, and the KMS. In the next chapter, we will focus on the non-cloud-based secret managers: HashiCorp Vault and CyberArk Conjur.

11

Exploring External Secret Stores

Previously, we worked with the cloud providers AWS, Azure, and GCP. We ran our application and integrated it with the secret providers offered on these platforms. We used the Secrets management facilities of each cloud provider and benefited from the ecosystem of tools that the cloud providers provides us with. This made it feasible to tackle concerns such as auditing high availability and disaster recovery. In this chapter, we shall explore external secret stores that are not part of a cloud provider's offerings.

We will cover the following topics:

- Overview of external secret store providers
- The different types of external secret stores, such as HashiCorp Vault, and CyberArk Secrets Manager
- Managing Secrets in an external secret store for Kubernetes

Technical requirements

To link concepts with hands-on examples, we are leveraging a series of tools and platforms commonly used to interact with the Google Cloud API and Kubernetes:

- **kubectl**: This is the command-line tool used for communicating with a Kubernetes cluster through the Kubernetes API (https://kubernetes.io/docs/reference/kubectl/).
- **minikube**: This is a local Kubernetes distribution used for Kubernetes learning and development. To install minikube on your system, you can follow the instructions from the official documentation (https://minikube.sigs.k8s.io/docs/start/).
- **Vault CLI**: This is used to interact with a HashiCorp Vault installation (https://developer.hashicorp.com/vault/docs/install).

- **jq**: This is a lightweight and flexible command-line JSON processor. It will help us extract the information needed from `kubectl` commands (`https://jqlang.github.io/jq/`).

- **Helm**: This is a package manager for Kubernetes that we will be using to simplify the deployment and management of Kubernetes resources (`https://helm.sh`).

Overview of external secret providers

By default, Secrets on Kubernetes are stored in **etcd** as mentioned in *Chapter 1, Understanding Kubernetes Secrets Management*. Storing Secrets on etcd comes with certain security concerns, as mentioned in *Chapter 7, Challenges and Risks in Managing Secrets*. Alternative forms of secret storage can help us harden our security and also segregate the concerns that come with secret usage. We will focus on the components that make it feasible to have external secret providers.

First, let us have a look at the available external secret store providers:

- AWS Secrets Manager

- Azure Key Vault

- GCP Secret Manager

- HashiCorp Vault

- CyberArk Conjur

The way these providers offer integration with Kubernetes might differ. A very popular approach to achieving integration with a secret store provider is through the Secrets Store CSI Driver.

Secrets Store CSI Driver

The Secrets Store CSI Driver makes it feasible to integrate Kubernetes Secrets through a **container storage interface** (**CSI**) volume. The Kubernetes Secrets Store interface is based on the Kubernetes CSI plugin. Through CSI, we can integrate external store providers to Kubernetes by implementing a CSI plugin, which can extend our cluster's storage capabilities without having to change the Kubernetes core code.

External secret store providers with CSI plugins

There are a handful of CSI provider plugins:

- AWS provider

- Azure provider

- GCP provider

- Vault provider

In the previous chapters, we focused on the CSI Secrets Store CSI Driver that came along with the cloud provider solutions. We mention a new provider, the Vault provider, which is HashiCorp's secret storage.

All the secret providers on the list give the option of high availability, and all secret providers provide auditing and logging. Those elements ensure data governance and security. Apart from the CSI Driver solution, there are also other approaches available for Secrets management integration. One of them is the Secrets Injector component, which we will cover next.

Secrets Injector

The Secrets Injector component offers another way to inject Secrets on an application and Secrets hosted on an external secret store provider.

Secret managers such as HashiCorp Vault and CyberArk Conjur support secret storage usage through the Sidecar Injector. Those sidecar injectors focus on the aspects of authorization and authentication when it comes to receiving the Secrets from the secret storage. Also, they tackle the integration with the Kubernetes workloads.

However, take note that injecting Secrets is not an action that always requires a sophisticated binary that interacts with Kubernetes. For example, let us consider GCP Secret Manager. There is no official binary that will receive the Secrets from Secret Manager and then attach them to the Pod. This does not prevent us from implementing a solution that will securely achieve the same result. We can utilize Workload Identity, as mentioned in *Chapter 10*, *Exploring Cloud Secret Store on GCP*. Through Workload Identity, our Kubernetes workloads can interact with Secret Manager. We can then use the client libraries of GCP Secret Manager, and through an initialization container, the Secrets can be mounted locally to the Pod.

This recipe can be applied to any other form of storage. The key element to note is the usage of Workload Identity; the security remained intact by utilizing it. We did not have to store any Secrets on etcd that would make it feasible to interact with Secret Manager. Instead, Kubernetes workloads would get assigned certain permissions to make it feasible to interact with Secret Manager.

In other forms of Secrets management, such as HashiCorp Vault, authentication and interaction with the secret storage are a bit different from what we have seen so far, yet the security qualities remain the same. Access to the Secrets is achieved in a secure and authorized way where the principle of least permissions is followed. We will examine this in the following chapter.

To summarize, we had an overview of the external Secrets Provider that we can use to inject our Secrets into Kubernetes. Going forward, we will focus on the HashiCorp Vault and its capabilities.

HashiCorp Vault

In the rapidly evolving landscape of distributed computing, securing sensitive information is paramount. Kubernetes, a leader in container orchestration, requires robust solutions to manage Secrets—sensitive data necessary for the proper configuration and operation of applications. HashiCorp Vault stands out as a central figure in addressing these challenges, providing a comprehensive suite of tools for secure Secrets management across Kubernetes clusters.

HashiCorp Vault offers a centralized, encrypted solution, ensuring that Secrets remain confidential and are never exposed in application code or configuration files. Its integration with Kubernetes not only simplifies Secrets management but also fortifies the security of containerized applications, introducing features such as dynamic Secrets, secure secret injection into Pods, and a Kubernetes-native authentication method. These features foster secure communications and secret retrieval between HashiCorp Vault and Kubernetes, enhancing flexibility, security, and efficiency in managing Secrets.

HashiCorp Vault's capability to dynamically generate short-lived credentials on demand distinguishes it from native Kubernetes Secrets, which are often stored unencrypted in etcd and become unwieldy as applications scale. HashiCorp Vault's approach minimizes the attack surface, enhances security, and addresses the potential mismanagement of Secrets.

Moreover, HashiCorp Vault's extensive audit logging ensures transparency and accountability, aiding compliance and facilitating swift responses to security incidents. By integrating HashiCorp Vault into Kubernetes deployments, organizations position themselves to achieve a robust, secure, and compliant containerized application environment, overcoming the limitations of native Kubernetes Secrets and elevating their Secrets management practices to the highest security standards.

There is an open source and an enterprise version, and we will focus on the open source version next.

Using HashiCorp Vault as a secret storage

HashiCorp Vault can be used as a secret storage; it can contain the Secrets of our application. This makes it feasible to host Kubernetes Secrets on Vault. This can be done in two ways: either having the Vault hosted outside of Kubernetes or hosting the Vault with Kubernetes.

Let us examine how we can integrate an external HashiCorp Vault with Kubernetes. For our needs, we shall use a minikube installation.

External Vault storage

We will proceed with creating a Vault instance, which will be run through a Docker container. We can run Vault using Docker Compose:

```
services:
  vault_node_1:
    image: vault:1.13.3
    container_name: vault_node_1
    ports:
      - "8200:8200"
    environment:
```

```
      VAULT_DEV_LISTEN_ADDRESS: "0.0.0.0:8200"
      VAULT_DEV_ROOT_TOKEN_ID: mytoken
      VAULT_LOG_LEVEL: debug
    volumes:
      - haproxy.cfg:/haproxy.cfg
```

We can run Vault using the following command:

```
$ docker compose up
```

Another solution is to run Vault by using a plain Docker command:

```
$ docker run -p 8200:8200 --rm -v haproxy.cfg:/haproxy.cfg  --name
vault_node_1  -e VAULT_DEV_ROOT_TOKEN_ID=mytoken -e VAULT_DEV_LISTEN_
ADDRESS=0.0.0.0:8200 -e VAULT_LOG_LEVEL=debug vault:1.13.3
```

There is no difference in the outcome of those two commands. Compose has the convenience of being just one file, but standalone docker commands also work as well. It is a matter of preference.

It is important to understand that we run Vault in development mode for debugging purposes. This is not a secure way to run Vault, which we will see in the *Development mode versus production mode* section of this chapter. Development mode will be used to make our example use case simpler.

Let us examine Vault. We specified the root token; this is a token with root permissions. We also set the level of logging to debug. This is to help us with troubleshooting our installation. The VAULT_ DEV_LISTEN_ADDRESS is the address to bind when in development mode. For now, this is sufficient to proceed with integrating with Kubernetes.

Installing Vault on Kubernetes

To be able to integrate Vault with Kubernetes, we need to install the Vault binaries. The easiest way to do so is through a Helm chart.

First, we shall acquire a reference for our Vault installation:

```
$ EXTERNAL_VAULT_ADDR=$(minikube ssh "dig +short host.docker.internal"
| tr -d '\r')
```

Then we will install Vault on Kubernetes:

```
$ helm repo add hashicorp https://helm.releases.hashicorp.com
$ helm repo update
$ helm install vault hashicorp/vault --set "global.
externalVaultAddr=http://$EXTERNAL_VAULT_ADDR :8200" --set="csi.
enabled=true"
```

We installed the Vault package on Kubernetes and set an external Vault address that Kubernetes will point to. Also, we enabled the CSI since we will show the CSI capabilities in another example. To check that our installation was successful, we can check whether the deployment of vault-agent-injector is in our cluster. By using kubectl, we can identify whether a vault-agent-injector deployment exists:

```
$ kubectl get deployment vault-agent-injector
NAME                    READY   UP-TO-DATE   AVAILABLE   AGE
vault-agent-injector    1/1     1            1           3h40m
```

Let us understand how the Vault Agent Injector works.

Vault Agent Injector

If we examine the Vault Agent Injector, we shall see that it uses a specific service account, vault-agent-injector. This component is responsible for changing the Pod specifications so agent containers can be included. These Vault Agent containers render Secrets from Vault to a shared memory volume.

On an initialization of a Pod that uses Vault Secrets, the following actions occur:

1.   The agent will identify the Pod that uses the Vault Secrets.

2.   The Pod specification will be changed and will include the Vault Agent containers.

3.   The Vault init container will fetch the Secrets and attach them to the Pod as shared memory volume.

4.   If the Secrets change in the Vault, the Vault Sidecar Injector will change the Secrets.

The vault-agent-injector Pod is assigned the vault-agent-injector-clusterrole role.

We can see the vault-agent-injector-clusterrole cluster role:

```
$ kubectl get clusterrole vault-agent-injector-clusterrole -o yaml

kind: ClusterRole
metadata:
...
  name: vault-agent-injector-clusterrole
rules:
- apiGroups:
  - admissionregistration.k8s.io
  resources:
  - mutatingwebhookconfigurations
  verbs:
  - get
  - list
  - watch
  - patch
```

The `vault-agent-injector` is registered to Kubernetes as a **mutating admission webhook**. Once a Pod is created with certain Vault annotations, `vault-agent-injector` will intercept the creation request and rewrite the Pod definition.

The Vault annotations would be like the following:

```
vault.hashicorp.com/agent-inject: 'true'
vault.hashicorp.com/role: 'webapp_admin_r'
vault.hashicorp.com/agent-inject-secret-credentials.txt: 'secret/data/
webapp/admin'
```

As we can see, we enable the injection method. Then, we specify the Vault role that will be used to fetch the Secrets and the Secrets that will be fetched:

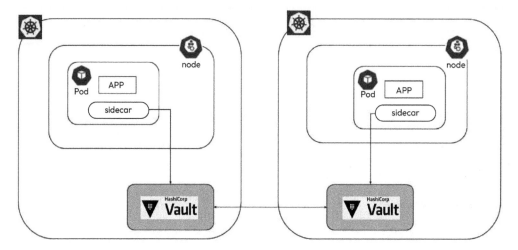

Figure 11.1 – Vault Injector and application hosted on Kubernetes

By rewriting the Pod definition, the Pod will now contain Vault Agent containers. The Vault Agent containers will then interact with Vault to retrieve the Secrets and inject them into the Pod.

Vault service account and Kubernetes authentication

For Vault to interact with Kubernetes, it must use a service account. By installing the Vault Helm package, a service account will also be created. The service account is named `vault`.

We need to create a token for that service account. From *Chapter 2, Walking through Kubernetes Secrets Management Concepts*, we know that in new versions of Kubernetes, we must create a secret for the service account by ourselves.

Let's create the secret for the service account. We will create a YAML file with the following specifications:

```
apiVersion: v1
kind: Secret
metadata:
  name: vault-sa-token
  annotations:
    kubernetes.io/service-account.name: vault
type: kubernetes.io/service-account-token
```

Next, we shall apply the YAML file:

```
$ kubectl apply -f vault-secret.yaml
```

The secret will be created, and we should be able to use it for Vault. Now we should configure Vault to enable the Kubernetes authentication.

Kubernetes authentication

We can authenticate Vault by using a Kubernetes service account token. This is the Kubernetes auth method. Essentially, we configure a Kubernetes service account token on Vault. Then, this service account token is used to interact with the Kubernetes API. To enable this, we need to have the auth method enabled on Vault.

The following steps should be executed:

```
# retrieve Kubernetes secret for the service account
$ VAULT_HELM_SECRET_NAME=$(kubectl get secrets --output=json | jq -r
'.items[].metadata | select(.name|startswith("vault")).name')
# retrieve service account token
$ TOKEN_REVIEW_JWT=$(kubectl get secret $VAULT_HELM_SECRET_NAME
--output='go-template={{ .data.token }}' | base64 --decode)
# retrieve Kubernetes certificate
$ KUBE_CA_CERT=$(kubectl config view --raw --minify --flatten
--output='jsonpath={.clusters[].cluster.certificate-authority-data}' |
base64 --decode)
# retrieve the Kubernetes host
$ KUBE_HOST=$(kubectl config view --raw --minify --flatten
--output='jsonpath={.clusters[].cluster.server}')
# point to local vault address
$ export VAULT_ADDR=http://0.0.0.0:8200
# login to vault using the root token
$ vault login mytoken
# enabled kubernetes authentication on vault
$ vault auth enable kubernetes
# write Kubernetes authentication configuration
```

```
$ vault write auth/kubernetes/config token_reviewer_jwt="$TOKEN_
REVIEW_JWT" kubernetes_host="$KUBE_HOST" kubernetes_ca_cert="$KUBE_CA_
CERT" issuer="https://kubernetes.default.svc.cluster.local"
```

Let us see how this works behind the scenes:

- A service account is configured on Vault. It has the permissions to interact with the Kubernetes API and execute TokenReview requests.

- A role is created on Vault with permissions to interact with a secret residing in Vault. The role is mapped to a Kubernetes service account.

- A Pod is created and gets assigned the service account we created in the previous step. The Vault Injector issues a request to Vault using the service account JWT in order to fetch the secret from Vault.

- Vault issues a TokenReview request to the Kubernetes API in order to validate the JWT token.

- Kubernetes validates the token.

- Vault checks whether the service account mapped to the token is mapped to a role with access to the secret requested.

- Vault responds with the secret value.

- The Vault Injector injects the secret into the Pod.

The following is a diagram of the flow we discussed so far:

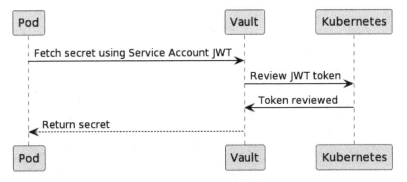

Figure 11.2 – Kubernetes auth flow

We configured Kubernetes authentication. One of the problems we will face is that $KUBE_HOST points to localhost; thus, the certificate is mapped to localhost. This can be an issue since Vault can access minikube through the Docker host address, thus a different address from localhost. For this reason, we shall use the proxy file we mounted previously. The port will have to change with the port of the $KUBE_HOST, which changes dynamically.

On another terminal, we shall execute the following commands and enable port forwarding:

```
$ KUBE_HOST=$(kubectl config view --raw --minify --flatten
--output='jsonpath={.clusters[].cluster.server}')
$ port=$(echo $KUBE_HOST | awk -F/ '{print $3}' | cut -d: -f2)
$ docker exec -it vault_node_1 sh
# apk add haproxy
# haproxy -f ./haproxy.cfg
```

Since this form of authentication involves many steps, auditing will help to increase our observability:

```
$ vault audit enable file file_path=/tmp/vault_audit.log
```

The audit log file at /tmp/vault_audit.log can be tailed:

```
$ docker exec -it  vault_node_1  tail -f /tmp/vault_audit.log
```

Since authentication is enabled and we have configured the service account needed, we should proceed and provide permissions for Vault to certain service accounts.

Vault policies and bindings

The benefit of using a secret provider such as Vault is the fact that we can store our Secrets and provide fine-grained policies.

For example, we shall store the following secret in Vault:

```
$ vault kv put secret/webapp/admin username='john.doe'
password='strong-password'
```

We would like to have a restrictive read-only policy for the secret.

Thus, we shall implement a policy with read-only permissions to the secret/webapp/admin secret:

```
$ vault policy write webapp_admin_r  - <<EOF path "secret/data/webapp/
admin" { capabilities = ["read"] } EOF
```

The policy is in place, so if we want certain workloads to be able to use this policy, we need to declaratively specify so. In our case, we shall have a Kubernetes service account mapped to a Pod that would require Secrets from Vault. The service account name would be simple-app. Our next step would be to bind the policy we created previously with that service account:

```
$ vault write auth/kubernetes/role/webapp_admin_r \
    bound_service_account_names=simple-app \
    bound_service_account_namespaces=default \
    policies=webapp_admin_r \
    ttl=24h
```

Now we should create that service account on Kubernetes:

```
$ kubectl create sa simple-app
```

This service account would be used by Vault Injector to inject the Secrets into the application. Provisioning the service account alone is not sufficient enough to interact with Vault. A cluster role binding is required:

```
apiVersion: rbac.authorization.k8s.io/v1
kind: ClusterRoleBinding
metadata:
  name: role-tokenreview-binding
  namespace: default
roleRef:
  apiGroup: rbac.authorization.k8s.io
  kind: ClusterRole
  name: system:auth-delegator
subjects:
  - kind: ServiceAccount
    name: simple-app
    namespace: default
```

auth-delegator is a role that allows delegated authentication and authorization checks. This way, the service account we configured on Vault can issue a TokenReview request for a JWT token that is bound to the simple-app service account.

Using Vault Secrets in an application

The simple-app service account will have the auth-delegator cluster role. The role enables delegated authentication and checks. Vault would be able to perform delegated authentication.

We shall create the application that will fetch the secret:

```
apiVersion: v1
kind: Pod
metadata:
  name: webapp
  labels:
    app: webapp
  annotations:
    vault.hashicorp.com/agent-inject: 'true'
    vault.hashicorp.com/role: 'webapp_admin_r'
    vault.hashicorp.com/agent-inject-secret-credentials.txt: 'secret/
data/webapp/admin'
spec:
  serviceAccountName: simple-app
```

```
    containers:
    - name: app
      image: nginx
```

The highlighted annotations used are crucial for `vault-agent-injector` to rewrite the Pod configuration so that the Vault initialization containers will take effect.

Once our application is up and running, we can now check the credentials:

```
$ kubectl exec -it webapp -c app -- cat /vault/secrets/credentials.txt
data: map[password:strong-password username:john.doe]
metadata: map[created_time:2023-10-08T19:23:50.814986175Z custom_
metadata:<nil> deletion_time: destroyed:false version:1]
```

Overall, we managed to interact with Vault in a secure way without having to mount any Vault-specific credentials to Kubernetes Secrets and thus on etcd. Instead, we relied on using the Kubernetes auth method supported by Vault. Now we can finally inject our credentials into the application by using the Vault sidecar container. However, Vault also supports another method of injecting Secrets into Kubernetes: the familiar CSI Driver method.

Vault and CSI Driver

Thanks to previous chapters, we are familiar with the Secret Store CSI Driver. Vault also enables us to use this approach. Using the CSI Driver is a different approach to mounting the Secrets from Vault on a Pod; however, it benefits from the same components. Since we have the Kubernetes auth method configured, we have the Vault authentication requirements tackled.

However, we do need to have the `secrets-store-csi-driver` package installed. We shall execute the following Helm commands:

```
$ helm repo add secrets-store-csi-driver https://kubernetes-sigs.
github.io/secrets-store-csi-driver/charts
$ helm install csi-secrets-store secrets-store-csi-driver/secrets-
store-csi-driver --namespace kube-system
```

The next step is to create `SecretProviderClass` pointing to the Secrets located in Vault:

```
apiVersion: secrets-store.csi.x-k8s.io/v1alpha1
kind: SecretProviderClass
metadata:
  name: vault-up-creds
  namespace: default
spec:
  provider: vault
  parameters:
    roleName: 'devweb-app'
```

```
    objects: |
    - objectName: "username"
      secretPath: "secret/data/devwebapp/config"
      secretKey: "username"
    - objectName: "password"
      secretPath: "secret/data/devwebapp/config"
      secretKey: "password"
```

The next step is to provision the app, which will use the CSI provider:

```
apiVersion: apps/v1
kind: Deployment
metadata:
  name: nginx-deployment
spec:
  replicas: 1
  selector:
    matchLabels:
      app: nginx
  template:
    metadata:
      labels:
        app: nginx
    spec:
      serviceAccountName: simple-app
      containers:
      - name: nginx-container
        image: nginx:latest
        ports:
        - containerPort: 80
        volumeMounts:
        - name: 'vault-up-creds'
      mountPath: '/mnt/secrets-store'
      readOnly: true
    volumes:
    - name: vault-up-creds
      csi:
        driver: 'secrets-store.csi.k8s.io'
        readOnly: true
        volumeAttributes:
          secretProviderClass: 'vault-up-creds'
```

We managed to securely integrate Vault with Kubernetes. We achieved this using the CSI and Vault Injector methods. There is another method to integrate Kubernetes workloads with Vault and this is by running an installation of Vault on Kubernetes.

Vault hosted on Kubernetes

In certain cases, a Vault cluster might be hosted on Kubernetes. It is an approach with several benefits. From a maintenance perspective, you take advantage of Kubernetes, and from a latency perspective, it can be faster, provided that the previous Vault installation was deployed on another network.

We shall do the installation through minikube.

We shall configure the values for the Vault installation:

```
cat > helm-vault-raft-values.yml <<EOF
server:
  affinity: ""
  ha:
    enabled: true
    replicas: 3
    raft:
      enabled: true
EOF
```

Due to running Vault on minikube, we do not have the option to run on multiple nodes. Thus, we disable the network affinity. Also, we shall run Vault with high availability enabled using three replicas:

```
$ helm repo add hashicorp https://helm.releases.hashicorp.com
$ helm repo update
$ helm install vault hashicorp/vault --values helm-vault-raft-values.
yml
```

By running Vault in a high availability mode, the Raft consensus algorithm is used.

Take note that Vault is installed using StatefulSet and the default number is 3 nodes.

If we check the logs, we shall see that Vault is not initialized:

```
$ kubectl logs -f vault-0
2023-10-11T21:01:25.268Z [INFO]  core: security barrier not
initialized
```

We now need to initialize Vault:

```
kubectl exec vault-0 -- vault operator init -key-shares=1
-key-threshold=1 -format=json > cluster-keys.json
```

This will create the `cluster-keys.json` file.

Let us see the contents of the cluster key:

```
{
  "unseal_keys_b64": [
    "the-unseal-key"
  ],
  "unseal_keys_hex": [
    "the-unseal-key-hex"
  ],
  "unseal_shares": 1,
  "unseal_threshold": 1,
  "recovery_keys_b64": [],
  "recovery_keys_hex": [],
  "recovery_keys_shares": 0,
  "recovery_keys_threshold": 0,
  "root_token": "root-token"
}
```

Our next step is to unseal the vault using the unseal key:

```
$ VAULT_UNSEAL_KEY=$(jq -r ".unseal_keys_b64[]" cluster-keys.json)
$ kubectl exec vault-0 -- vault operator unseal $VAULT_UNSEAL_KEY
```

Then we need to join the nodes one by one:

```
$ kubectl exec -ti vault-1 -- vault operator raft join http://vault-0.
vault-internal:8200
$ kubectl exec -ti vault-2 -- vault operator raft join http://vault-0.
vault-internal:8200
```

By joining the nodes on the cluster, the leader election process should start taking place.

Now we have to unseal the other nodes:

```
$ kubectl exec vault-1 -- vault operator unseal $VAULT_UNSEAL_KEY
$ kubectl exec vault-2 -- vault operator unseal $VAULT_UNSEAL_KEY
```

Now that unsealing has been done, we can start adding data to Vault.

A port forward on Kubernetes should be effective:

```
$ kubectl port-forward vault-0 8200:8200
```

Next, execute the following commands:

```
#point Vault CLI to localhost
$ export VAULT_ADDR=http://0.0.0.0:8200
# extract vault root token
$ VAULT_ROOT_TOKEN=$(jq -r ".root_token" cluster-keys.json)
#login with root token
$ vault login $VAULT_ROOT_TOKEN
# use the kv-v2 secrets engine on path secret
$ vault secrets enable -path=secret kv-v2
# put secret
$ vault kv put secret/webapp/config username="static-user"
password="static-password"
```

Let us stop forwarding to vault-0 and forward to another node:

```
$ kubectl port-forward vault-1 8200:8200
```

We also evaluate whether we can fetch the Secrets:

```
$ vault kv get secret/webapp/config
```

As expected, we got our Secrets:

```
$ vault kv get secret/webapp/config
...
====== Data ======
Key          Value
---          -----
password     static-password
username     static-user
```

The Secrets were stored and replicated through the node.

Take note that in this example we enabled the kv-v2 engine. The engine allows us to have multiple versions of Secrets. We will examine this functionality in the following section.

We read through an overview of running Vault on Kubernetes, which covered aspects of running Vault in production mode. Therefore, it is worth noting the differences between running Vault in development mode and in production mode.

Development mode versus production mode

We have run Vault so far in development mode. Development mode has certain characteristics:

- Lack of high availability
- Unsealed by default
- Single unseal key
- Initialized by default
- Data stored in memory

When it comes to production, things should be different.

Production mode

In production mode, high availability should be in place. This is achieved with the Raft protocol. When Vault is run in production, we do not have a standalone Vault instance but a Vault cluster based on the Raft protocol. This comes with the benefit of high availability; if a Vault node goes down, the requests can be served by another node that is available. Also, we can have performance standby nodes, nodes that are used to serve read requests, thus achieving horizontal scalability on read operations.

Another thing that is much different in production mode is the initialization. When a Vault cluster is created it must be initialized.

Seal and unseal

To be able to use a Vault installation, Vault needs to be initialized so that the storage backend will be prepared to receive data.

During the initialization, the following happens:

- A root key is generated
- The root key is stored in the storage backend
- The root key is encrypted
- The root key is stored in its encrypted form

Since the root key is encrypted, it cannot be used; it needs to be decrypted. In order to decrypt a root key, an unseal key is needed.

The unseal key is not distributed as a single key. It uses Shamir's secret-sharing algorithm (https://en.wikipedia.org/wiki/Shamir%27s_secret_sharing). The unseal key is divided into parts called *shares*, and those shares are spread throughout the cluster. For the key to be reassembled, it requires several shares to be reassembled, which is called the **threshold**. Supposing an attacker steals some shares. It will not be possible to reconstruct the unseal key if the shares stolen are less than the threshold. By using Shamir's secret sharing algorithm, Vault becomes more resilient to attacks that aim to acquire an unseal key.

When we unseal a vault, we use the unseal keys to retrieve the root key unencrypted. Then, the root key will reside unencrypted in the Vault memory. Vault, by using the root key, will be able to decrypt the encryption key needed to store data in Vault.

When we run Vault in production mode, the initialization is manual. The initialization is executed using the `vault operator init` command. We can specify the number of shares—the unseal keys. As a result, we shall have printed some unseal keys and a root token. The unseal keys will be used to reassemble the root token. The root token is a token to which the root policy is attached. It is a token that can perform operations using the root key.

In the case of an intrusion, it is feasible to seal the vault. By sealing, the root key will be purged from Vault's memory, and the vault will no longer be able to decrypt the data residing in its storage. Furthermore, operations and Vault services will stop.

High availability

As we have seen by installing Vault on Kubernetes, we had three instances deployed by default in StatefulSets. This is because of Raft. Vault is a distributed system and Raft is the consensus algorithm used. The minimum number of nodes is three. With three nodes, a failure of one node can be tolerated, provided the other two nodes continue operating. To calculate the node tolerance, use the formula *(n-1)/2*, where *n* is the number of total nodes. For example, on a Vault installation consisting of five nodes, Vault will continue to be operational if two nodes fail. Once Vault is up and the nodes achieve consensus, data is written to the leader. The leader must replicate the data written to the followers.

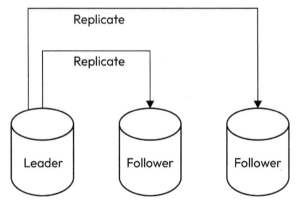

Figure 11.3 – Replication of data

Take note that if a write operation is tried on a follower, Vault will respond to the caller with the leader address. This way, the data will be written to the leader.

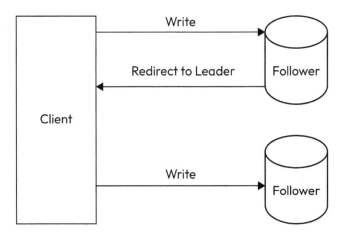

Figure 11.4 – Client redirect

Raft on Vault tackles the problem of state synchronization, thus enabling the option of integrated storage. However, Vault can be backed by various forms of external storage.

Storage

Vault has various options for storage. There are options for external storage, which include databases such as Cassandra, DynamoDB, and more. Those options provide all the benefits that come with the underlying external storage. For example, in the case of DynamoDB, Vault can benefit from the backups, auditing, high availability, and all the other features that come with DynamoDB.

The other storage that is recommended is integrated storage. Integrated storage is maintained by HashiCorp. It is collocated with the host; this makes operations more efficient due to avoiding network hops. Also, by using integrated storage, the operational complexity is reduced and extra expertise on external storage is not required.

KV-2 vs KV-1 storage engine

The kv Secrets engine is used to store Secrets in the physical storage in Vault. The latest version of kv, KV version 2, offers versioning on secret storage. By default, 10 versions of a secret are retained. The number is configurable. The older versions of a secret can be retrieved. Versioning increases storage costs. Deleting a version marks it as deleted, but the version is not physically deleted; it can be undeleted. To force a version's physical deletion, the destroy command needs to be used.

Here is an example of the destroy command:

```
$ vault kv destroy -mount=secret -versions=5 secret/webapp/admin
```

The first version of the kv engine, KV version 1, does not have the versioning feature; thus, the storage needs are less than for KV version 2.

Policies

The principle of least permissions is crucial to ensuring the security of our Secrets. This is achieved by Vault policies.

By using policies, we can specify access privileges. Take, for example, the policies we created previously to fetch the Secrets from Vault on a Kubernetes application. We created the policy devwebapp, which will provide read capabilities to the secret/devwebapp/config path. This policy was attached to the service account of the Kubernetes application that would use that secret. Thus, the tokens generated for that service account would be able to read only the secret specified.

To summarize, we had an overview of HashiCorp Vault and how it can be integrated with Kubernetes. Next, we will focus on another secret manager provider: CyberArk Conjur.

CyberArk Conjur

Conjur from CyberArk is a Secrets management solution. It has a commercial and an open source version.

Conjur as a solution comes with the following benefits:

- **Role-based access control (RBAC)**
- Logging and auditing
- Integration with Kubernetes
- High availability

Let us take a closer look at Conjur and see how it achieves these qualities.

How Conjur works

Conjur requires the following components:

- Reverse Nginx proxy
- Conjur application
- Database

The reverse proxy is used to handle the TLS termination. It sits in front of the Conjur application. The Conjur application is a Ruby-based application and is responsible for securely storing Secrets. This application is backed by a PostgreSQL database.

High availability

Conjur uses Raft to make high availability possible. It has a leader–follower architecture. The master will serve inbound traffic. In case of a master failure, a follower instance will be promoted to master.

Server keys

Conjur uses a data key, a Conjur UI key, and SSL keys. Those keys are generated during the Conjur server initialization plaintext. They should be encrypted to harden the initialization. This happens through the usage of a master key.

By using the master key, the keys are encrypted.

Before using the Conjur services, we need to unlock the keys using the master key. Once the encrypted keys are unlocked using the master key, they will reside on the Linux keyring and memory-based file system. Conjur offers the option to use AWS KMS or a hardware security module as a master key.

Storage

For storing Secrets, Conjur is backed by a database. Conjur uses PostgreSQL to store the Secrets. Conjur benefits from all the features that come with a PostgreSQL database. A PostgreSQL database comes with many features, such as replication, auditing, and fine-grained permissions.

For example, a secret stored on Conjur can be found on the PostgreSQL database by querying the Secrets table:

```
# SELECT*FROM secrets;
 resource_id             |version |value|expires_at
 ------------------------+--------+-----+------------
 acccount:variable:test|1        |\x4..|
 (1 row)
```

This secret is unusable since it is encrypted. In case of a breach, the names of the Secrets would be leaked but not the actual value of the Secrets since the decryption key is needed.

Versioning

Conjur also has the secret versioning feature. It keeps the last 20 versions of a secret.

Policies

By using Conjur policies, we can define security rules that describe which roles have permissions to perform certain operations on a Conjur resource.

Here's an example of a Conjur policy:

```
- !policy
  id: ExamplePolicy
  body:
  - !host webApp
  - !variable secretVar
  - !permit
    role: !host webApp
    privileges: [read, execute]
    resource: !variable secretVar
```

As we can see, the `ExamplePolicy` policy provides to the non-human identity `webApp` the permission to read the `secretVar` variable.

Audit logs

As we have seen in previous chapters, audit logs are crucial when it comes to Secrets management.

From the documentation, we can see what an audit log in JSON format looks like:

```
{
  "subject@43868": {
    "resource": "demo:group:security_ops"
  },
  "policy@43868": {
    "version": "1",
    "id": "demo:policy:root"
  },
  "auth@43868": {
    "user": "demo:user:admin"
  },
  "action@43868": {
    "operation": "add"
  },
  "PROGRAM": "conjur",
  "PID": "e9c07c05-4dc2-4809-b7e1-43f5d3a20599",
  "MSGID": "policy",
  "MESSAGE": "demo:user:admin added resource demo:group:security_ops",
  "LEVEL": "notice",
  "ISODATE": "2020-04-14T20:40:24.806+00:00",
  "FACILITY": "auth"
}
```

The preceding log has all the information that we need to identify what happened on our Conjur server. `action` displays the action that took place, `auth` displays the entity that executed the action that took place, and `subject` displays the resource affected.

Kubernetes integration

Conjur has many options for enabling Kubernetes integration. One of them is the Kubernetes Authenticator Client.

Kubernetes Authenticator Client

Conjur has the Kubernetes Authenticator Client. The Kubernetes application that uses Conjur Secrets has a sidecar container with a Conjur client. The client using the service account will authenticate with Conjur. Then, Conjur will issue a temporary token. The sidecar container will use that temporary token to retrieve the Secrets.

In this section, we learned more about the secret manager Conjur. We identified its features and how it can integrate with Kubernetes. Those features, along with the features that we focused on in the previous chapters, form the standards for managing Secrets using an external secret store.

Qualities for securely managing Secrets

As we have seen, there are certain qualities when it comes to storing external Secrets. In this chapter, we took a deep dive into the HashiCorp Vault and how it integrates with Kubernetes. We also had a look at another Secrets management provider, Conjur.

A secret manager needs to have certain qualities:

- High availability
- Encryption of data
- Secure access
- Versioning
- RBAC
- Integration with Kubernetes
- Auditing

Those qualities are essential to ensuring the secure and robust storage of an application's Secrets.

High availability

High availability is required to ensure our data is safe. It can protect us from losing any data in case of a service outage. It ensures business continuity. External secret stores such as Vault and Conjur achieve high availability by utilizing Raft, the popular consensus method. By having a consensus method, the cluster approach for availability is feasible; we can add multiple nodes to different data centers, which will form a cluster and share workloads. Thanks to this choice, in case of a failure, data is distributed in a way that can tolerate failures.

Encryption of data

The data in an external secret store should be encrypted. The encryption keys that encrypt the data in the external secret store should also be encrypted. As we have seen previously, providers achieve this by implementing mechanisms such as Shamir's secret sharing or by using a master key to encrypt the data encryption keys. Then, the data encryption keys are used to encrypt the actual data.

Secure access

Access is secured with proper authentication methods and the principle of least privilege. We can achieve this with policies. External secret stores such as Vault and Conjur give us the option of policies. With policies, we can specify the operations that an identity can perform on a secret resource. This allows us to create fine-grained permissions that minimize the risks that come with overprivileged accounts that interact with the Secrets storage.

Versioning

All the secret store providers we worked with throughout this book offered versioning. Versioning is crucial in preventing accidental deletion and enabling smooth rotation. Secrets, by their nature, are sensitive, which makes rotation a necessity. Having a versioning of Secrets enables developer teams to proceed with the secret rotation operations in a robust and resilient way.

Integration with Kubernetes

As we can see, integration with Kubernetes is achieved using the least permissions needed, and we did not store any sensitive keys in etcd. Instead, HashiCorp Vault or Conjur were managed through Kubernetes service accounts.

Secrets were injected into our applications without having to store them in etcd. Also, we did not have to store any Secrets that could communicate with the secret storage.

Auditing

Auditing is crucial for Secrets management. Through auditing, we achieve a record of activity towards the resources that reside on an external secret store. In all the options for external Secrets storage, auditing capabilities are present. In case of a breach or any malevolent action, auditing can help us identify the exposure and take remediation actions. Auditing can also help in debugging as well as ensure that the system operates properly.

Summary

In this chapter, we took a deep dive into HashiCorp Vault, how it integrates with Kubernetes, and the different methods that can be used to access the Vault Secrets through Kubernetes workloads. We used Secrets from Vault either through the `vault-agent-injector` method or through the CSI Driver. Furthermore, we performed an installation of Vault on Kubernetes and identified the qualities for a Vault production deployment. We also learned about another Secrets provider, CyberArk Conjur, and its capabilities. In the next chapter, we will focus on the overall use cases of Secrets and the different approaches that we can follow for integrating with external secret stores. Also, we will take a deep dive into the approaches to integration with external secret stores.

12

Integrating with Secret Stores

Kubernetes provides a basic system for managing Secrets, but it is not typically seen as secure enough for sensitive data such as passwords, tokens, or keys, especially in production settings. To address this, integrating advanced Secrets management tools into Kubernetes is vital. These tools enhance security through encryption and offer centralized management of sensitive information. This surpasses the native capabilities of Kubernetes Secrets, leading to a more robust and compliant security stance. In this chapter, you will learn how to integrate Secrets management tools with Kubernetes. The chapter will cover how to configure external secret stores in Kubernetes and explore the different types of external secret stores that can be used. You will gain an understanding of the security implications of using external secret stores and how to use them to store sensitive data using different approaches such as init containers, sidecars, CSI drivers, operators, and sealed Secrets. The chapter will also cover the best practices for using external secret stores and how they can impact the overall security of a Kubernetes cluster. In this chapter, we're going to cover the following main topics:

- Configuring external secret stores in Kubernetes

- Integrating with external secret stores

- Security implications and best practices

- Practical and theoretical balance

Technical requirements

To link concepts with hands-on examples, we are leveraging a series of tools and platforms commonly used to interact with external Secrets management and Kubernetes:

- **minikube**: It runs a single-node Kubernetes cluster inside a **virtual machine** (**VM**) on your computer. Get it set up using the guide at `https://minikube.sigs.k8s.io/docs/start/`.

- **Helm**: This is a package manager for Kubernetes that will simplify deployments. Check out the Helm installation guide for setup instructions at `https://helm.sh/docs/intro/install/`.

- **kubectl**: This is the Kubernetes command-line tool. Instructions for its installation are available at `https://kubernetes.io/docs/tasks/tools/install-kubectl/`.

- **External Secrets management tool**: While various tools can be utilized for the purpose of our demonstrations, it's recommended to have Hashicorp Vault. The official guide for its installation is found at `https://www.vaultproject.io/docs/install`.

Integrating secret stores with Kubernetes

As we've explored in previous chapters, Kubernetes has its own Secrets management capabilities. However, when operating at scale or with specific security requirements, the native Kubernetes Secrets may fall short. The sheer diversity of Secrets management tools available, as previously discussed, alludes to this need. But why integrate them with Kubernetes?

Integrating third-party tools with Kubernetes offers the following benefits:

- **Operational consistency**: For organizations that already use tools for applications outside Kubernetes, integration provides a uniform Secrets management experience across the board.

- **Enhanced security features**: Many external tools offer advanced features such as secret rotation, granular access controls, and multi-layered encryption methods that aren't readily available or require additional configurations in native Kubernetes.

- **Scalability and performance**: At scale, the management of a large number of Secrets may become complex using only Kubernetes native Secrets. External tools, designed for high-volume operations, can effectively address this.

- **Advanced audit trails**: In an environment of tougher regulations and increasing cyber threats, having a thorough audit capability is essential, not a luxury. Many tools come equipped with comprehensive logging and alerting functions.

- **Detailed audit capabilities**: These capabilities ensure regulatory compliance, improve security, increase accountability, detect unusual activities, support informed decision-making, provide legal evidence, enhance operational efficiency, build customer trust, reduce insider threats, and enable historical analysis for future improvements.

- **Cross-platform compatibility**: With the rise of hybrid and multi-cloud strategies, secret managers can offer consistent Secrets management across different cloud platforms, making it easier to manage Secrets in such heterogeneous environments.

While we've recognized the capabilities of various cloud secret stores and third-party secret stores in previous chapters, this chapter aims to bridge the gap to focus on integration. The primary focus is to showcase how these secret stores can be seamlessly integrated with Kubernetes, leveraging the best of both worlds.

Through the subsequent sections, we'll dive deep into the mechanics of these integrations, offering both a theoretical and practical understanding. Each method, from Kubernetes extensions to Pod lifecycle mechanisms, will illustrate different strategies and approaches for this integration. By the end of this chapter, our goal is to provide you with a robust set of strategies and insights, empowering you to make choices that align seamlessly with your unique operational requirements.

Configuring external secret stores in Kubernetes

The decentralized nature of Kubernetes and its dynamic workloads necessitate a robust Secrets management solution. This section provides insights into the general configuration process and delineates two predominant paradigms for secret consumption within Kubernetes.

The following are the general configuration steps:

1. **Selection of secret store**: Begin by choosing a Secrets management tool that suits organizational needs, factoring in aspects such as security requirements, scalability, compliance standards, team familiarity, and more. Options abound, ranging from cloud-native solutions such as AWS/ GCP Secrets Manager and Azure Key Vault to tools such as HashiCorp Vault and CyberArk.

2. **Initialization and connecting to Kubernetes**: Once the secret store is selected, proceed with its initialization. Deploy it either within the Kubernetes cluster or alongside it based on architectural preferences, ensuring smooth connectivity between the store and Kubernetes.

3. **Handle authentication and authorization**: Establish robust and secure communication channels between Kubernetes and the secret store. Mechanisms could encompass IAM roles, tokens, service accounts, or client certificates. Concurrently, put in place fine-grained authorization controls to ensure that only entitled services or applications access designated Secrets.

4. **Determine secret retrieval and consumption method**: Delve into how the Secrets will be consumed. Decide if Secrets from the external store will be converted into native Kubernetes Secrets or if they will be fetched directly from the external store when required.

5. **Test the configuration**: Before rolling out the integration in a production environment, conduct thorough testing. Verify secret retrieval, consumption, and other configured functionalities to ensure they operate as intended.

6. **Monitor and auditing**: As the final step, implement monitoring mechanisms to oversee access to Secrets. Augment this with logging and auditing tools to swiftly detect unauthorized access attempts or potential breaches.

Completing these general configuration steps lays a strong foundation for secure and efficient Secrets management within your Kubernetes environment. With the secret store now integrated, authenticated, and authorized, you're set to proceed to the next phase, ensuring a seamless and secure consumption of Secrets by your applications.

Secret consumption in Kubernetes

When integrating an external secret store, two primary paradigms dominate secret consumption within Kubernetes:

- **Convert to native Kubernetes Secrets**: Translating Secrets from external stores into native Kubernetes Secrets allows the leveraging of Kubernetes-native methods for Secrets management and access. It provides the benefit of caching, minimizing the need for frequent external requests. Additionally, it eliminates a critical point of failure. However, there are challenges such as redundancy and ensuring synchronization between the two secret storage locations.

- **Directly fetch from external store**: Directly retrieving Secrets ensures applications get the most recent versions, cutting down on the need to synchronize. It also leads to a cleaner audit trail. Nevertheless, this method might introduce latency due to external fetch operations and create a direct dependency on the external store.

To summarize, the process of configuring an external secret store in Kubernetes is fundamental to constructing a scalable and secure cloud-native infrastructure. A clear comprehension of the configuration steps and the various paradigms of secret consumption sets the stage for an effective Secrets management strategy. Future sections will provide a more in-depth exploration of these topics and the accompanying mechanisms.

Integrating with external secret stores

The integration of external secret stores with Kubernetes is a critical component of securing your applications and protecting sensitive data. This section explores various mechanisms and patterns that can be used to seamlessly integrate external secret stores with your Kubernetes clusters, enhancing security and management efficiency.

Kubernetes extensions and API mechanisms

Kubernetes provides a variety of extensions and API mechanisms that can be leveraged to connect and interact with external secret stores. In this part, we will delve into the available options and guide you on how to utilize them effectively for Secrets management.

Admission controllers and mutating webhooks for Secrets in Kubernetes

Kubernetes provides a rich set of tools for controlling and modifying behavior within its environment. Among them, *admission controllers* and *mutating webhooks* play a pivotal role in enhancing the operational and security aspects of Kubernetes clusters. Especially when it comes to Secrets management, these tools can be game-changing.

Admission controllers are parts of the Kubernetes control plane that govern and enforce how the cluster is used. They intercept requests to the Kubernetes API server before the persistence of the object but after the request is authenticated and authorized. By doing so, admission controllers have the ability to take specific actions, such as rejecting a request or modifying the object before it's stored. There are several built-in admission controllers, but for specific requirements such as Secrets management, you might need custom controllers.

Mutating webhooks come into play when we want the flexibility provided by admission controllers but with custom logic. They allow you to run custom code (or a custom function) when specific resources are created or modified. This is incredibly valuable for Secrets management, as you can programmatically modify Kubernetes resources; for example, you can inject secret references into Pods at the time of creation.

Consider a scenario where you don't want developers to explicitly define Secrets within the manifest. Using a mutating webhook, you can set up a system where developers only specify a label or annotation. The webhook then intercepts the Pod creation request, identifies the label or annotation, and injects the required secret reference, thus abstracting away the direct interaction with Secrets.

Here's an illustrative example of setting up a mutating webhook for secret injection:

```
apiVersion: admissionregistration.k8s.io/v1
kind: MutatingWebhookConfiguration
metadata:
  name: secret-injector-webhook
webhooks:
  - name: secret-injector.example.com
    clientConfig:
      service:
        name: secret-injector-service
        namespace: default
        path: "/mutate"
      caBundle: [CA_BUNDLE]
    rules:
      - operations: ["CREATE"]
        apiGroups: [""]
        apiVersions: ["v1"]
        resources: ["pods"]
```

Let's break down this configuration:

- The webhook is named `secret-injector.example.com`.

- The `clientConfig` specifies the service that handles the webhook. In this case, the service is named `secret-injector-service`.

- The `rules` section defines when this webhook is invoked. Here, it's set up to run when a Pod

- is created.

When a new Pod gets created, the request is intercepted by our webhook. The service `secret-injector-service` then processes this request, checks for specific labels or annotations, and decides whether to inject secret references.

The combination of admission controllers and mutating webhooks provides a robust mechanism to streamline and enforce best practices for Secrets management. By offloading Secrets management concerns to these tools, developers can focus on their application logic while ensuring that Secrets are handled in a secure and compliant manner.

In conclusion, when looking to enhance the Secrets management capabilities within your Kubernetes clusters, consider leveraging admission controllers and mutating webhooks. They not only help maintain the sanctity of the cluster but also automate and enforce best practices for handling sensitive data.

Custom resource definitions in Secrets management

Kubernetes allows for the extensibility of its API through the use of **custom resource definitions** (**CRDs**). CRDs empower cluster operators to introduce new resource types in Kubernetes without the need to modify the core Kubernetes code base. When dealing with Secrets, especially those stored outside of a Kubernetes cluster in external systems such as AWS Secrets Manager or HashiCorp Vault, CRDs can offer a more Kubernetes-native approach to managing and accessing them.

Defining an ExternalSecret CRD

A CRD definition for an external secret might look something like the following:

```
apiVersion: apiextensions.k8s.io/v1
kind: CustomResourceDefinition
metadata:
  name: externalsecrets.k8s.example.com
spec:
  group: k8s.example.com
  versions:
    - name: v1
      served: true
      storage: true
  scope: Namespaced
  names:
    plural: externalsecrets
    singular: externalsecret
    kind: ExternalSecret
    shortNames:
      - esec
```

Once you've defined the CRD, the next logical step is to create instances of this new resource type (`ExternalSecret`). However, just defining and creating the CRD doesn't give it functionality. To make the ExternalSecret resource meaningful, you need a custom controller that understands how to interpret and act upon these resources.

Using the ExternalSecret CRD

Assuming you have a secret named database-password stored in AWS Secrets Manager, you might define an ExternalSecret resource that references it as follows:

```
apiVersion: k8s.example.com/v1
kind: ExternalSecret
metadata:
     name: my-database-password
spec:
backendType: awsSecretsManager
data:
  - key: database-password
    name: dbPassword
region: us-west-1
```

Here's a breakdown of this resource:

- metadata.name: This is the name assigned to this ExternalSecret within Kubernetes. It doesn't necessarily have to match the name in AWS Secrets Manager.

- spec.backendType: This denotes the external Secrets manager to use; in this case, it's AWS Secrets Manager.

- spec.data: This is a list that indicates the Secrets to fetch.

- key: This is the name or identifier of the secret in AWS Secrets Manager.

- name: This is the name the secret will take when presented to Kubernetes Pods.

- spec.region: This specifies the AWS region where the secret resides.

Upon applying the following resource:

```
kubectl apply -f my-external-secret.yaml
```

A custom controller observing ExternalSecret resources would do the following:

1. Detect the creation of a new ExternalSecret.

2. Understand from the specification that it should communicate with the AWS Secrets Manager in the us-west-1 region.

3. Authenticate with AWS Secrets Manager (assuming it has the necessary permissions).

4. Retrieve the database-password secret.

5.   Present this secret to Kubernetes Pods under the name `dbPassword`. This could be by creating a native Kubernetes secret, setting it as an environment variable, or placing it in a `tmpfs` volume depending on the controller's design.

In essence, CRDs combined with custom controllers provide a powerful mechanism to extend Kubernetes's capabilities. For Secrets management, CRDs allow Kubernetes to naturally integrate with external secret storage solutions, making the process of fetching and using Secrets seamless for end users.

Kubernetes API extensions: custom API server

Building a custom API server allows us to define our API behaviors, including interactions with external secret stores. A Pod can request a secret through the custom API, and this API server can fetch it from an external store, process it, and return it. However, running and maintaining a custom API server isn't trivial. You'd need to set it up, ensure it's secure, and potentially handle scaling and failover.

Please note that this is a simplified example focusing on the conceptual configuration:

```
apiVersion: v1
kind: Pod
metadata:
  name: custom-api-server
spec:
  containers:
  - name: custom-api-server
    image: my-custom-api-server:latest
    ports:
    - containerPort: 443
    volumeMounts:
    - mountPath: /etc/custom-api-server
      name: config
  volumes:
  - name: config
    configMap:
      name: custom-api-server-config
```

For a custom API server to work with the main Kubernetes API server and external secret storages, it needs specific settings in its configuration, `custom-api-server-config`. This includes how it will verify who is allowed to access it, known as authentication, and the rules for how it communicates, called API specifications. Typically, this setup uses either service-based or role-based authentication. Service-based authentication checks the identity of the service requesting access, while role-based authentication looks at the user's or service's role to decide access. A common example is using IRSA roles in AWS, where Kubernetes services get special permissions to access AWS resources securely.

This method provides seamless interaction with external secret stores, especially for teams more familiar with `kubectl` than with, say, Hashicorp Vault's CLI. By extending the API, users can stay in their familiar environment. However, as powerful as it is, just extending the API does not complete the loop. You need additional components or procedures to ensure safe and efficient consumption of the Secrets by the Pods. This could be through agents, controllers, or other orchestration mechanisms that watch for these custom or converted Secrets and make them available to Pods.

The Kubernetes extensions and API mechanisms offer a flexible and powerful means to integrate external secret stores, providing a variety of options to suit different use cases and requirements. Understanding how to leverage these tools is key to effective Secrets management within Kubernetes.

Pod lifecycle and manipulation mechanisms

Managing Secrets throughout the lifecycle of a Pod is essential for maintaining security and operational efficiency. This section focuses on the mechanisms that Kubernetes provides for injecting and managing Secrets in conjunction with the Pod lifecycle.

Init containers

Init containers run before application containers and can be used for setup tasks such as fetching Secrets from an external store. If your application needs a configuration file populated with Secrets before it starts, an init container can fetch those Secrets, populate the configuration, and store it in a shared volume.

Here's a sample configuration:

```
apiVersion: v1
kind: Pod
metadata:
  name: app-with-init-container
spec:
  initContainers:
  - name: fetch-secrets
    image: secret-fetcher:latest
    volumeMounts:
    - name: config-volume
      mountPath: /config
  containers:
  - name: main-app
    image: my-app:latest
    volumeMounts:
    - name: config-volume
      mountPath: /config
  volumes:
```

```
- name: config-volume
  emptyDir: {}
```

By incorporating this sample init container configuration, you can ensure that your application has access to the necessary Secrets before it starts.

Sidecars

Sidecars run alongside the main container in a Pod and can be used to dynamically manage Secrets during the Pod's lifecycle. If your application needs to periodically refresh its Secrets without restarting, a sidecar can fetch the latest Secrets and update a shared configuration or notify the main application.

Here's a sample configuration:

```
apiVersion: v1
kind: Pod
metadata:
  name: app-with-sidecar
spec:
  containers:
  - name: main-app
    image: my-app:latest
    volumeMounts:
    - name: config-volume
      mountPath: /config
  - name: secret-refresher
    image: secret-refresher:latest
    volumeMounts:
    - name: config-volume
      mountPath: /config
  volumes:
  - name: config-volume
    emptyDir: {}
```

Sidecars in Kubernetes enhance Secrets management by running alongside the main container, enabling dynamic updates of Secrets without needing to restart the application, as illustrated in the provided sample configuration.

DaemonSets

DaemonSets ensures that all (or some) nodes run a copy of a Pod, making them suitable for node-level tasks, such as setting up node-wide Secrets or Secrets management tools. If you have a node-level application (for example, a logging agent) that requires certain Secrets, you can use a DaemonSet to ensure each node fetches its own Secrets.

Here's a sample configuration:

```
apiVersion: apps/v1
kind: DaemonSet
metadata:
  name: node-level-agent
spec:
  selector:
    matchLabels:
      name: node-level-agent
  template:
    metadata:
      labels:
        name: node-level-agent
    spec:
      containers:
      - name: agent
        image: my-agent:latest
        env:
        - name: NODE_SECRET
          valueFrom:
            secretKeyRef:
              name: node-secret
              key: secret-key
```

By utilizing DaemonSets for such node-level operations, you ensure a consistent and secure distribution of Secrets across your entire Kubernetes cluster.

Environment controllers

Different from CRDs, environment controllers don't seek to expand the Kubernetes API. Instead, they dynamically manage environment variables directly within the Pod's context. The advantage is direct integration at the Pod level, avoiding the need for additional CRD management or controller infrastructure specific to a new CRD. For applications that read Secrets from environment variables, and if you want to avoid storing these Secrets in Kubernetes directly, an environment controller can fetch and inject these Secrets just before the Pod starts, avoiding the need for the application or another container to fetch them.

Imagine we're using a custom controller that watches `EnvSecret` CRD resources. Here's a sample configuration:

```
apiVersion: mycontroller/v1
kind: EnvSecret
metadata:
  name: database-creds
```

```
spec:
  externalRef: db-credentials-in-vault
  target:
    envVarName: DB_CREDS
    podSelector:
      matchLabels:
        app: my-app
```

This hypothetical EnvSecret CRD resource instructs the controller to fetch db-credentials-in-vault from an external store and populate it into the DB_CREDS environment variable for Pods with the label app: my-app.

Effectively managing Secrets throughout the Pod lifecycle ensures that applications have access to the necessary sensitive information when they need it while maintaining a high level of security.

Specialized Kubernetes patterns – SealedSecrets

SealedSecrets is a Kubernetes controller and tool for one-way encrypted Secrets. It's designed for developers to encrypt a secret and submit it to the control plane (typically in a Git repository and through **continuous integration and continuous delivery (CI/CD)**. Kubernetes administrators have the decryption key and, upon seeing the encrypted secret (a SealedSecret), the controller decrypts it into a regular Kubernetes secret. It enhances security by ensuring that actual secret values are not directly stored in a Git repository but kept in an encrypted format instead.

The brilliance of SealedSecrets is in its simplicity: Secrets are encrypted in a way that only the cluster itself can decrypt, allowing for Secrets to be safely stored alongside the application's configuration, typically in version control.

Let's walk through the distinct phases of the SealedSecrets process:

1. **Setup**: Install the SealedSecrets controller and its kubeseal CLI tool

2. **Encrypt**: Use kubeseal to encrypt a secret, which creates a SealedSecret

3. **Deploy**: Apply the SealedSecret via kubectl, just like any other Kubernetes resource

4. **Decryption**: The SealedSecret controller, running in the cluster, decrypts the SealedSecret and creates a standard Kubernetes secret

The primary benefit of using SealedSecrets in DevOps is its ease of use. It allows developers to keep their application's configuration and Secrets (in an encrypted form) under version control together safely. However, it's crucial to note that SealedSecrets are not exactly the same as regular Kubernetes Secrets. When decrypted, SealedSecrets turn into standard Kubernetes Secrets within the cluster. These Secrets are then only accessible to the workloads that have the required permissions.

Let's briefly explore the creation and application of SealedSecrets and how they're used in Pods:

1. **Creating a SealedSecret**:

   Here is a quick example of creating a simple Kubernetes secret.

   ```
   apiVersion: v1
   kind: Secret
   metadata:
     name: my-secret
   type: Opaque
   data:
     password: [base64_encoded_value]
   ```

   Encrypt this secret using `kubeseal`:

   ```
   kubeseal < secret.yaml > sealed-secret.yaml
   ```

   The resultant `sealed-secret.yaml` is as follows:

   ```
   apiVersion: bitnami.com/v1alpha1
   kind: SealedSecret
   metadata:
     name: my-secret
     namespace: default
   spec:
     encryptedData:
       password: [encrypted_value]
   ```

2. **Applying the SealedSecret**:

   By applying the `sealed-secret.yaml` file via `kubectl`, the SealedSecret controller will decrypt it and create a regular Kubernetes secret named `my-secret` in the specified namespace.

3. **Usage in Pods**:

   Once the SealedSecret is decrypted and the regular secret is available, Pods can reference this secret just like any other, for example, to mount it as a volume or use it to set an environment variable:

   ```
   apiVersion: v1
   kind: Pod
   metadata:
     name: my-app
   spec:
     containers:
     - name: app
       image: my-app:latest
       env:
       - name: PASSWORD
   ```

```
valueFrom:
  secretKeyRef:
    name: my-secret
    key: password
```

In essence, SealedSecrets facilitates the encrypted storage and management of Secrets outside the cluster, while the in-cluster controller ensures their safe decryption and transformation into accessible Kubernetes Secrets when required. It harmoniously bridges the gap between the operational need for secret encryption and the practical use of these Secrets within the Kubernetes ecosystem.

Secret Store CSI Driver for Kubernetes Secrets

The Secret Store CSI Driver provides an advanced solution for integrating external Secrets management platforms with Kubernetes. This robust mechanism aims to enhance the security and efficiency of handling Secrets in Kubernetes workloads.

Understanding the CSI driver for Secrets management

The **Container Storage Interface (CSI)** is a critical standard for connecting various storage systems to orchestrators such as Kubernetes. In the realm of Secrets management, the Secret Store CSI Driver acts as this connecting bridge:

- **CSI driver**: Fundamentally, this is an interface between Kubernetes and numerous external storage systems. It has the responsibility of dynamically provisioning Secrets. In a world where timely access to Secrets can be crucial, the capability this driver offers can be invaluable.

- **Integration mechanism**: The driver, identified as `secrets-store.csi.k8s.io`, empowers Kubernetes to fetch and mount multiple Secrets, keys, and certificates from high-grade external secret stores. These are then made available to Pods as a volume. When connected, the encapsulated data is mounted into the Pod's file system. This direct access ensures applications can readily consume the Secrets.

CSI driver stands as a vital bridge between Kubernetes and external storage solutions. Facilitating the seamless and secure provisioning of Secrets, keys, and certificates ensures timely access and efficient integration.

Secrets CSI Driver's unique aspects

The Secret Store CSI Driver boasts several distinct features:

- **Dual architecture**: The driver amalgamates the CRD and DaemonSets. The CRD steers the custom behavior and the interaction with the external secret stores. On the other hand, DaemonSets ensures a copy of the driver is operational on each node in the cluster. This architecture ensures Secrets are uniformly available across the cluster.

- **Direct mounting**: In a departure from traditional methods, this driver fetches Secrets and mounts them right into the Pods using a `tmpfs` in-memory file system. This approach ensures Secrets aren't written to node disks, enhancing security.

- **Node-level interface**: Because it operates at the node level with the Kubernetes CSI interface, the driver necessitates root user privileges on each host.

The Secret Store CSI Driver stands out with its innovative dual architecture, direct in-memory secret mounting, and node-level operation, necessitating root privileges and ensuring a uniform, secure approach to Secrets management across Kubernetes clusters. Here is a sample configuration to demonstrate the end-to-end usage of the Secret Store CSI Driver:

1. **Deploying Secret Store CSI Driver**:

   For a quick start with the Secret Store CSI Driver in Kubernetes, you can use Helm 3 for installation:

   I.   Begin by adding the driver's Helm repository with the following command:

   ```
   helm repo add secrets-store-csi-driver https://kubernetes-
   sigs.github.io/secrets-store-csi-driver/charts
   ```

   II. Then, install the driver in the `kube-system` namespace:

   ```
   helm install csi-secrets-store secrets-store-csi-driver/
   secrets-store-csi-driver --namespace kube-system
   ```

   The exact deployment steps can differ depending on your Kubernetes environment, but you typically have the option to use helm charts or raw YAML files. These are available in the official repository, which you can find at `https://github.com/kubernetes-sigs/secrets-store-csi-driver`.

2. **Declaring a SecretProviderClass**:

   This is the central object that tells the driver where and how to fetch the Secrets:

   ```
   apiVersion: secrets-store.csi.x-k8s.io/v1alpha1
   kind: SecretProviderClass
   metadata:
     name: my-secret-provider
   spec:
     provider: [PROVIDER_NAME]  # e.g., azure, vault
     parameters:
       # Your specific provider parameters here
   ```

3. **Usage in a Pod**:

   Once the `SecretProviderClass` is set, you can reference it in your Pod configuration:

   ```
   apiVersion: v1
   kind: Pod
   ```

```
    metadata:
      name: my-pod
    spec:
      containers:
      - name: my-container
        image: my-image
      volumes:
        - name: secrets-volume
          csi:
            driver: secrets-store.csi.k8s.io
            readOnly: true
            volumeAttributes:
              secretProviderClass: "my-secret-provider"
      volumeMounts:
      - name: secrets-volume
        mountPath: "/mnt/secrets"
```

The provided example configuration outlines the steps to deploy the driver, declare a SecretProviderClass, and incorporate it into a Pod. Moving forward, let's dive into the advantages and limitations of this approach.

Advantages and limitations of the Secrets CSI Driver

The Secret Store CSI Driver, while immensely powerful, comes with both strengths and challenges:

- **Advantages**:

  - **Unified access**: Using a standard interface, the driver can fetch Secrets from multiple enterprise-grade external stores

  - **Enhanced security**: Direct mounting to tmpfs ensures Secrets are never persisted on node disks

  - **Dynamic updates**: Depending on the external store's capabilities, Secrets can be updated dynamically, ensuring workloads have access to the latest data

- **Limitations**:

  - **Complex setup**: The dual nature (CRD and DaemonSet) can make the initial setup more complex

  - **Node-level access**: Requiring root access on every node can be seen as a security concern in certain environments

  - **Provider dependencies**: Some features might be dependent on the capabilities of the external secret store

For comprehensive details, best practices, and community support, always refer to the official documentation, found at `https://secrets-store-csi-driver.sigs.k8s.io/`. For those interested in contributing, understanding its architecture, or exploring its detailed capabilities, the GitHub repository for the project is a valuable resource (Secret Store CSI Driver on GitHub, found at `https://github.com/kubernetes-sigs/secrets-store-csi-driver`).

In conclusion, the Secret Store CSI Driver marks a significant advancement in Kubernetes' ability to manage Secrets. Adopting it can lead to more secure and efficient Secrets management, though like all tools, its correct implementation is crucial.

Service mesh integration for secret distribution

In the evolving world of Kubernetes, a *service mesh* has emerged as a crucial overlay to handle inter-service communications. Its primary value proposition lies in abstracting the complexity of service-to-service interactions, offloading developers from having to embed this logic in the application code. When it comes to secret distribution, especially in the context of certificates and tokens, a service mesh plays a pivotal role. To summarize, a service mesh is a configurable infrastructure layer for microservice applications that makes communication flexible, reliable, and fast. It's implemented through lightweight network proxies deployed alongside application code without the application needing to be aware.

Secrets in service mesh – certificates and tokens

When we talk about Secrets in the context of a service mesh, we're mostly referring to the following:

- **Certificates**: These are used to establish trust between services in the mesh. **Mutual TLS (mTLS)** often gets employed to ensure both client and server services can trust each other. The service mesh automates the provisioning and rotation of these certificates.

- **Tokens**: For certain authentication and authorization scenarios, tokens (such as JWTs) might be used. These can be generated, validated, and rotated by the service mesh, ensuring applications don't have to handle this complexity.

The service mesh simplifies and secures the management of certificates and tokens through automation. Within the service mesh, the handling and distribution of Secrets are both secure and dynamic, adhering to a well-established and commonly practiced procedure throughout their entire lifecycle:

1. **Dynamic secret creation**: A service mesh can integrate with external **certificate authorities (CAs)** or even have its built-in CA. On-demand, certificates are generated for services when they join the mesh.

2. **Secret distribution**: Once generated, these certificates (or tokens) get securely distributed to the relevant services. This distribution is done through the sidecar proxies that accompany each service instance in the mesh.

3. **Rotation and renewal**: A key benefit of using a service mesh is its capability to automate the rotation of Secrets. This feature enhances security by regularly updating these sensitive credentials. After a predefined period, Secrets are renewed and older ones are invalidated, all without any downtime or manual intervention.

4. **Revocation**: In scenarios where a service might be compromised, the service mesh can quickly revoke the associated Secrets, mitigating potential damage.

The service mesh automates the entire process, from creating and distributing certificates and tokens on-demand to managing their rotation and revocation, ensuring a secure and efficient operation with minimal manual intervention required.

Service meshes in action – Istio

While there are multiple service mesh implementations available, **Istio** stands out as a prominent example.

For its certificate management, Istio uses a component called **Citadel**. It acts as the CA, generating, distributing, rotating, and having the capability to revoke certificates for services in the mesh. With its built-in capabilities, Istio's Citadel ensures that the mTLS communication within the mesh remains secure.

The following is an example configuration for enabling mTLS in Istio:

```
apiVersion: "security.istio.io/v1beta1"
kind: "PeerAuthentication"
metadata:
  name: "default"
  namespace: "foo"
spec:
  mtls:
    mode: STRICT
```

Istio, as a leading service mesh implementation, utilizes its Citadel component not only for robust certificate management to secure mutual TLS communication; it also extends its capabilities to include authentication, identity provisioning, and policy enforcement, making it a comprehensive solution for managing security within the service mesh architecture.

Benefits and considerations

Service meshes, when integrated into Kubernetes, bolster security through automated certificate management and enable mTLS for all communications. This ensures uniform application of security policies across the cluster. However, the added layer of sidecar proxies introduces latency and brings challenges to monitoring and maintenance.

For organizations already utilizing or planning to utilize a service mesh, incorporating it for Secrets management, especially for certificates and tokens, becomes compelling. Such integration simplifies Secrets management, ensuring secure transmission, appropriate scoping, and regular rotation. Yet, it's crucial to recognize that while service meshes excel in managing certificates and tokens, they aren't a one-size-fits-all solution for all secret types.

In sum, when a service mesh is present in your Kubernetes setup, leveraging it for managing certificates and tokens can streamline operations and enhance security. However, it shouldn't be seen as a complete replacement for comprehensive Secrets management.

In conclusion, a service mesh enhances the Kubernetes ecosystem's security landscape, especially around secret distribution in the form of certificates and tokens. While the benefits are manifold, like with any technology, a thorough understanding and diligent implementation are key to reaping its full potential.

Broker systems in Secrets management

Within the expansive terrain of IT security, especially when discussing the realm of Secrets management, the term **broker system** emerges as an essential player. Acting as intermediaries, these brokers act like traffic cops, ensuring that applications get what they need, but only after verifying their *identity*.

The following can help you understand how broker mechanisms work:

- **Request**: An application needing a secret sends a request to the broker.
- **Validation:** The broker validates the request, often verifying the sender's identity and authorization.
- **Fetch and transmit**: Once validated, the broker retrieves the secret from the store and securely sends it to the application.
- **Audit and log**: All transactions, be they requests or fetches, are duly logged for auditing. This design ensures applications sidestep the intricacies of directly engaging with different secret stores; they merely need to interface with the broker.

Consider the following example. Suppose service `foo` needs to connect to a specific database. Instead of directly fetching the database credentials, the following occurs:

1. `foo` sends a request: `I need credentials for DB1.`
2. The broker checks whether `foo` has the right permissions for `DB1`
3. Upon confirmation, the broker fetches and hands over the credentials

Throughout this process, `foo` remains agnostic to the exact secret storage location and the retrieval method. It safely obtains necessary database credentials through a broker, which validates permissions and retrieves the information, ensuring a secure access process.

Broker mechanisms versus secretless brokers

It's easy to conflate the two given the similar terminology, but they function distinctly. Secretless brokers go one step further; they establish connections on behalf of applications without ever revealing the secret to the application.

Essentially, this is how they differ:

- **Broker mechanisms**: They deliver Secrets to applications after validations
- **Secretless brokers**: They use Secrets to facilitate a direct connection, keeping the Secrets hidden

Thought bubble – brokers and service mesh

At this juncture, it's worth drawing a parallel with service mesh. A service mesh employs proxies to control and manage traffic between services in a microservices architecture. If you think about it, isn't this proxy acting like a broker? Indeed, the service mesh's proxy ensures secure communication between services, potentially managing certificates, tokens, and sometimes other Secrets. However, its primary focus isn't Secrets management, but facilitating secure service-to-service communication.

Why do brokers still matter?

While secretless brokers and service meshes are making headway, traditional broker systems remain invaluable. They're flexible, work with a vast array of applications, provide centralized control for secret distribution, allow granular access, and often bridge the gap for legacy systems. Their role isn't just retrieval but also secret governance and lifecycle management.

Exploring the realm of integrating external secret stores with Kubernetes, this section shed light on essential mechanisms and patterns vital for secure and efficient Secrets management. We kicked off with Kubernetes extensions and API mechanisms, illustrating how these tools can be seamlessly woven into your Secrets management strategy, followed by an in-depth look at Pod lifecycle and manipulation mechanisms, ensuring that Secrets are securely managed throughout a Pod's lifecycle. The journey continued with specialized Kubernetes patterns, highlighting SealedSecrets as a paradigm of enhanced security, and delved into the world of service mesh integration, showcasing its prowess in secure secret distribution and service-to-service communication. The discussion was rounded off with broker systems in Secrets management, emphasizing their role in creating a secure, intermediary layer between applications and secret stores and ensuring a decoupled, flexible management system. Altogether, these subsections collectively forge a comprehensive guide, empowering teams to securely and efficiently manage Secrets in Kubernetes while navigating the complexities of external secret integration.

Security implications and best practices

As Kubernetes gains traction, integrating it with external secret stores comes with specific advantages, such as specialized encryption and audit capabilities. However, this approach also brings its own set of challenges and security implications.

Here's a list of them:

- **Dependency on external systems**: Relying on external secret stores means introducing an additional layer of complexity and dependency. Any downtime or compromise in the external store can directly impact the applications running in the Kubernetes cluster.

- **Data transit exposure**: Transferring Secrets from the external store to Kubernetes could expose them if the transmission isn't properly secured, for example, if it lacks end-to-end encryption.

- **Privilege escalation through brokers or intermediaries**: Brokers or sidecars fetching Secrets can become potential attack vectors. A malicious actor gaining access to one of these can potentially siphon Secrets from the external store.

- **Configurations and access policies**: Incorrect configurations or overly permissive access policies in the external secret store can inadvertently expose sensitive Secrets.

- **Versioning and secret rotation challenges**: If not managed properly, syncing secret versions between Kubernetes and the external store can be challenging, leading to potential mismatches or usage of outdated Secrets.

Integrating Kubernetes with external secret stores can be challenging. Ensuring the security and integrity of Secrets in Kubernetes necessitates a set of robust practices. Here, we outline the key best practices to consider:

- **Secure the data transit**: Always use encrypted channels (such as TLS) when transferring Secrets from the external store to Kubernetes. Ensure both ends of the communication authenticate each other.

- **Restrict and monitor access**: Implement fine-grained access controls in the external secret store. Only allow specific entities (such as certain brokers or sidecars) to fetch Secrets and monitor their activities.

- **Secret rotation and sync**: Periodically rotate Secrets in the external store and ensure there's a mechanism to propagate these changes efficiently into Kubernetes. This avoids stale Secrets and potential vulnerabilities.

- **Harden broker or intermediary systems**: If using brokers, sidecars, or any other intermediary system to fetch Secrets, ensure they're secure, monitored, and run with the least privilege possible.

- **Back up the external store**: Regularly back up the external secret store. In the event of a compromise or failure, this ensures Secrets can be restored and services can be brought back online quickly.

- **Audits and anomaly detection**: Use the auditing capabilities of the external secret store. Monitor for any unusual access patterns or anomalies that could indicate a breach or misconfiguration.

By acknowledging these implications and adhering to best practices, Kubernetes administrators can effectively and securely leverage the strengths of external secret stores.

Practical and theoretical balance

When integrating Kubernetes with external secret stores, striking the right balance is crucial. This balance isn't just about the technical aspects; it spans scalability, auditability, interoperability, and even cost implications. The goal is to create a robust, scalable, and secure environment that doesn't compromise usability or cost efficiency.

Security remains paramount. You must ensure that Secrets aren't exposed during transit or at rest. External dependencies can introduce vulnerabilities if not properly managed, and a single compromise could lead to a domino effect, endangering multiple systems. Always ensure encrypted communications and choose secret stores with strong security postures.

Usability and the user experience are often seen as the other side of the security coin. A system that's too cumbersome might lead to workarounds or shortcuts, negating the security benefits. Moreover, when evaluating how to apply these considerations in practice, it's critical to understand the optimal usage of the various mechanisms. Pod lifecycle-based methods, such as init containers and sidecars, naturally align with direct fetch methodologies without converting to Kubernetes-native Secrets. In contrast, Kubernetes extensions and API mechanisms, although versatile, are inherently more suited for conversion to Kubernetes resources.

Granular access is crucial for modern applications. Not every application or service requires access to all Secrets. Properly implemented granular access minimizes the risk if a particular service is compromised. Legacy systems can't always be ignored or replaced immediately. Therefore, any solution must consider how to integrate or coexist with older systems that might not have been designed with modern security practices in mind. Handling external dependencies is a delicate task. Depending too much on external systems can introduce fragility into the infrastructure. It's essential to evaluate the reliability of these systems and have contingencies in place.

Understanding failure and recovery models is important, as it's a matter of when, not if, failures will occur; thus, having comprehensive backup and restoration strategies in place is imperative to restoring Secrets in the event of data corruption or loss. Addressing the potential secret leak blast radius is vital. Understand the implications of a breach: what happens if a node or an entire cluster is compromised? Minimize the potential damage by compartmentalizing and isolating Secrets as much as possible. Auditability and monitoring ensure the traceability of secret access. Comprehensive logs and real-time alerts help in identifying and rectifying suspicious activities swiftly.

The scalability of the secret store must align with your organizational growth. As clusters and deployments grow, the secret store should seamlessly handle increased traffic. Lifecycle management involves managing Secrets throughout their entire lifecycle—creation, updates, rotations, and deletions—and seamlessly integrating these processes into CI/CD pipelines.

In our multi-cloud era, interoperability is non-negotiable. Solutions must support diverse environments, ensuring compatibility across different cloud providers. Costs extend beyond direct financial implications. Consider operational costs, potential breach-related costs, and latency-related costs, ensuring the overall cost-efficiency of the solution. Geographic redundancy becomes essential for global operations, ensuring low latency and high availability from any location worldwide. Ease of transition ensures future flexibility. Avoid being locked into a particular solution by favoring those designed with open standards.

Lastly, adhere to regulatory and compliance requirements specific to your industry, ensuring the secret store's compliance with standards such as ISO 27001, PCI-DSS, and HIPAA.

Summary

Exploring the integration of Kubernetes with external secret stores reveals essential methods and patterns for secure and efficient Secrets management. We've delved into key mechanisms, including Kubernetes extensions, Pod lifecycle manipulations, and innovative tools such as the Secret Store CSI Driver, showcasing Kubernetes' adaptability and commitment to security.

Service mesh and broker mechanisms play crucial roles in balancing robust security with application agility, acting as intermediaries for secret distribution and decoupling applications from direct secret access. Achieving this balance requires attention to granular access controls, legacy systems, and the potential impacts of secret leaks, alongside the need for scalability, monitoring, and compliance.

In conclusion, this intricate journey towards integrating Kubernetes with external secret stores is about creating a resilient and secure operational environment, ensuring a scalable and sustainable future for organizations navigating the Kubernetes ecosystem.

Building on our exploration of integrating Kubernetes with external secret stores, the next chapter presents an end-to-end story of secret lifecycle management in a production environment. This will encompass practical applications, challenges, and solutions, illustrating a comprehensive approach to managing Secrets securely and efficiently in real-world scenarios.

13

Case Studies and Real-World Examples

In this chapter, we will see real-world examples of how Kubernetes Secrets are used in production environments. The chapter will cover case studies of production Secrets management in Kubernetes and lessons learned from real-world deployments. Additionally, you will learn about managing Secrets in CI/CD pipelines and integrating Secrets management into the CI/CD process. The chapter will also cover how to manage Secrets in pipelines using Kubernetes tools and the best practices to secure CI/CD Secrets management. We will expand on the following topics:

- Real-world examples of how Kubernetes Secrets are used in production environments
- Secrets management from a CI/CD perspective
- Lessons learned from real-world deployments
- Managing the Secrets' lifecycle end to end in the Kubernetes production system

Technical requirements

To link theory with practice, we are leveraging a series of tools and platforms commonly used to interact with the Google Cloud API and Kubernetes:

- **gcloud CLI**: This is a set of tools used to create and manage Google Cloud resources (`https://cloud.google.com/sdk/gcloud#download_and_install_the`)
- **kubectl**: This is the command-line tool used for communicating with a Kubernetes cluster through the Kubernetes API (`https://kubernetes.io/docs/reference/kubectl/`)
- **minikube**: This is a local Kubernetes distribution used for Kubernetes learning and development. To install minikube on your system, you can follow the instructions from the official documentation (`https://minikube.sigs.k8s.io/docs/start/`)

- **kubeseal**: The kubeseal client is a utility that assists us with our interactions with a `sealed-secrets` installation on Kubernetes (`https://github.com/bitnami-labs/sealed-secrets#kubeseal`)

- **argocd**: This is a command-line utility that simplifies interactions with Argo CD (`https://argo-cd.readthedocs.io/en/stable/cli_installation/`)

Real-world examples of how Kubernetes Secrets are used in production environments

So far, we have seen some different approaches to managing Kubernetes Secrets. We will proceed and see examples of how Secrets are managed in a production environment. We will compare some different approaches, identifying their differences and looking at the pros and cons.

Qualities of Secrets management in production

When it comes to Kubernetes Secrets management in production, regardless of the approach taken, certain qualities need to be satisfied. These qualities make our production deployment robust and secure. The qualities are as follows:

- High availability

- Disaster recovery

- Encryption

- Auditing

Let us deep dive into each one of them.

High availability

Kubernetes is highly available; we saw how in *Chapter 1, Understanding Kubernetes Secrets Management*. A secret stored in Kubernetes will be stored on etcd, and etcd nodes are part of the Kubernetes cluster. If one etcd node goes down, the Secrets will still be present on the other etcd nodes. This ensures that Kubernetes will continue to operate with all the Secrets functioning. Eventually, once the missing etcd node is up, it will resume operations along with the other nodes. High availability ensures the robustness of Kubernetes in scenarios where a node is lost. Apart from the plain unavailability of a node, high availability should also tackle the risk of a data center going down. All the nodes of a Kubernetes cluster should not be hosted in the same data center; instead, the nodes of the cluster should be spread through different data centers. If connectivity to a data center is lost, or if a data center has an issue, the nodes hosted on the other data centers will be able to carry over. However, we might encounter more extreme scenarios, scenarios where instead of a node or a data center becoming unavailable, an entire region becomes disconnected. In those cases, being able to perform disaster recovery in another region is crucial.

Disaster recovery

In *Chapter 6, Disaster Recovery and Backups,* we focused extensively on disaster recovery. When it comes to Secrets, it is crucial to have a disaster recovery plan in place. From a Secrets management perspective, the disaster recovery scenarios will vary on the decisions taken on managing Secrets. Secrets can be managed either on Kubernetes etcd or through external secret storage.

Secret storage using etcd

The approach taken to implement disaster recovery on a Kubernetes cluster will heavily influence the disaster recovery of Secrets that are managed through etcd.

We have the following options:

- Cluster created on demand in another region

- Standby Kubernetes cluster in another region

- Active-active Kubernetes clusters in multiple regions

The option of creating a cluster on demand in another region can be achieved with internal tooling such as keeping backups of etcd or by using tools such as Velero. In the case of a cloud provider, for example, GCP, you can duplicate a Kubernetes cluster with the click of a button.

In maintaining a standby cluster or active-active clusters, many of the choices are heavily dependent on how you perform deployments on Kubernetes. CI/CD is crucial. For example, for your standby cluster to be functional, your CI/CD job might need to push Secrets to two clusters. You might also follow the GitOps model. When it comes to the GitOps model, you might utilize a tool such as Argo CD. In those cases, the standby Kubernetes cluster can be updated by pulling the changes from a Git repository. This way, the Secrets are applied to the available clusters without the need to push the secret changes directly to the cluster.

When it comes to Kubernetes and disaster recovery, there are various options, as we saw in *Chapter 6, Disaster Recovery and Backups.*

External secret store

With an external secret store, disaster recovery is managed by the secret store itself and its features. All the cloud-based Secrets store options we examined supported either cross-regional availability or the option for cross-region replication. Azure Vault and Google Cloud Secret Manager provide cross-region availability, and AWS Secrets Manager provides cross-region replication. In HashiCorp Vault Enterprise, there is also the option of cross-region replication.

Encryption

Encryption is crucial. We had a deep dive into encryption in *Chapter 3, Encrypting Secrets the Kubernetes-Native Way.* On every Kubernetes installation, it is crucial to follow encryption at rest, considering disk storage as well as the encryption of etcd Secrets.

Auditing

We have seen in *Chapter 5*, *Security, Auditing, and Compliance*, why auditing matters and why it is needed in the first place. On every cloud provider we have worked with, the option of auditing was always present. Auditing is also available on HashiCorp Vault and CyberArk Conjur.

We focused on and had an overview of the qualities that need to be in place when it comes to Secrets management in production. Next, we shall focus on how Secrets management and CI/CD come together and the risks to avoid.

Secrets management from a CI/CD perspective

Managing Secrets in CI/CD pipelines is an interesting concept. In previous chapters, we focused primarily on the Git-based concept of Secrets management and the secret-storage-based Secrets management. We have not mentioned manual secret persistence to Kubernetes. There are many reasons for that:

- You lose track of your Kubernetes deployment needs
- Dependencies are not visible
- No clear depiction of what is applied
- Not compatible with infrastructure as code

Next, we will focus on interacting with Secrets on our CI/CD pipelines.

Integrating Secrets management into your CI/CD process

Your CI/CD strategy will differ significantly depending on the approach taken for managing Secrets.

Git-based Secrets management

By managing Secrets through a Git-based approach, CI/CD should be able to interact with the components involved.

Depending on the encryption mechanism, you need to have credentials configured on the CI/CD account that will be able to interact with the KMS system that encrypts the credentials or a Kubernetes service account that can decrypt the Secrets.

Let us examine the case of sealed Secrets, a concept we learned about in *Chapter 12*, *Integrating with Secret Stores*, where a fine-grained Kubernetes role and a Kubernetes service account should be created. The reason is that the sealing operation happens inside the cluster. The sealed secret can then be stored on Git. To retrieve the actual value, you need to decrypt it through the cluster. The sealing operation can also happen offline; in this case, more steps are needed to make sure that the encryption key is securely handled.

External secret store and Workload Identity

So far, we have worked with Microsoft Azure Key Vault, Google Cloud Secret Manager, and AWS Secrets Manager. All of them support the integration of Workload Identity and GitHub Actions.

The traditional way to interact with a cloud component on a CI/CD pipeline was by attaching the credentials of the cloud provider on the CI/CD job. This practice increases security risks. The credentials, such as a service account or a key secret, are static credentials; if compromised and without a proper logging or audit system, these could be used for an extended period, creating a silent breach.

Workload Identity is a more secure solution. With Workload Identity, we can assign to a CI/CD job fine-grained permissions toward a cloud component. Workload Identity is not supported by all CI/CD providers out there; however, there is a strong adoption of the Workload Identity approach and it is expected to become the norm.

By using Workload Identity, a CI/CD job can have temporary credentials to interact with a cloud provider's secret store. Since we have now had an introduction to Workload Identity, we will proceed and see it in action using GCP.

GitHub Actions and GCP Workload Identity integration

One of the issues with CI/CD jobs interacting with cloud components is the permissions. Traditionally, this is resolved by uploading credentials to the CI/CD job variables with all the risks this solution can introduce, which we will cover later in this chapter.

GitHub Action supports **OpenID Connect** (**OIDC**). Through OIDC, it is possible to authenticate between cloud providers and GitHub, using short-lived tokens. This way, we avoid the need for storing long-lived cloud Secrets in GitHub.

In *Chapter 10, Exploring Cloud Secret Store on GCP*, we integrated a GKE cluster with GCP's Secret Manager, so we are already familiar with GCP as a platform. Imagine the scenario of our CI/CD jobs needing to interact with Secret Manager, which is integrated with GKE.

Without the support of OIDC, we would have to store a GCP service account key to the CI/CD job. Thanks to OIDC, we can set up the authentication from GitHub to GCP using Workload Identity Federation.

First, we will have to configure an identity pool:

```
$ gcloud iam workload-identity-pools create "ga-ksm-pool"
--project="${GCP_PROJECT_ID}" --location="global" --display-
name="GitHub actions Pool"
```

Then, we include GitHub as an identity provider:

```
$ gcloud iam workload-identity-pools providers create-oidc "github" \
--project="${GCP_PROJECT_ID}" \
--location="global" \
```

```
--workload-identity-pool="ga-ksm-pool" \
--display-name="Github provider" \
--attribute-mapping="google.subject=assertion.sub,attribute.
repository=assertion.repository" \
--issuer-uri="https://token.actions.githubusercontent.com"
```

The identity pool is provisioned, and GitHub is one of the identity providers. The next step is to bind a service account on GCP to a GitHub repository:

```
$ gcloud iam service-accounts create github-service-account
--project="${GCP_PROJECT_ID}"
$ project_number=$(gcloud projects list --filter="$(gcloud config
get-value project)" --format="value(PROJECT_NUMBER)")
$ gcloud secrets add-iam-policy-binding ksm-secret
--member="serviceAccount:github-service-account@${GCP_PROJECT_ID}.iam.
gserviceaccount.com" --role=roles/secretmanager.viewer
$ gcloud secrets add-iam-policy-binding ksm-secret
--member="serviceAccount:github-service-account@${GCP_PROJECT_ID}.iam.
gserviceaccount.com" --role=roles/secretmanager.secretAccessor
$ gcloud iam service-accounts add-iam-policy-binding "github-service-
account@${GCP_PROJECT_ID}.iam.gserviceaccount.com" \
--project="${GCP_PROJECT_ID}" \
--role="roles/iam.workloadIdentityUser" \
--member="principalSet://iam.googleapis.com/projects/${project_
number}/locations/global/workloadIdentityPools/ga-ksm-pool/
attribute.repository/${github_organisation_or_username}/${github_
repositoryname}"
```

Through this configuration, we allow authentications from the Workload Identity provider to impersonate the desired service account. Also, note that when we specified the Workload Identity pool as a member, we specified the GitHub repository where we shall host the actions that would require GCP access.

We are set up to proceed with the GitHub job configuration:

```
name: Read from Secret Manager
on:
 push:
  branches:
   - 'main'
jobs:
 run:
  name: 'get secret'
  permissions:
   id-token: write
   contents: read
  runs-on: 'ubuntu-latest'
  steps:
```

```
 - id: 'auth'
   uses: 'google-github-actions/auth@v1'
   with:
     workload_identity_provider: 'projects/{project-id}/locations/
global/workloadIdentityPools/ga-ksm-pool /providers/github'
     service_account: 'github-service-account@${GCP_PROJECT_ID}.iam.
gserviceaccount.com'
 - id: fetch
   run: |-
     curl -H 'Bearer: ${{ steps.auth.outputs.access_token }}'
https://secretmanager.googleapis.com/v1/projects/project-name/secrets/
secret-name/versions/latest:access
```

On the GitHub Actions console, we should be able to see the job successfully creating a token and authenticate upon the Workload Identity instance created, as well as receiving a secret from Secret Manager. Obviously, this way of authentication can be applied even when we want to interact with GCP.

Take note that the preceding steps print the secret on purpose since they serve as an example of how GitHub Actions and GCP Workload Identity integrate. You should not print any retrieved Secrets on the CI/CD console, as we shall mention later in the chapter.

In a nutshell, by utilizing Workload Identity, we can avoid storing long-lived credentials in a CI/CD job configuration. Also, we establish seamless integration with the cloud provider and make it easier to interact with cloud provider components such as Secret Manager on GCP.

Vault as an external secret store

As we have seen from the integration of Vault with Kubernetes, a token is needed to be able to interact with Vault. When we use a long-lived token, we face the risk of compromise. For this reason, instead of using a Vault token directly, we can proceed with the method of JWT with GitHub OIDC tokens.

Each GitHub action receives an auto-generated OIDC token. We can configure trust between a GitHub Actions workflow and Vault using the OIDC provider of GitHub.

A similar concept was Kubernetes authentication. We were taking the JWTs, originating from a Kubernetes service account, and using them to retrieve Secrets from Vault. Since Vault had already established trust with our Kubernetes cluster, it could validate the Secrets and return the credentials.

A similar process happens with the GitHub OIDC provider and the HashiCorp integration.

Executing CI/CD pipelines on Kubernetes

Another way to securely integrate CI/CD pipelines with a Kubernetes secret store is to run the pipeline inside Kubernetes. The CI/CD jobs run inside Kubernetes, so the credentials and other Kubernetes components are not exposed outside of our premises.

Many major cloud providers, such as GitHub Actions and GitLab, provide the option to manage CI/CD pipeline orchestration on GitHub and GitLab but execute the CI/CD jobs inside Kubernetes. There are numerous benefits to that approach.

By running a CI/CD job on-premises, you make it possible for the CI/CD job to interact with resources that reside only on-premises. For example, supposing a HashiCorp Vault installation is in a private network that is not publicly accessible. To integrate the Vault instance with an external CI/CD provider, we must make the Vault instance publicly accessible, which increases our security concerns.

By running a pipeline on-premises, that is not the case. Running CI/CD pipelines inside Kubernetes can harden the security of our CI/CD pipelines. Tekton is a very popular open source framework that enables us to create CI/CD systems in a Kubernetes installation.

Moving on, there is another approach to continuous delivery, which is through the GitOps model. Let us see how the GitOps model works by running an example with Argo CD.

GitOps

GitOps is a set of practices that is used to manage infrastructure and application configurations via a Git-centric approach. Argo CD follows the GitOps model. It monitors a Git repository that we specify and ensures that the application is in the desired state. Argo CD is a Kubernetes controller that monitors the running infrastructure and compares it with the infrastructure specified in the Git repository.

We can understand the model by doing a simple Argo CD installation:

```
$ kubectl create namespace argocd
$ kubectl config set-context --current --namespace=argocd
$ kubectl apply -n argocd -f https://raw.githubusercontent.com/
argoproj/argo-cd/v2.5.8/manifests/install.yaml
```

We can now port forward so that we can interact with Argo CD without the need to expose the service through an ingress:

```
$ kubectl port-forward svc/argocd-server -n argocd 8080:443
```

In another session, we can retrieve the default admin autogenerated password, in order to log in to `argocd`:

```
$ argocd admin initial-password -n argocd
$ argocd login 127.0.0.1:8080 --username admin --password ***-**
--insecure
```

We can now create an application; we shall use the examples in the Argo CD repository (`https://github.com/argoproj/argocd-example-apps`):

```
$ argocd app create guestbook --repo https://github.com/argoproj/
argocd-example-apps.git --path guestbook --dest-server https://
kubernetes.default.svc --dest-namespace default
```

An application is now running based on a deployment file in another Git repository.

Let us examine GitOps and its compatibility with the Secrets management methods we have seen so far:

- Sealed Secrets can be supported without extra effort since the sealed Secrets controller will be able to apply any new Secrets distributed through Git.

- Solutions driven by external secret storage are not affected since the secret information resides on another component.

- Helm Secrets support depends on the tool used for GitOps. Argo CD can support Helm Secrets; however, it requires modifications to facilitate the encryption and decryption of Secrets that are distributed through Helm charts.

Now that we have had an overview of Secrets management and CI/CD, let us proceed with the risks that come with the integration of CI/CD and Secrets.

Risks to avoid with Secrets in CI/CD pipelines

A CI/CD pipeline can be subject to various risks when it comes to Secrets. It is quite easy to misconfigure a CI/CD pipeline, which can lead to problems such as leaking sensitive information, running overprivileged pipelines, and supply chain attacks.

Leaking Secrets in a pipeline

Leaking Secrets in a pipeline is easier to accidentally do than you'd think. CI/CD pipelines by default treat secret information differently from other configuration variables. Take, for example, a GitHub Actions workflow. If we try to print a secret in a job, the secret will be masked, and thus the information will not be leaked. This is not enough. By changing the pipeline's configuration, we can persist the secret value in a file. This makes it possible to print the file and retrieve the secret information. To make matters worse, CI/CD pipelines keep the job history and logs. In certain cases, the history cannot be erased or will be erased after some time.

Another way that a secret can be leaked is by making it part of the artifacts generated by the CI/CD pipeline. In this situation, the Secrets can be downloaded through the CI/CD UI.

These examples of misconfigured pipelines can lead to security incidents. The secret information has been leaked and so it needs to be rotated.

Production Secrets

Another risk is using the same Secrets used in a production workload with a CI/CD pipeline. A secret in a production environment is used to perform different operations from the ones that take place in a CI/CD environment. Having a production secret on a CI/CD environment can lead to code that might run with more privileges than the ones needed if the CI/CD is misconfigured, and its usage might affect an actual production system. In the case of a secret leak, the risk impact is much greater when using a dedicated secret for a CI/CD job.

Malevolent contributions

CI/CD can be a target for attackers trying to steal Secrets. A pull request on a repository that triggers a pipeline gives a variety of options for the pull request author to retrieve the secret value. For these cases, it is essential to protect the CI/CD jobs that interact with sensitive information. Branches should be protected, and certain pipelines should be segregated to enable fine-grained permissions and prevent access from individuals who might try to retrieve secret information through CI/CD jobs.

In open source projects, contributions might have the purpose of stealing Secrets or being part of a supply chain attack attempt. We can use GitHub Actions as an example, where workflows from forks do not have access to Secrets. Also, to prevent any abusive behavior on pull requests, GitHub Actions gives the option to approve workflow runs from public forks (`https://docs.github.com/en/actions/managing-workflow-runs/approving-workflow-runs-from-public-forks`).

Untrusted software

A pipeline can be as secure as the software that is used to implement it. Throughout the internet, there is a wide variety of CI/CD software utilities, ranging from libraries to Docker containers. These software components can be outdated, exposing the pipeline to security vulnerabilities, or some of them might have been compromised by an attacker with the goal of a supply chain attack.

Take, for example, a Jenkins plugin or a GitHub workflow action that reads the Secrets from a pipeline and sends them to an external location. The same can happen with any utility that is not trusted or has even been compromised.

Software should be used only from trusted sources, and its authenticity should be verified, for example, using hash-based verification. Also, the software used in the pipelines should be the latest software that incorporates the necessary security patches.

Pipelines with extra privileges

CI/CD is essential for every company that needs to build, test, and release software. Since it has a crucial role, it is expected to interact with Secrets that might be shared by a Kubernetes installation. Secrets privileges that exceed the scope of a CI/CD job can cause serious incidents in the case of a leak or misconfiguration.

Take, for example, a CI/CD job used for testing purposes interacting with an external secret storage used by a Kubernetes cluster. Suppose this job deletes Secrets from the secret storage, targeting a staging environment. However, the permissions assigned to the pipeline are broad enough to enable the deletion of Secrets in a production environment. A pipeline misconfiguration can lead to data loss or even a production outage.

Now that we have had an overview of the risks associated with Secrets and CI/CD integration, let us proceed with identifying the best practices.

Best practices for secure CI/CD Secrets management

We had an overview of CI/CD jobs interacting with Kubernetes Secrets. To ensure that we are secure, we need to follow certain practices:

- Do not commit clear text Secrets
- If using tokens, rotate them and make them short-lived
- If an OICD-based integration is possible, use it, as it is more secure
- Moving pipelines to Kubernetes on-premises hardens security
- The principle of least privilege should be followed
- Use dedicated Secrets for testing
- Do not use the same Secrets for testing and production

So far, we have focused on the ways to handle Kubernetes Secrets in production and the integration of Kubernetes Secrets and CI/CD. Next, we will focus on a case study for implementing a Secrets system within an organization.

Lessons learned from real-world deployments

Let us now look at how we can interact with Secrets on Kubernetes and what we should and should not do when we interact with Secrets on Kubernetes.

Case study – Developing Secrets management

As more organizations embrace container orchestration, the following case study illustrates the journey toward establishing a robust system for Secrets management within an organization.

The Keywhiz Secrets management system at Square

Keywhiz is a system that Square developed to keep important digital keys and passwords, such as those used to secure websites, safe and in one place. This system is beneficial as the organization previously lacked secure methods for storing these Secrets. Keywhiz makes sure that only the right parts of Square can get to these Secrets when they need to, using secure connections.

Deep dive into Keywhiz's secret system

Let us dive deep into Keywhiz to see how Square built the system end to end.

Business justification

Square built Keywhiz with the idea that important Secrets should be hard to reach. They shouldn't pop up in places where just anyone can see them, such as on a developer's computer or the internet. Only the specific parts of Square that need these Secrets should be able to get them. This is especially true for services that use secure connections to protect data. Instead of using many steps or other services to get to these Secrets, Square's services can get them directly. Even for special cases, such as when they need to use extra secure hardware, Keywhiz has a way to handle it.

Keywhiz also focuses on not having too many Secrets scattered around, which can be risky. By keeping them all in one system, it's easier to keep track of them and make sure they are safe. Plus, this system lets Square check on the health of their digital keys and passwords, for instance, to see whether they are strong enough or need to be changed soon.

It's important for Square to know when and how a secret is used. So, Keywhiz keeps a detailed record of every time a secret is accessed. This isn't something you can do if you just drop the Secrets onto servers as files. Although there are tools that can help keep an eye on this, they require extra work to set up.

Keywhiz is made to work with a lot of different services at Square. It has been set up to handle a wide range of needs, from securing websites to handling databases.

The reliability of this system is key. It has to work all the time because Square's services rely on these Secrets to run.

The system is also designed to be easy to use. If it wasn't, people might try to take shortcuts, which could be less safe.

Finally, Keywhiz separates the process of changing keys from updating software. This means that Square can update its security without having to change the whole system, which makes things safer and more flexible.

Categorizing and centralizing the store Secrets

Square's Keywhiz system takes the security of its digital Secrets seriously. It begins by organizing these Secrets into clear categories. This isn't just about keeping things tidy—it's about knowing exactly which part of Square's system needs which Secrets to operate. From there, all Secrets are kept in one central place. This means they're not scattered across different spots where they could be forgotten or, worse, fall into the wrong hands.

But what makes Keywhiz stand out is how it locks up these Secrets. Before a secret is saved in Square's databases, it gets wrapped up in a layer of encryption—like putting a letter into a safe that only certain people can open. This involves a specific type of encryption known as **AES-GCM** (`https://en.wikipedia.org/wiki/Galois/Counter_Mode`). It's recommended by the **National Institute of Standards and Technology** (**NIST**) in their Special Publication 800-38D as a preferred method for block cipher (`https://en.wikipedia.org/wiki/Block_cipher`) modes of operation, focusing on **Galois/Counter Mode (GCM)** and **Galois Message Authentication Code (GMAC)**. Each secret gets its own unique encryption key, created using a method known as **HKDF** (https://en.wikipedia.org/wiki/HKDF), a simple **key derivation function (KDF)** based on the HMAC message authentication code, which is a way to make sure that even if one key is discovered, the others remain safe. Square uses hardware security modules to contain derivation keys.

Now, when it comes to delivering these Secrets, Keywhiz makes sure that only the right parts of Square's system, which they call *clients*, can get to them. The structure of access control revolves around three key elements: clients, groups, and Secrets. A "client" refers to any certificate that gains access to Secrets. These clients can belong to multiple groups, which are collections of clients. For a client to access a particular secret, the secret must be associated with at least one of the groups to which the client belongs. Typically, Keywhiz organizes this by creating three main types of groups: one for each service on a specific server, one for each distinct service, and a universal group that includes all clients.

Before, people tried other ways to keep Secrets safe, such as mixing them into the code where programs are written or manually adding them to servers. But these ways are risky—the Secrets can accidentally get shared with the world or get lost. Even trying to keep Secrets safe using systems that manage server settings isn't ideal because those systems are meant to share their information across the company, which is not what you want for your Secrets.

PKI as a source of the truth for authentication

Public key infrastructure (PKI) is central to Square's authentication process. It's like a verification system that ensures that only the right parts of Square's network can access the Secrets they need. To establish this trust, Square uses mTLS and X509 certificates, which are digital proofs of identity for services. Square simplifies this task with **certstrap**, a straightforward certificate management tool. This tool helps Square create its own certificate authorities, which you can think of as digital ID offices. With certstrap, Square can issue these digital IDs to its services, ensuring each one is recognized and trusted within its network.

certstrap allows Square to avoid the complexities of traditional tools such as OpenSSL. It enables Square to create a chain of trust where each service's identity is verified and secured. This verification is crucial for Square, as it keeps communication between services secure, ensuring that Secrets are only accessed by authorized entities within the company.

Authorization data model

In Square's Keywhiz system, authorization—deciding who gets access to what—is a structured process. Here's how Square has set it up:

- Clients are parts of Square's systems, such as a service or an application, that need access to Secrets to work properly. They prove who they are with something called a client certificate. It's like an ID card for systems.

- Secrets are the sensitive bits of information that clients need to do their jobs, such as configuration files or passwords. Each secret has a unique name so there are no mixups, and they can't be changed once they're set. However, Square can keep multiple versions of a secret if updates are needed.

- Groups act as a meeting point for clients and Secrets. Think of groups as tags or labels. Square labels the clients and the Secrets with these group tags. When a client and a secret have the same group tag, the client can see and use the secret. It's Square's way of organizing which parts of their system can access which Secrets.

- Users are the people who manage Keywhiz at Square. They're the ones setting up the system and deciding which clients and Secrets get which group tags. They log in to Keywhiz with secure methods, and after they're in, they need a special code from Keywhiz to keep doing their work securely.

Square's Keywhiz manages access through a structured authorization model of clients, Secrets, groups, and user management, maintaining secure and orderly permissions.

Secrets distribution

Square also maintains a Keywhiz client implementation called **Keysync**. Keysync is a program that connects to Square's Keywhiz server securely and asks for the Secrets it needs to keep Square's services running. It uses something called **mTLS**—a way of communicating securely—to make sure everything is safe and private.

Once Keysync gets these Secrets, it keeps them in a secure area of the server's memory called **tmpfs**. This is a temporary space that doesn't save anything once the server is turned off. So, if there's a power cut or the server has to be restarted, those Secrets don't get left behind where they could be seen by others.

The neat thing about Keysync is that it's built to handle unexpected problems. If there's an issue with the Keywhiz server, Keysync will still have the Secrets it previously downloaded, so Square's services can keep working without interruption. It's only after a full server reboot that Keysync needs to get all the Secrets again.

To handle these Secrets, Square's administrators have an admin CLI that allows them to type commands directly into the system to add, remove, or change Secrets as needed. It's a straightforward way for them to keep everything up to date and to check on the health of the Secrets management system without having to navigate through complicated interfaces.

Keysync, the CLI for Square's Keywhiz interface, ensures the secure and confidential delivery of Secrets across different scenarios.

Challenges and lessons of Keywhiz from a third-party view

Given that Keywhiz was deprecated on September 18, 2023, and is no longer maintained, reflecting on the challenges and lessons it presented during its service is insightful. The recommendation to transition to HashiCorp Vault highlights the need for robust and actively supported Secrets management solutions.

Centralized management with Kubernetes cases is hard

One of the core challenges Keywhiz faces in Kubernetes Secrets management is the inherent complexity of centralized management in a highly distributed and dynamic environment such as Kubernetes. Kubernetes environments often require a more flexible and decentralized approach to Secrets management. Although Keywhiz offers centralized control and strong encryption for Secrets, it may not be optimally configured for the decentralized and ephemeral nature of Kubernetes workloads.

For example, in Kubernetes, it's essential to have a Secrets management solution that can handle the dynamic creation and deletion of Secrets, in line with the ephemeral nature of Kubernetes Pods and Services. Secrets management in Kubernetes also requires tight integration with Kubernetes' **role-based access control** (**RBAC**) and the ability to manage Secrets across multiple clusters and namespaces efficiently.

While Keywhiz excels at centralized Secrets management, providing strong encryption and a secure way to distribute Secrets to various services and platforms, adapting these capabilities to the specifics of Kubernetes can be challenging. Kubernetes environments often benefit from tools such as HashiCorp Vault, which offers extensive Kubernetes integration, including dynamic Secrets, integration with Kubernetes service accounts for authentication, and the ability to define fine-grained access control policies for Secrets.

A Secrets management system is not just one system but a whole ecosystem

Keywhiz's role in an organization's ecosystem extends beyond its function as a standalone Secrets management tool. Its effectiveness relies heavily on its integration with the company's existing workflows, policies, and organizational culture. This scenario illustrates that the efficacy of a Secrets management system is not determined solely by its technical capabilities but by how well it aligns with and supports the broader operational context of the organization.

For instance, consider a healthcare organization that adopts Keywhiz to manage sensitive data, such as patient records and login credentials for internal systems. In this setting, while Keywhiz serves as the repository for these Secrets, its utility is dependent on seamless integration with the organization's existing healthcare information systems. This integration could involve syncing with employee directory services to manage access based on roles and departments. It would also entail aligning with healthcare compliance standards, where Keywhiz's audit trails and encryption capabilities become critical in meeting regulatory requirements. In this way, Keywhiz becomes an integral part of the organization's overall data security framework, influencing and being influenced by various factors beyond the immediate scope of secret storage.

Lack of auditing as a story

A notable limitation of Keywhiz is its approach to auditing, especially considering how it handles secret distribution. Keysync works as a client where Secrets are downloaded as `tmpfs` files, which are then used by applications. However, this model does not inherently provide detailed auditing data for each action taken on these Secrets, and specifically, it lacks visibility into whether applications are actively using the downloaded Secrets, as this interaction occurs client-side and is not directly observable by the Keywhiz server.

This leads to potential gaps in the auditing process, such as the following:

- Identifying the specific user or service that accessed a secret

- Recording the precise timestamp of each access

- Understanding the nature of the access, such as whether the secret was read, modified, and so on

- Detecting the IP address or machine from which the secret was accessed

The Keysync process does not reflect the real-time requirements for Secrets associated with applications, leading to challenges in maintaining a continuous and comprehensive audit trail. This gap can impact the ability to fully document the lifecycle of secret access within an organization, making it difficult to trace all interactions with sensitive data.

Managing the Secrets lifecycle from end to end in a Kubernetes production cluster

The previous chapter covered a broad range of topics, but there was a noticeable disconnect between the concepts discussed and practical examples for managing Secrets in a production environment. In this section, we will narrow our focus and delve into the end-to-end management of Secrets within a Kubernetes production cluster, offering a more practical, application-oriented perspective.

In exploring the management of Secrets in such an environment, we recognize that the process involves more than just secure storage. We shift our focus from mere storage repositories to a comprehensive view of Secrets usage throughout the system's lifecycle. Secrets are integral to operational processes, embedded in the workflows that drive an organization's digital operations.

The challenge lies in effectively managing the entire lifecycle of Secrets, from inception to decommissioning, with a rigorous emphasis on precision and security. This comprehensive approach is essential for organizations committed to high security and operational standards. Managing Secrets effectively is about understanding their generation, distribution, revocation, and decommissioning within the dynamic Kubernetes ecosystem. This section will guide you through the nuanced and vital role of Secrets management in maintaining a secure and efficient digital infrastructure.

Finalizing your decision on comprehensive Secrets lifecycle management

When it comes to managing Secrets in a Kubernetes production environment, adopting a holistic and comprehensive approach is paramount. Secrets lifecycle management extends far beyond the mere aspect of secure storage, encompassing a range of critical processes from the initial provisioning to the final decommissioning and revocation.

Provisioning involves the creation or generation of Secrets in a secure and controlled manner, ensuring that they are strong and unique and that they comply with organizational security policies. The storage phase requires a robust and secure repository, such as HashiCorp Vault or cloud Secrets stores, ensuring that Secrets are encrypted at rest and protected from unauthorized access. Distribution is a delicate operation, where Secrets must be securely transmitted to the required services or applications, ensuring integrity and confidentiality throughout transit.

Decommissioning comes into play when Secrets are no longer required, necessitating a secure process to retire them, ensuring that they cannot be reused or exploited. Finally, revocation is a critical step in the lifecycle, particularly in instances of compromise or when a secret's integrity is in doubt. A swift and efficient revocation mechanism ensures that access is immediately cut off, mitigating potential damage.

Embracing a comprehensive Secrets lifecycle management approach ensures that Secrets are not just securely stored but are also properly managed throughout their entire lifecycle. This end-to-end perspective is not just a best practice but an organizational necessity to ensure the integrity of the Secrets and, by extension, the entire production system. As we delve deeper into each of these aspects in the subsequent sections, the overarching importance of a holistic approach to Secrets management in Kubernetes will become increasingly clear, highlighting its role as a critical component in the broader security and operational landscape of the organization.

High SLAs as the key to business sustainability

Maintaining high **service-level agreements** (**SLAs**) is vital for Secrets management within Kubernetes environments, emphasizing system reliability and availability as foundational aspects of business sustainability. This is particularly important in production environments where downtime or security breaches could have significant financial and operational implications.

To achieve this high level of reliability, businesses need to implement strong monitoring and alerting systems. Regular stress testing of the Secrets management system is also essential to identify and address potential vulnerabilities, ensuring the system can handle various operational stresses and maintain its SLA commitments.

In the context of cloud Secrets storage, providers typically offer committed SLAs that meet the requirements of most use cases. However, for self-deployed Secrets management systems, different approaches are necessary to evaluate and ensure SLAs, especially when secret retrieval is critical for system infrastructure and platform usage.

One strategy to ensure high SLAs is the active-active replication model used by solutions such as HashiCorp Vault. This model provides continuous synchronization across multiple active systems, enhancing fault tolerance and availability. However, it's not the only approach.

Alternative methods, such as using a secure Redis configuration for buffered Secrets, can offer temporary availability (e.g., for a few hours) and enhance platform reliability. In this scenario, Secrets are stored as encrypted ciphertext in Redis, which acts as a temporary buffer. This method not only secures the

Secrets but also provides an additional layer of reliability, ensuring that Secrets are available during critical periods or in the event of primary system failures.

Overall, the approach to maintaining high SLAs in Secrets management should be tailored to the specific needs and architecture of the Kubernetes environment.

Emergency recovery – backup and restore

In Kubernetes production clusters, crafting an effective emergency recovery plan for Secrets management is essential. A robust recovery plan is key to quickly restoring operations in the event of data losses, system failures, or security incidents, thereby minimizing downtime. This proactive approach ensures that the Secrets management system can swiftly recover from unexpected disruptions, thus maintaining the continuity of the production environment.

Regular backups play a critical role in safeguarding the integrity and availability of Secrets and configurations. These backups form the foundation for a reliable recovery mechanism, ensuring that there's a dependable process for retrieving sensitive information and configurations following unforeseen data loss, hardware failures, or security breaches.

For further details and insights on this topic, you may refer to *Chapter 6, Disaster Recovery and Backups*.

Not just storing but provisioning Secrets

Provisioning and storing Secrets are critical steps in managing Secrets within a Kubernetes environment, acting as the initial point of entry and a significant opportunity to enforce secure usage models. By controlling the origin of Secrets and clearly defining their target resources, organizations can establish a robust framework for long-term Secrets management.

When provisioning Secrets, it's imperative to ensure transparency and traceability. Enforcing a clear and standardized process for secret creation helps in tracking where Secrets come from, their intended purpose, and their targeted resources. This practice aids in maintaining an organized Secrets inventory, making it simpler to manage and audit over time.

In terms of storing Secrets securely in Kubernetes, adopting best practices such as encryption at rest and in transit, using dedicated service accounts, and implementing role-based access controls is essential. Organizations should leverage Kubernetes' native capabilities, such as Namespaces and NetworkPolicies, to provide additional layers of isolation and protection.

A key aspect of ensuring long-term success in Secrets management is to enforce the use of specific secret types. Kubernetes supports various secret types, each tailored to specific use cases. By mandating the use of these types, organizations can benefit from Kubernetes' built-in validation mechanisms, ensuring that Secrets conform to the expected structure and reducing the risk of misconfigurations. For instance, enforcing a secret type of `kubernetes.io/dockerconfigjson` for storing Docker registry credentials ensures that the secret's content adheres to the expected format, reducing the risk of runtime errors.

Furthermore, utilizing specific secret types aids in creating a self-descriptive and more manageable environment. Developers and administrators can easily understand the purpose and usage of a secret based on its type, enhancing overall clarity and reducing the potential for mistakes. This practice also simplifies auditing and compliance processes, as it becomes straightforward to track and report on the usage of different types of Secrets across the Kubernetes cluster.

Incorporating these practices into the provisioning and storage phases of Secrets management sets a solid foundation for secure and efficient secret handling. It ensures that Secrets are created, stored, and used in a manner that aligns with security best practices, providing a significant return on investment in terms of security, compliance, and manageability. By enforcing clear standards and utilizing Kubernetes' native capabilities, organizations can create a robust and resilient Secrets management environment, ready to support their applications securely and efficiently.

Secrets rotation

The rotation of Secrets stands as a crucial practice in maintaining a secure Kubernetes environment, primarily due to the inherent security implications tied to static, long-lived credentials. Secrets, once compromised, can serve as gateways for malicious entities, leading to unauthorized access and potential data breaches. To mitigate such risks, implementing the periodic rotation of Secrets is necessary, ensuring that even if a secret were to be compromised, its lifespan would be limited, thereby reducing the potential damage inflicted.

However, the task of rotating Secrets is not without its challenges, especially when dealing with a large number of Secrets distributed across various services. This is where automation steps in, offering a streamlined and efficient solution. By leveraging automated systems, organizations can ensure timely rotations, aligning with best practices and compliance requirements. These systems work by periodically updating Secrets and credentials, distributing the updated versions to the respective services, and ensuring the outdated Secrets are retired securely.

It is crucial to note that while automation plays a significant role in Secrets rotation, there may be exceptional cases where certain Secrets are exempt from rotation due to technical constraints or specific use cases. In these situations, it is imperative to maintain transparency and clear documentation, marking these Secrets accordingly to ensure visibility. Despite the exemption, a robust incident response plan must be in place, guaranteeing that if a security incident were to occur, these exempted Secrets could be rotated in a timely manner, mitigating potential risks and securing the environment. This comprehensive approach to Secrets rotation ensures not only the security of the Secrets themselves but also the resilience and integrity of the entire Kubernetes ecosystem.

Handling secret updates and rotation

Handling secret updates and rotations is a crucial aspect of maintaining security. As recommended by NIST, regularly rotating Secrets is essential to minimize security risks.

Our approach to updating Secrets involves several methods:

- **Monitoring and reloading**: We continually monitor for secret changes, updating them in application memory to ensure the latest values are used.

- **Keyring mode**: This involves maintaining multiple versions of Secrets to prevent downtime. It's important to monitor which version is in use and phase out older ones timely.

- **Restart as reload method**: Implement an automatic system to restart Pods when Secrets change, possibly using Kubernetes jobs or other tools to detect changes and initiate restarts.

Each application's needs dictate the chosen method, focusing on the following:

- **Timely secret consumption**: Depending on the server's capability to handle multiple values

- **Graceful secret changes**: Ensuring applications manage new Secrets smoothly, without losing state or causing downtime

- **Downtime avoidance**: For applications that can't afford downtime, use strategies such as multiple Pod replicas and rolling updates

- **Monitoring and alerting**: Keep a robust system to monitor Secrets and Pods, with alerts for secret rotations and Pod restarts

This strategy aims for both security and operational efficiency, adapting to various application requirements on secret rotation.

Sample Kubernetes manifest for automated secret rotation

The following is a simplified example to illustrate how you might set up a Kubernetes job to trigger Pod restarts upon secret rotation:

```
apiVersion: batch/v1
kind: Job
metadata:
  name: secret-rotator
spec:
  template:
    spec:
      containers:
      - name: secret-rotator
        image: user-implemented-rotator-image
        env:
        - name: VAULT_ADDR
          value: "http://vault:8200"
        - name: SECRET_PATH
          value: "secret/my-app"
```

```
        - name: KUBERNETES_NAMESPACE
          valueFrom:
            fieldRef:
              fieldPath: metadata.namespace
        - name: POD_SELECTOR
          value: "app=my-app"
      restartPolicy: Never
  backoffLimit: 0
```

Here is a diagram showing the additional Secrets rotation job:

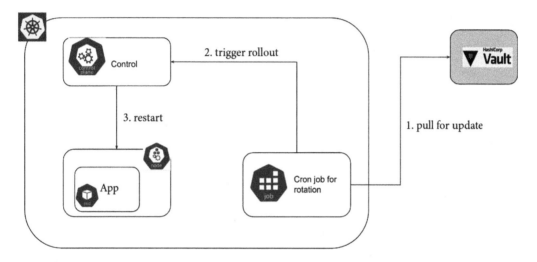

Figure 13.1 – Cron job for secret rotation

In this example, the job runs a container that watches for secret rotations in Vault and restarts the relevant Pods in Kubernetes when a rotation is detected. This ensures that the init containers for the affected Pods run again, fetching the latest version of the Secrets. By adopting such strategies, you ensure that your applications remain secure with up-to-date Secrets while minimizing downtime and maintaining a robust and resilient deployment.

Authorization sprawl issue

In Kubernetes, managing access to Secrets requires careful attention due to the delicate balance involved.

The **authorization sprawl** issue in Kubernetes arises when permissions are set too broadly, often unintentionally, leading to significant security risks. This often occurs with RBAC configurations that are not adequately tailored, resulting in users or services gaining more privileges than necessary.

Certainly, solutions such as Kubernetes RBAC and integration with identity management solutions are well known, but the real issues include the following:

- How to enforce compliance and prevent users from exploiting or circumventing the configuration source

- How to effectively monitor and promptly revoke any policy violations

- How to audit configuration-based access policy changes and understand their impact

A typical misconfiguration in Kubernetes RBAC might unintentionally allow unexpected groups to access all Secrets:

```yaml
# serviceaccount.yaml
apiVersion: v1
kind: ServiceAccount
metadata:
  name: myapp-sa
---
# role.yaml
kind: Role
apiVersion: rbac.authorization.k8s.io/v1
metadata:
  name: myapp-role
rules:
  - apiGroups: [""]
    resources: ["pods", "secrets"]
    verbs: ["get", "watch", "list", "create", "update", "delete"]
---
# misconfigured-role-binding.yaml
kind: RoleBinding
apiVersion: rbac.authorization.k8s.io/v1
metadata:
  name: myapp-role-binding
roleRef:
  apiGroup: rbac.authorization.k8s.io
  kind: Role
  name: myapp-role
subjects:
  - kind: ServiceAccount
    name: myapp-sa
```

In this example, the myapp-sa service account is created with overly broad access to Pods and Secrets. The myapp-role-binding role binding exacerbates the issue by referencing myapp-

`role`, which grants full access to these resources. As a result, `myapp-sa` is endowed with more permissions than necessary, posing a risk of unauthorized access to sensitive data.

Addressing this issue requires the implementation of fine-grained access controls that precisely define permissions for each role and user, adhering to the principle of least privilege. This entails granting only the level of access required for users to perform their specific tasks. Regular reviews and updates of RBAC policies are also essential.

Tagging, labeling, and masking on the client side

Within a Kubernetes environment, the approach to managing Secrets should be holistic, accounting for not just how Secrets are stored but also how they are managed and interacted with on the client side. Tagging, labeling, and masking Secrets become pivotal in this context. The rationale behind adopting these practices is grounded in their ability to enhance security, manageability, and adherence to compliance standards. By tagging and labeling Secrets, teams embed essential metadata that elucidates the secret's purpose, associated resources, and lifecycle stage. This metadata becomes a powerful tool, aiding in implementing granular access controls and simplifying the tracking of secret usage across the system.

When it comes to implementation, these practices should be seamlessly integrated into the development and deployment workflows. Developers and operators should be encouraged, or even mandated, to include relevant tags and labels as part of their deployment configurations, ensuring that every secret is appropriately annotated from the outset. Masking, on the other hand, involves obscuring secret values in logs or UIs to preclude accidental exposure, which is a common risk, especially in debugging scenarios. Systems need to be configured to automatically recognize and redact sensitive information, a task that can be achieved through pattern recognition, checksums, or the explicit marking of sensitive fields in the application's logging configuration.

In the long term, the payoff of these practices is substantial. The wealth of metadata provided through tagging and labeling facilitates a robust and continuous audit trail, allowing teams to track and manage Secrets effectively over extended periods. This is crucial not just for day-to-day operational integrity but also for meeting stringent security and compliance requirements. Any unauthorized access or modifications can be quickly identified and rectified, ensuring that the organization's Secrets management strategy is both secure and resilient. Meanwhile, masking ensures that even in scenarios where logs or UIs are exposed, the confidentiality of secret values is maintained, mitigating the risk of accidental exposure.

By adopting these client-side practices, organizations lay down a foundation for a comprehensive Secrets management strategy, ensuring that Secrets are managed, tracked, and protected end to end within their Kubernetes environments. This approach not only fortifies the organization's security posture but also ensures that its Secrets management practices are aligned with industry best practices and compliance standards.

Auditing and monitoring on the server side

On the server side of Secrets management, regular auditing and robust monitoring play crucial roles in maintaining a secure and compliant Kubernetes environment. Auditing serves as a necessary practice for ensuring that all interactions with Secrets—be they accesses, modifications, or deletions—are meticulously recorded and reviewed. This practice is fundamental not just for maintaining the integrity of the Secrets themselves but also for verifying that all access patterns adhere to established security policies and compliance requirements. By implementing comprehensive auditing, organizations create a secure trail of evidence, facilitating accountability and transparency across all operations involving sensitive information.

To achieve this level of oversight, it is imperative to utilize both techniques and tools that are tailored for robust auditing and monitoring. This includes implementing solutions that can provide real-time alerts and detailed access logs, ensuring that any anomalous or unauthorized activities are promptly detected and addressed. Tools such as audit logs in Kubernetes, and monitoring solutions such as Prometheus or Grafana, can be configured to work seamlessly within the environment, providing teams with the visibility they need to safeguard their Secrets. Additionally, integrating these tools with existing **security information and event management** (SIEM) systems can further enhance the organization's capability to correlate events, identify patterns, and respond to potential threats swiftly and effectively.

The importance of consistent auditing for security and adherence to regulations, along with strategies and instruments to enhance thorough auditing, guarantees the proper monitoring of access and changes to Secrets.

Ensuring secure Secrets distribution

Ensuring the secure distribution of Secrets within a Kubernetes environment is paramount, as insecure practices can lead to severe vulnerabilities and security breaches. When Secrets are distributed in plain text at rest, whether within the host's filesystem or within a container's environment, they become susceptible to unauthorized access and potential exploitation. This vulnerability is especially concerning if an attacker gains access to the host or container, as they could easily retrieve and misuse these Secrets.

Understanding and establishing clear security boundaries is critical in mitigating these risks. Organizations must take a proactive stance, implementing stringent controls and adopting a principle of least privilege to minimize the blast radius in the event of a security incident. This approach involves restricting access to Secrets, ensuring that only the necessary parties have access and that Secrets are not unnecessarily exposed.

Building a trust chain during the Secrets distribution process is essential in maintaining the integrity and confidentiality of the Secrets. This involves verifying the authenticity and integrity of the Secrets at every step of the distribution process, from the moment they are generated or retrieved from the Secrets store, through their transmission, and finally, to their consumption by the intended services or applications. Various measures can be implemented to ensure this trust chain, including the use of encryption during transit, secure injection methods for Secrets delivery, and utilizing trusted platforms and identities for access control.

Decommissioning and revoking Secrets

Decommissioning and revoking Secrets are critical aspects of Secrets lifecycle management, ensuring that outdated, compromised, or otherwise unnecessary Secrets are removed promptly and securely. Implementing best practices for decommissioning involves safely retiring Secrets and ensuring that they are purged from both the Secrets store and any environments where they may reside. This process must be thorough and systematic to prevent any potential security risks associated with lingering Secrets.

Integration of Secrets management into broader service decommission workflows is paramount. As services are retired or replaced, the associated Secrets should simultaneously undergo decommissioning. This ensures a cohesive and streamlined process, reducing the risk of oversight and potential security vulnerabilities. By embedding Secrets considerations directly into service decommissioning processes, organizations can enforce consistency and adherence to security protocols.

Revocation protocols play a critical role in both proactive and reactive Secrets management. Proactively, Secrets should be rotated and revoked according to predefined schedules or triggers, such as the expiration of a certificate or the end of a service's lifecycle. Reactively, in the event of a security incident or discovery of a compromised secret, immediate revocation is necessary to mitigate risks and prevent unauthorized access. Establishing clear and efficient revocation protocols ensures that teams can respond swiftly, minimizing the potential impact of a security breach.

Together, these practices fortify the Secrets management lifecycle, ensuring that Secrets are not only generated and used securely but are also retired and revoked with equal diligence. This comprehensive approach enhances the overall security posture of the Kubernetes environment, safeguarding sensitive information and maintaining the integrity of the production system.

Responsibility, on-call support, penetration testing, and risk evaluation

The effective management of Secrets within a Kubernetes production environment necessitates a clear delineation of responsibilities, robust on-call support structures, and an ongoing commitment to security through penetration testing and risk evaluation.

Responsibility and on-call support

The team managing the deployment platform must clearly define and distribute the responsibilities associated with both Secrets distribution and Secrets store management. This encompasses not only the initial setup and distribution of Secrets but also their ongoing management, updates, and rotation. On-call responsibilities are a critical component of this, ensuring that there is always a knowledgeable and capable team member available to address any issues that may arise, ranging from access issues and misconfigurations to potential security incidents. These team members must be well versed in both the configuration and debugging of the Secrets management tools and the broader Kubernetes environment to effectively address and resolve incidents. Additionally, they should be actively involved in enhancement efforts, working to continuously improve the system's stability, security, and efficiency.

Penetration testing and risk evaluation

The regular penetration testing of the production Secrets store is paramount in identifying and mitigating potential security risks. This proactive approach to security helps in uncovering vulnerabilities, assessing the robustness of access policies, and evaluating potential paths through which Secrets could be exposed. The results of these penetration tests should feed directly into the organization's broader risk evaluation efforts, helping to build a comprehensive understanding of the system's security posture and guiding informed decisions around risk mitigation.

Penetration testing should not be a one-time effort but rather an ongoing practice, continuously evolving to address new threats and vulnerabilities as they emerge. It should cover various aspects of the Secrets management lifecycle, from the initial provisioning of Secrets, through their storage, distribution, and eventual decommissioning.

By integrating these practices into the organization's overall risk evaluation framework, teams can ensure that they are not only addressing immediate threats but also building a resilient system capable of withstanding future challenges. This comprehensive approach to responsibility, on-call support, penetration testing, and risk evaluation forms a critical component of maintaining a secure and efficient Secrets management framework within Kubernetes production environments.

Summary

In this chapter, we delved into the intricacies of managing Kubernetes Secrets within production clusters. We highlighted the qualities necessary for effective Secrets management and examined various deployment strategies and their integration with CI/CD processes. Additionally, we explored a detailed case study on Keywhiz, which provided a thorough understanding of Secrets management development, emphasizing a holistic approach that covers the entire lifecycle of Secrets management.

The next chapter will offer a synthesis of the insights and knowledge we've gained throughout the book. It will also cast a forward-looking perspective on the evolution and future trends in Kubernetes Secrets management.

14

Conclusion and the Future of Kubernetes Secrets Management

This handbook provided you with the fundamental components to secure your container orchestration platform, serving as a reference to continuously improve your security posture while having observed the needs of external solutions to enhance or address the current Kubernetes design when it comes to Secrets management.

In this last chapter, we are going to cover the following main topics:

- The current state of Kubernetes and what it brings to Secrets management

- The future brought by the Kubernetes projects and how to influence it

- How to stay up to date with the latest trends and practices

The current state of Kubernetes

With the widespread adoption of Kubernetes, this handbook shows solutions that can leverage Kubernetes native constructs as an internal vault solution as well as external ones from Azure, AWS, GCP, and HashiCorp. A combination of the two might be required to improve the security posture when managing Secrets for both the platform components and applications.

These solutions serve as safeguards to sensitive information stored within Kubernetes clusters and revolve around the principle of storing, managing, and distributing API keys, passwords, and certificates with no or limited security exposure safely and securely.

Native solutions

The Kubernetes project uses **Kubernetes Enhancement Proposal (KEP)** to document the design changes with the targeted releases for the alpha, beta, and **general availability (GA)** of these sets of changes.

The KMS provider

KEP has been documenting security changes concerning the native Kubernetes Secrets management since version 1.25 with the following themes:

- Implement seamless key rotation
- Introduce health checks for reliability
- Improve performance without compromising resilience and security
- Improve end-to-end observability between the Kubernetes API server, the KMS plugin, and the KMS with auditing capabilities

These improvements are in sync with the challenges we have observed and mitigated through this handbook, improving and helping to maintain a Kubernetes cluster's security posture.

At the time of writing, the latest release of Kubernetes is 1.28. It brings a set of improvements regarding the native Secrets management, as documented within *KEP-3299, KMSv2 Improvements*:

- Here are the changes:

  - Deprecation of the previous KMSv1 feature in favor of KMSv2; this change leads toward the GA of KMSv2, which is scheduled in version 1.29.

  - Implementation of a new **Data Encryption Key (DEK)** when enabling the KMSv2KDF feature gate or the generation of a new DEK per encryption. This change provides the operation team with an optional behavior that can be enabled to comply with regulations where the default KMSv2 behavior of generating a single DEK at the Kubernetes API server startup time is not acceptable.

Here is the KEP 3299 GitHub link: `https://github.com/kubernetes/enhancements/blob/master/keps/sig-auth/3299-kms-v2-improvements/README.md`.

See the *Key value data* section in *Chapter 3, Encrypting Secrets the Kubernetes-Native Way*, for an overview of the technical evolution between the KMSv1 and KMv2 implementations.

Note that KMSv2 is still considered *beta* in version 1.28 of Kubernetes and is targeted for a GA status with version 1.29 (at the time of writing).

The CSI Secrets Store

CSI Secrets Store could be considered an external solution to Kubernetes due to its dependency on an external vault service. However, the CSI Secrets Store is:

- Based on the **Container Storage Interface** (**CSI**) architecture which is a native Kubernetes interface

- Carried over by a Kubernetes project's **Special Interest Group** (**SIG**)

- Leveraging native Kubernetes API objects without the need for an agent, a sidecar container, or non-native Kubernetes patterns

Here is the link to the CSI Secrets Store project: `https://secrets-store-csi-driver.sigs.k8s.io/`.

Not only this model can ease the injection of Secrets from an external vault into applications, but it can also synchronize Secrets as native Kubernetes Secret objects if needed.

> **Sync Secret capability**
>
> When using the Sync Secret feature, the CSI Secrets Store will synchronize external Secrets as native Kubernetes Secret objects which requires setting up an encryption of data at rest to ensure the sensitive data payloads from these objects are encrypted.
>
> See the *Key value data* section from *Chapter 3, Encrypting Secrets the Kubernetes-Native Way*, for an overview of the different options.

Like with Kubernetes's `kms` provider, the CSI Secrets Store is following the same minimal requirements to embrace a DevSecOps model, which includes the following:

- A native CSI model for the platform team to implement a simple connectivity towards external vault services

- A self-service model via the native Kubernetes API objects for application teams to consume Secrets

- Metrics, logging, and secret auto-rotation, to comply with security regulations and frameworks

- Visibility from a roadmap perspective and the current implementation status, which is available here: `https://secrets-store-csi-driver.sigs.k8s.io/design-docs`

The CSI Secrets Store project is an elegant and native solution that is getting more and more popular and even becoming fully integrated within enterprise Kubernetes distributions such the Red Hat OpenShift version 4.14.

External solutions

In the previous section, we looked at the Kubernetes project's roadmaps for its native solutions since they are open source. However, that is something difficult to do here as not all the solutions are open source.

The external solutions that we have reviewed within this handbook are the most common ones as they lead their segment or are native to the cloud providers.

Like the Kubernetes projects, these ecosystem solutions are rapidly evolving to support more patterns and improve business continuity planning, but more importantly, improve the security posture for both the platform and applications running on it.

Due to the plethora of solutions, let's zoom in on just one example at the time of writing. A recent addition from HashiCorp, called Vault Radar, provides scanners to identify Secrets being leaked or hard coded within the application code. Vault Radar offers remediation paths for security exposures and prioritizes these by ranking by risks.

When it comes to improving and maintaining a security posture and with the increased adoption of multi-cloud architecture, identifying such sprawl of sensitive information is critical to reducing surface attacks.

The future state of Kubernetes

When thinking about the future state of a piece of software or a solution, there are two considerations:

- The desires or needs that are linked to specific, future, and missing use cases
- The existing roadmap, its relationship with the current architecture, and how to include future enhancements

As we've observed in this handbook, there is not one software to address all needs. It often involves combining multiple projects and composing a solution toward our end goal while managing Secrets for both the Kubernetes platform and applications running on it. As such, let's have a solution-driven overview of what we would expect for the future.

Food for thought and enhancements

Starting with the native stack offered by the Kubernetes project, the proposed changes and roadmap are documented in KEP-3299. The same goes for the design documents from the SIG in charge of CSI Secrets Store.

Generally speaking, and with all respect to Kubernetes' API-driven design, the following topics would be greatly welcomed:

- **Native encryption**: While Kubernetes provides encryption providers, the actual engines, such as `aesgcm` and `aescbc`, come with a set of challenges that relatively complexify the implementation, exposing their encryption keys or the lack of a commercial version of a KMS plugin to provide enterprise support and services. This change could also help with not only encrypting the sensitive data payload stored in `etcd` but any other data payload from API objects. A deployment definition, as an example, can provide enough valuable information about the platform and applications to be exploited by malicious attackers.

- **Dynamic secret**: The ability to update the secret based on specific scenarios, which is a requirement to comply with most, if not all, regulations and frameworks. Efforts on that matter are being considered within the following initiatives:

  - KEP-3299 has priority in terms of automating the rotation of the encryption to reduce potential attacks

  - CSI Secrets Store triggers an update of the secret payload when the external source is changing.

  - While both previous points could observe and act on the life cycle of key or secret, auditing the actual usage and uniqueness of a secret payload would be greatly appreciated to reduce the sprawl of the same payload across multiple platforms and applications, thus leading to large-scale exposure when the related payload is compromised

- **Offload all API objects data to an external vault service**: Due to the relative burden on the operation teams to secure `etcd` so that it doesn't have potential security exposures, what about replacing this data store with an external vault that leverages the Kubernetes KMS plugin provider? This would greatly ease the burden in terms of knowledge, the cost in terms of time and knowledge, and maintenance.

- **Network-Bound Disk Encryption (NBDE) for etcd**: While offloading to an external vault service could lead to complex solutions to guarantee resilient access to the external vault service, a similar approach to NBDE could help secure the `etcd` data store. The premise of such a solution is to have multiple service instances (at least three for obvious high-availability requirements) bound to a defined network segment and to hold a part of the encryption key within the boundaries of a defined network segment. Using such an encryption key service model along with the **Trusted Platform Module** (**TPM**) would enable Kubernetes encryption providers such as `aesgcm` and `aescbc` to be safer than they are today with limited external services to be deployed.

- **Enrich the logging capabilities**: With **security information and event management** (**SIEM**) systems, a more detailed view of the security posture could be provided from a secret-related point of view. This is often a request from enterprise organizations that want to leverage the power of a centralized logging system to correlate events and quickly audit potentially impacted systems during a security incident response, especially considering the sprawl of objects in multi-platform and multi-cloud architecture.

These are five examples that you could think of after reading this handbook and implementing the shared solutions.

How to share your thoughts

We all have ideas to improve the usability and requirements to support the organization's survival. Like the five previous examples, these might not be part of any request for enhancements, roadmap, or design documents from any software projects and vendors yet.

So, how can we influence the development? The general rule is to open an issue or a ticket to express your enhancement request.

For proprietary solutions, this would be translated by contacting the vendor and asking to open a ticket related to your enhancement, which might (or might not) find its way to the vendor's engineering organization. At this stage, the evolution of such a request is about the same as following the activity of a black hole.

For open source projects, including Kubernetes, the process is much more open. First, it is recommended to discuss your thoughts with the appropriate SIG on Slack or at meetups. This will allow you to discover if a similar workstream is currently in progress to which you can contribute or if it is a good idea to introduce it to the Kubernetes project development teams.

At this stage, the next step is to create a new issue on the Kubernetes repository. Let's look at GitHub issue #111532 concerning the default behavior of the Kubernetes API server regarding the `EncryptionConfiguration` API object:

What would you like to be added?

The current behavior of the EncryptionConfiguration API for the provider list is order-based, so the API server must be restarted for it to acknowledge a newly defined order.

As an example, let's consider moving from this definition:

```
apiVersion: apiserver.config.k8s.io/v1
kind: EncryptionConfiguration
resources:
  - resources:
      - secrets
    providers:
      - identity: {}
      - kms:
          name: myKmsPlugin
          endpoint: unix:///tmp/myKmsPlugin.sock
          cachesize: 100
```

Moving to the following one will require the API server to be restarted:

```
---
apiVersion: apiserver.config.k8s.io/v1
kind: EncryptionConfiguration
```

```
resources:
  - resources:
      - secrets
    providers:
      - kms:
          name: myKmsPlugin
          endpoint: unix:///tmp/myKmsPlugin.sock
          cachesize: 100
      - identity: {}
```

With proposal #111405, the necessary construct enables this implementation.

Why is this needed?

The current behavior is the source of disruption from a service perspective, requires a user with elevated privileges, and does not allow the KMS provider's plugin capabilities to be leveraged within the context of the managed Kubernetes offering (no access to the control plane nodes).

This change will improve the following aspects:

- *Day 2 operations; move the EncryptionConfiguration API to a regular CRUD API object*
- *Resilience and service continuity by avoiding having to restart the API server*
- *The usage of the KMS provider plugin to manage Kubernetes offerings*

> **Note about GitHub issue #111532**
> This example is an as-is extract from this book's GitHub repository without language fixing or formatting applied.

The template is simple – a clear explanation of the what and the why with clear example(s) and, if you can, the how with the code to illustrate the change.

The Kubernetes SIG authentication in charge of the KMSv2 implementation picked up GitHub issue #111532 and addressed the request for enhancement by implementing the code change from GitHub #111919. The outcome of this change is the configuration being reloaded without the need to restart the Kubernetes API server when the `EncryptionConfiguration` API object is modified.

The following links will provide you with direct access to the resources so that you can contribute to the Kubernetes project:

- How to reach out to the Kubernetes community: `https://kubernetes.io/community/`
- The Kubernetes GitHub organization: `https://github.com/kubernetes`
- The Kubernetes SIGs: `https://github.com/kubernetes-sigs`

- GitHub issue #111532 used as an example: `https://github.com/kubernetes/kubernetes/issues/111532#issue-1321971248`

- GitHub issue #111919 used to address enhancement #111532: `https://github.com/kubernetes/kubernetes/issues/111919`

While it might seem rather intimidating to introduce an issue for such a large project, the open source communities around Kubernetes have been building a safe space for anyone to share their ideas and experiences. Now, it is your turn to contribute!

Continuous improvement

This handbook took a continuous improvement approach by considering the DevSecOps best practices. When designing, architecting, implementing, and securing any platform or software, various principles should be considered. Let's take a look.

Skill acquisition

Most security exposures are linked to a lack of knowledge or awareness. One of the DevSecOps principles is cross-team collaboration so that members can share their experiences and discoveries as they all share the same responsibilities to ensure secure systems for their end users and customers.

Participating in training, webinars, and meetups should be a priority for any organization to understand the importance of security and to improve its security posture.

Finally, contribute to open source projects by sharing experience, knowledge, code, and ideas that will contribute back to your organization.

Start early, fail fast, and iterate

Most organizations still tend to consider a waterfall approach when it comes to building infrastructure with limited innovation.

While this project methodology is more than valid for many domains, waiting until the last moment to implement a solution could lead to significant delays with suboptimal outcomes or worse, a project failure.

Another reason to consider adopting such a methodology is limited innovation for the last two decades in building new platforms. As a result, the adoption of Kubernetes is often done with the relics of legacy patterns, which has led to suboptimal implementation or additional burdens for both the application and operation teams.

A good practice for cloud-native platforms such as Kubernetes is to start the implementation early with all the stakeholders involved and learn alongside the project with continuous feedback on success, failures, and future improvements. This will lead to a hybrid project model that fits both the waterfall and agile project management styles so that it suits the enterprise's needs for planning and accelerated delivery.

Automation as a strategy and Everything as Code (EaC)

Most security breaches are related to a lack of automation. When teams are working on security topics or incidents, they often perform the tasks on systems, document them in tickets, and the effort stops there.

As a best practice, every single action toward implementing a system should be codified, reviewed through a source revision system, and automated. This includes the activities of all teams as they are all responsible from a security standpoint for both existing procedures and future ones that are linked to incidents or newly discovered vulnerabilities.

From there, constant drift detection needs to be in place to guarantee all systems are retrofitted with the latest security remediations.

A good practice is to consider **Everything as Code (EaC)** for automating your infrastructure, application, governance, compliance, and security. When doing so, the entire stack, from the hardware up to the application running in containers, along with the business continuity plan, can be part of your **continuous integration and continuous delivery (CI/CD)** pipelines. This approach will serve as the gatekeeper against deploying critical applications on unsafe platforms.

Threat modeling

Threat modeling identifies potential security threats and vulnerabilities early on in the implementation and deployment of platforms and applications. The security team should be part of the core team of each domain to help discover what could go wrong and plan the relevant mitigations.

By leveraging a collaboration culture with the appropriate tooling, threat modeling helps to create a proactive security posture, thereby reducing and even preventing major security issues before they become real.

Incident response

While implementing all these solutions as preventive measures, security incidents will occur or later happen. The DevSecOps practices include a response plan to simplify how security incidents are handled as soon as they are detected. The security team will train the organization by defining its roles, communication channels, and the required actions to contain and mitigate the security exposure.

The incident response should not just be a documented process but a regular exercise to be randomly triggered and can be gamified like a Locked Shield to upskill the teams when they're experiencing a cyberattack.

Here is a link illustrating an annual Lock Shield scenario at an international level: `https://ccdcoe.org/exercises/locked-shields/`.

Summary

Congratulations – you've made it! You've read this handbook, which acts as a reference for any organization adopting Kubernetes and is concerned with the topic of Secrets management. Often considered under control from a legacy platform perspective, it is a completely different story when it comes to Kubernetes as the leading cloud-native container platform.

The handbook provides a comprehensive walkthrough with technical examples about how to address the challenges, respond to the questions of business continuity, and provide the necessary considerations about auditing and compliance. But all these will not make much sense if they're considered as an endgame with a one-time implementation approach instead of adopting a DevSecOps mindset.

While most consider DevSecOps as a buzzword, it is a fundamental shift that organizations can embrace to rapidly learn and adopt new technologies. This method calls for cross-collaboration between all teams supporting an organization's infrastructure. By fostering a culture of *sharing is caring*, the tasks of automating the security policies, checks, and remediations will become an organic activity without the need to consider security as a bottleneck to innovation.

Adopting the culture, process, and technology shared in this handbook will allow organizations to deliver value faster to their customers in a more secure, reliable, and compliant way.

Technology is easy and should not be a substitute for organizational change. Hopefully, this book helped you with selecting the appropriate toolset to manage your Secrets and sparked your transformation journey of infusing a culture of DevSecOps and continuous change.

Index

S

www.packtpub.com

Subscribe to our online digital library for full access to over 7,000 books and videos, as well as industry leading tools to help you plan your personal development and advance your career. For more information, please visit our website.

Why subscribe?

- Spend less time learning and more time coding with practical eBooks and Videos from over 4,000 industry professionals

- Improve your learning with Skill Plans built especially for you

- Get a free eBook or video every month

- Fully searchable for easy access to vital information

- Copy and paste, print, and bookmark content

Did you know that Packt offers eBook versions of every book published, with PDF and ePub files available? You can upgrade to the eBook version at packtpub.com and as a print book customer, you are entitled to a discount on the eBook copy. Get in touch with us at customercare@packtpub.com for more details.

At www.packtpub.com, you can also read a collection of free technical articles, sign up for a range of free newsletters, and receive exclusive discounts and offers on Packt books and eBooks.

Other Books You May Enjoy

If you enjoyed this book, you may be interested in these other books by Packt:

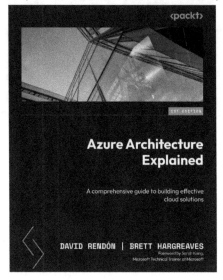

Azure Architecture Explained

David Rendón, Brett Hargreaves

ISBN: 978-1-83763-481-1

- Implement and monitor cloud ecosystem including, computing, storage, networking, and security

- Recommend optimal services for performance and scale

- Provide, monitor, and adjust capacity for optimal results

- Craft custom Azure solution architectures

- Design computation, networking, storage, and security aspects in Azure

- Implement and maintain Azure resources effectively

Mastering Elastic Kubernetes Service on AWS

Malcolm Orr, Yang-Xin Cao (Eason)

ISBN: 978-1-80323-121-1

- Understand Amazon EKS architecture and how every component works
- Effectively manage Kubernetes cluster on AWS with Amazon EKS
- Build a Docker image and push it to AWS ECR
- Efficiently scale and provision resources leveraging Amazon EKS
- Dive deep into security and networking with Amazon EKS
- Understand Fargate serverless and apply it to the workload

Packt is searching for authors like you

If you're interested in becoming an author for Packt, please visit `authors.packtpub.com` and apply today. We have worked with thousands of developers and tech professionals, just like you, to help them share their insight with the global tech community. You can make a general application, apply for a specific hot topic that we are recruiting an author for, or submit your own idea.

Share Your Thoughts

Now you've finished *Kubernetes Secrets Handbook*, we'd love to hear your thoughts! Scan the QR code below to go straight to the Amazon review page for this book and share your feedback or leave a review on the site that you purchased it from.

`https://packt.link/r/1-805-12322-X`

Your review is important to us and the tech community and will help us make sure we're delivering excellent quality content.

Download a free PDF copy of this book

Thanks for purchasing this book!

Do you like to read on the go but are unable to carry your print books everywhere?

Is your eBook purchase not compatible with the device of your choice?

Don't worry, now with every Packt book you get a DRM-free PDF version of that book at no cost.

Read anywhere, any place, on any device. Search, copy, and paste code from your favorite technical books directly into your application.

The perks don't stop there, you can get exclusive access to discounts, newsletters, and great free content in your inbox daily

Follow these simple steps to get the benefits:

1. Scan the QR code or visit the link below

https://packt.link/free-ebook/9781805123224

2. Submit your proof of purchase
3. That's it! We'll send your free PDF and other benefits to your email directly

www.ingramcontent.com/pod-product-compliance
Lightning Source LLC
LaVergne TN
LVHW081519050326
832903LV00025B/1540